REES HOWELLS

LIFE OF FAITH

Intercession, Spiritual Warfare
And Walking in the Spirit

Christian Principles, Addresses, Teaching & Testimonies
from an Intercessor & Missionary

MATHEW BACKHOLER

Rees Howells, Life of Faith, Intercession, Spiritual Warfare and Walking in the Spirit: Christian Principles, Addresses, Teaching & Testimonies from an Intercessor & Missionary

Scripture quotations unless otherwise stated are taken from the New King James Version (NKJV). Published by Thomas Nelson, Inc. Copyright © 1982 by Thomas Nelson, Inc. Used by permission. All rights reserved.

Authorised Version (A.V.) also known as the King James Version (K.J.V.) 1611.

Revised Version (R.V.), 1881, 1885, also known as the English Revised Version (E.R.V.).

ISBN 978-1-907066-64-1 (hardback)

British Library Cataloguing In Publication Data
A Record of this Publication is available from the British Library
First Published in November 2022 by ByFaith Media

JESUS CHRIST is LORD

Rees Howells c.1908, at the time of his village ministry

Contents

Contents of Photos

Contents of Photos

Contents of Photos

Jesus said, "Every scribe instructed concerning the Kingdom of Heaven is like a householder who brings out of his treasure things new and old" (Matthew 13:52).

'Deliver those who are drawn toward death and hold back those stumbling to the slaughter. If you say, "Surely we did not know this," does not He who weighs the hearts consider it? He who keeps your soul, does He not know it? And will He not render to each man according to his deeds?' (Proverbs 24:11-12).

'Now faith is the substance of things hoped for, the evidence of things not seen. For by it the elders obtained a good testimony' (Hebrews 11:1-2).

WRITING from Brynamman, South Wales, the Rev. Rees Howells sends me some particulars of a new Bible College upon which he has been led to embark. A valuable property, which would admirably meet the purposes of such a school, is on offer, and, in addition, " the services of the best men in the country " are available. Mr. Howells is convinced that this is a momentous time in the history of Wales; " God has given the vision, and if we are obedient to it, we may soon see the day when hundreds of young people will be turned out for the ministry who will stand four-square on the Word of God." Mr. Howells and his wife feel called to relinquish their work as foreign missionaries in order to devote themselves to this new enterprise. Although Wales is called the " Land of Revivals," Mr. Howells says they have no monuments of faith that will speak to the coming generations, and he is very anxious to see such a monument set up in the proposed Bible College.

Newspaper article 31 October 1923, written by Rees Howells and published on the nineteenth anniversary of the *Welsh Revival (1904-1905). *See Appendix A. The new Bible College which will be a monument of faith in the Land of Revivals – Wales: "God has given the vision, and if we are obedient to it, we may soon see the day when hundreds of young people will be turned out for the ministry who will stand four-square on the Word of God."

When the Lord made me to abide for a soul, I did nothing else. If, after the Holy Spirit said to me: "Build Me a College," I did everything else, but failed to build a college, I should be condemned. It was a College I had to build. The one thing He gives me to do is the one thing that I do. Anything else I do not count – Rees Howells.

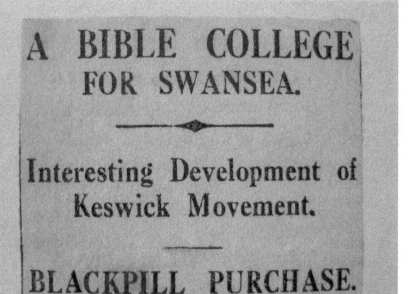

Newspaper clipping from October 1923

I would always be tested and come to the place that I could not do it myself. Then I would ask the Holy Spirit to do it through me. When I was called to build a College, it was only natural that I should receive thousands of pounds. The Lord saw the danger. He caused me to leave the Mission and shut myself up in my room away from people. For ten months I went through the Bible, spending from 6am to 5pm, in my room, and having only one meal a day – Rees Howells.

Introduction

As a student at the Bible College of Wales (and later a staff member) my contemporaries and I often wondered why there were only two books about the life of Rees Howells and the Bible College of Wales, one from Norman Grubb (1952), and the other from Doris M. Ruscoe (1983). After all, Rees and his wife Lizzie (also known as Elizabeth) had done so much within Christendom, alongside his team of faithful intercessors at the College, who also helped train and thrust forth more labourers into the harvest fields of the world.

On the second floor of Derwen Fawr Mansion, the floor in which all the Howells' family had lived was a locked room. The second floor was out of bounds to students, unless they had a valid reason to be there. When paying your fees you were encouraged to use the backstairs, originally the servants stairs which came up from the larder area. Once, coming down from the third floor onto the main landing on the second floor, I was accosted by "Mr Samuel" as he was known (Samuel Rees Howells) wanting to know what I was doing. I explained that I was on an errand for Mair Davies (in her 80s) and that it was easier and quicker for me to cover three floors than her. "Ok bach," was the reply, a term of Welsh affection, and off I went.

But what was behind that locked door? I later asked Miss Ruth Williams, Mr Samuel's personal secretary and the matriarchal figure of Derwen Fawr and was told, "Nothing, just paperwork." I later discovered when Alan K. Scotland was the Director of the Bible College of Wales, called by the Holy Spirit and commissioned by Mr Samuel, that it was the undisturbed "BCW Archives" as I refer to them. These contained boxes, shelves and filing cabinets of paperwork, documents, letters, account books, diaries, tapes, historical objects, books, deeds, maps, booklets, photos, newspaper clippings, and other ephemera.

Whilst working on various Samuel Howells, Rees Howells and Bible College of Wales related books over more than a decade, my research and that of my brother, Paul, led us to some intriguing letters from 1964 to 1966, which details the backstory of an unpublished manuscript. This has more than doubled in length and become *Rees Howells, Life of Faith, Intercession, Spiritual Warfare and Walking in the Spirit* (2022). Inside the manuscript was also a testimony from a former student who spoke at the College in 1961. From the available evidence we can deduce a date of no later than 1963 for its inception and its 'completion' in 1966, though it lay semi-dormant for such a time as this. The following excerpts from letters to or from Samuel Howells relate to this unpublished manuscript.

23 January 1964: From Peter D. Smith, Chairman Publication Committee of Christian Literature Crusade (C.L.C.), Fort Washington, Pennsylvania, USA. To Samuel Howells of the Bible College of Wales, Swansea: '...We understand from Norman P. Grubb that you are working on a manuscript based on notes prepared by your late father, Rees Howells.

'Mr Grubb suggested that we contact you in case you did not have a publisher in view. We have had good success over here with the book REES HOWELLS INTERCESSOR. In view of this we would be happy to consider your manuscript when ready, with an eye to publishing here. On the other hand, if you are thinking of approaching either C.L.C. London or Lutterworth Press, please bear in mind that we often prepare joint editions with them [USA and UK] and this is just as convenient.

'Of course, it may well be that you are not yet ready for a publisher and in this case we just wish to let you know that we are interested in anything from your pen at any time...'

3 February 1964: From Samuel Howells, Bible College of Wales, Swansea, to Mr Smith: '...In reply to your reference to the manuscript prepared by father, I am afraid that as yet it is not ready for publication. When this stage is reached we will certainly get in touch with you concerning the matter...'

7 February 1964: From Norman Grubb to Samuel Howells, from Fort Washington, USA: 'My dear Samuel, just returned from the Presidential Prayer Breakfast. A magnificent witness, all speakers pointing to Christ. The President [Lyndon B. Johnson] gave a deeply earnest word on prayer and how important he thought this Annual Breakfast was as a testimony to the nation and the world that that our only hope and source of wisdom is in God. Most of the Cabinet were there with him, also the Chief Justice, and hundreds of Senators, Congressman etc...

'I would be delighted to go over [Geoffrey] Crane's notes, and if we feel it's of the Lord to go forward with publishing, I will certainly help in that. As you see, I had already mentioned it to Peter Smith...'

1 December 1966: From Samuel Howells to Rubi (the nickname for Norman Grubb): '...We are most grateful for your help with this manuscript again. Our prayer is that it may prove to be a blessing to folk just as has been the case with the biography.

'We want you to deal with it freely and please be drastic whether [sic] necessary. Although you say you are not a grammarian or stylist, I can assure you that you are far better in this respect than any of us here.... We have done our best to improve it from what it was when handed in by Geoffrey [Crane], and really it has been quite a job, and undoubtedly there is still room for further improvement.

'I had a talk with Geoffrey recently and he intimated that for certain sections of this work plenty of material was available and whereas for others, only a little. Where there was enough material it was possible that they were linked by association of ideas; where there was little material; a looser arrangement naturally had to suffice. Please, however, rearrange this material just in the way you think will prove to be the best order.

'Geoffrey also said that you already have the Compiler's Note. We want you to alter this also wherever you think it is needful to do so. And just a final word about the whole manuscript, if, after going over it again, you do not think it is quite suitable for publication [at this time], just say the word and we shall fully understand. We leave everything then to your leading and discretion.'

15 December 1966: From Samuel Howells to Rubi (Norman Grubb): '...We are glad that the C.L.C. folk have raised the point concerning the name that is to be attached to the new work. We are firmly of the opinion that it is your name that should be used for this purpose and none else. Geoffrey has assured one that he does not want to occupy any prominent position in this respect, but of course if you do want to mention his name somewhere that will be quite in order. We are convinced that it was the fact you allowed your name to be used as the author of the biography [*Rees Howells Intercessor,* 1952] that caused the book to circulate so widely. I am afraid that very few of us will have realised what it meant for you to identify yourself with it at that time, especially in view of the intense opposition there was to the writing of the biography in many quarters.'

Many members of the Worldwide Evangelisation Crusade (WEC) advised Norman Grubb against associating himself with Rees Howells' biography from 1950-1952. However, Grubb first suggested it to Rees in September 1936 in a letter. After the death of C.T. Studd in 1931, WEC was in a 'helpless condition' wrote Norman Grubb, financially and some members were trying to oust Grubb from leadership to take control, whilst others were telling him to close the mission because it was so weak! Yet it was Rees Howells' advice, friendship (from 1928 onward), prayers and financial support that helped keep the WEC afloat and grow into an international movement with an annual influx of new recruits. In 1935, thirty new BCW graduates trained in the life of faith, committed to the Every Creature Commission, joined WEC as missionaries.[1]

Continuation of the above letter, 15 December 1966: 'The Lord, however, has abundantly honoured this step which you took and we shall always be grateful to you for what you did. As I have already mentioned, it is our desire for your name to be attached to this again, provided of course that you agree to such an arrangement.'

19 December 1966: Samuel Howells to Rubi (Norman Grubb), '...We entirely agree with your suggestion of eliminating certain of the sayings because they would be quite unintelligible to the ordinary reader who is not conversant with the background. The biography has unquestionably made a tremendous impact on thousands of people, but here there was continuity and a general theme was maintained throughout. This would naturally grip the reader's attention, and as a result they would find it difficult to leave the book until they had finished reading it. But we appreciate that it is quite different with this present work and here undoubtedly the main difficulty lies. It would be a real pity if we were to do the wrong thing at the present juncture, and thereby detract in some way from the biography.

'I was wondering therefore whether it would be better to postpone the completion and publication of this until some time later so that we may all have a further opportunity to reflect and pray over the matter. There is really no urgency and perhaps it could be left until you are over in Britain possibly next summer. As you know, all we desire in the whole affair is God's will....'

The Bible College of Wales,
Derwen Fawr,
Swansea.
15th December 1966.

My dear Rubi,

I was glad to receive your letter dated December 5th, and to know mine had reached you safely. We trust by now that the manuscript also has arrived, and that you have been able to make something of it.

We are glad that the C.L.C. folk have raised the point concerning the name that is to be attached to the new work. We are all firmly of the opinion that it is your name that should be used for this purpose, and noone else. Geoffrey has assured one that he does not want to occupy any prominent position in this respect, but of course if you do want to mention his name somewhere that will be quite in order. We are convinced that it was the fact that you allowed your name to be used as the author of the biography that caused the book to circulate so widely. I am afraid that very few of us will have realised what it meant for you to identify yourself with it at that time, especially in view of the intense opposition there was to the writing of the biography in many quarters. The Lord however, was abundantly honoured this step which you took and we shall always be grateful to you for what you did. As I have already mentioned, it is our desire for your name to be attached to this again, provided of course that you agree to such an arrangement.

Recently we received a very interesting letter from missionary friends in Rhodesia, and they wrote: "The other day a missionary and an African believer came to visit us at our compound here. We could see that this African brother was truly a Spirit-filled man, and through his ministry the Saviour was revealed in every meeting in a most wonderful manner. Some of these meetings reminded us of those precious times which we had in the Bible College years ago. In the course of conversation we asked this dear national as to the manner in which he was brought to the Lord, and he answered: 'I was well and truly born again many years ago in the south coast of Natal'. We then mentioned to him about Mr. Rees Howells, and of the way that he had been wonderfully used as a missionary in Rhodesia and in other parts of South Africa, and asked him, 'Have you ever read the book Rees Howells Intercessor?' His eyes lit up and he turned to his missionary friend and said, 'Do you remember the man that I told you was my spiritual father, and who was a great blessing to me over the course of the years? Well, this person was brought into a real relationship with God, and into the fulness of the Spirit at the time when Mr. Howells visited our station in 1917'. Of all the people who have come to our station, or indeed we have known since the days we were in the College, we have never heard a person who seemed to live and walk with God as this man did. We don't think we will ever forget the blessing the Holy Spirit through him brought to us here, and we trust that this is just a beginning of the real outpouring of the Holy Spirit in this area. Quite a number have surrendered themselves to God in these past months, and the African brother told us the morning he went away that he came up here in real weakness, and wondered what would take place, but he knew as the Holy Spirit began revealing the things of the Lord Jesus in the meetings that he was ministering to a prepared people. To the Lord be all the praise and honour".

A letter from Samuel Howells to Rubi (Norman Grubb) of WEC, 15 December 1966. The second paragraph discusses the name to be attached to the manuscript, as quoted earlier.

The last paragraph of the above letter: 'Recently we received a very interesting letter from missionary friends in Rhodesia, and they wrote: "The other day a missionary and an African believer came to visit us at our compound here. We could see that this African brother was a truly Spirit-filled man, and through his ministry the Saviour was revealed in every meeting in a most wonderful manner. Some of these meetings reminded us of those precious times which we had in the Bible College years ago..." The man was converted many years ago in the south coast of

Natal when Rees Howells visited in 1917, and brought 'into the fullness of the Spirit.' The man stated that Rees Howells was his spiritual father who had been a great blessing to him over many years. The missionary continued: 'Of all the people who have come to our station, or indeed we have known since the days we were in the College, we have never heard a person who seemed to live and walk with God as this man did. We don't think we will ever forget the blessing the Holy Spirit through him brought here, and we trust that this is just a beginning of the real outpouring of the Holy Spirit in this area....'

In 2011, I was with Richard and Kristine Maton at their home in Blackpill, Swansea. My brother and I were in the process of publishing *Samuel, Son and Successor of Rees Howells* by Richard Maton (2012). This was a book the Holy Spirit told me (ByFaith Media) to publish some years before, which was submitted to Richard Maton in writing, who, in-turn passed it on to Alan K. Scotland who commissioned the book. In Blackpill, we were having fellowship, discussing work, book related issues and other spiritual matters when Richard Maton handed me a manuscript. I was reminded of that locked room on the second floor of Derwen Fawr, filled with the archives in the time of Miss Ruth Williams. Richard commissioned me to publish the work, if I was led to do so. It was *Go Through the Gates: Selections from Addresses of Rees Howells, Late Director of the Bible College of Wales*. Richard explained that it was compiled and edited by Mr Geoffrey Crane, a man who had helped mentor Richard when he joined the College community in 1957 and became a teacher at Emmanuel Preparatory School, and later Principal of BCW. Richard spoke very highly of "Mr Crane." He joined BCW as a student in 1936 or 1937 and later became a teacher at Emmanuel School. He was in charge of Missionary Press, later known as Emmanuel Press, for some in-house BCW publications and for vital work for missionaries.[2]

I kept the manuscript of *Go Through the Gates* for nearly a decade and pondered it in my heart as Mary did in Bethlehem (Luke 2:19), after the shepherds heard the angel talk of a Babe wrapped in swaddling clothes and came to seek Him. I occasionally flicked through a few pages, dipping in and out but never read it for ten years. If I did, I might have been tempted to publish it straightaway. In addition, I did not want to distract from the first two books about Mr Samuel, *Samuel, Son and Successor of Rees Howells* by Richard Maton and *Samuel Rees*

Howells, A Life of Intercession (2012) by Richard Maton, Paul Backholer and myself. I waited fifteen years for permission from the Holy Spirit to publish *God Challenges the Dictators* (2020), thus ten years for this book was a short wait! Whilst working on *Rees Howells, Vision Hymns of Spiritual Warfare, Intercessory Declarations* (2021), I asked the Holy Spirit which book I was to work on next. *"Go Through the Gates,"* was the reply, but I also knew this was not to be the title. I committed the work to God and sought guidance from the Holy Spirit, as to how best to proceed. The Word of God declares: 'Commit your works to the Lord and your thoughts shall be established' (Proverbs 16:3), and 'commit your way to the Lord, trust also in Him and He shall bring it to pass' (Psalm 37:5). Amen.

Geoffrey Crane was the compiler and editor of the original 1960s manuscript of just under 31,000 words. The original layout of the manuscript would have worked for a textbook but not for a non-fiction book. There were lots of headings, subheadings, numbers, Roman numerals and underlining, reminiscent from my days at school. All of this has been stripped away and much has been added, taking this work to more than 86,000 words.

I have also included more than seventy digitally enhanced black and white photos; many have never been published before, or have not seen the light of day in more than a century!

Rees Howells' first language was Welsh (as was Lizzie's, his wife), though he mostly spoke and taught in English at the Bible College of Wales. Only from 1936 could welsh people defend themselves in court in the Welsh language. All of Rees Howells' messages were dictated from English by his secretaries and from a number of staff members. Some of Rees Howells' sentences in English appear clunky, or back to front, because on occasions he would invert syntax (the grammatical arrangement of words in sentences). Therefore the grammar is not perfect, but to correct it in full would take away the authentic voice of Rees Howells. Norman Grubb in an unpublished introduction to the biography wrote: '...He never was home in English, and often the turns he gave to phrases sound strange to English ears. I have endeavoured to smooth out phrases and sentences which might distract an ordinary reader by their construction, so that the attention may be concentrated on the message....'

A. J. Russell of London was a journalist and author, who helped edit, proofread and promote *God Challenges the Dictators* (1939). He was a friend of Rees Howells and his Literary Agent. In a letter regarding the manuscript, dated 14 November 1939, A. J.

Russell wrote: '...This kind of argumentative narrative needs smaller paragraphs to retain attention than a novel. It is important.' And, 'A number of these sentences were inverted and these I took the liberty of returning to their feet.' What Rees Howells said in College meetings was transcribed exactly how he spoke, and much of Rees' authentic style of preaching, teaching and talking can be found within this book.

Rees Howells did not expound on systematic theology but preached and taught on certain themes or topics. At other times he focused on 'plots' from the Bible, which he related to real-time events, especially during World War Two. Stories of the prophets and the battles they encountered or the Patriarchs, their callings, experiences and life-lessons.

Some of the themes in different chapters are the words of Rees Howells taken from various College meetings and compiled together. Many of the full sermons, transcribed into the College meeting notes reveal this stop-start preaching. Often sermons would end abruptly and prayer would begin, or a hymn or chorus had to be sung. A student or staff member would be asked to give their testimony of financial deliverance, an answer to prayer, a healing, or the latest wireless news from World War Two would be received and corporate prayer would take a new direction or greater intensity. At other times the Holy Spirit would give a word of knowledge, a prophetic utterance and the sermon would take a new twist or the supplications would be focused in a more specific direction. The following day or weeks later the news from the wireless would catch up with the prayers from the College!

Speech marks have been omitted as the majority of the sentences and paragraphs are the very words of Rees Howells. To include them after each new sentence with a new line would begin to make the work feel messy, whilst to indent the text is wasted page space throughout an entire book. Scriptures, words and sentences that are in parenthesis/square brackets were not part of the original teaching or sermons, however, sometimes the Scripture reference was included, and the text has been added to aid the reader. At other times a Scripture reference was given and I have added an explanation of the biblical story or incident in round brackets.

Quotes and additional facts in boxes are not words from Rees Howells, but the anecdote or contemporary quote is relevant to the subject matter. I have included other facts and figures or historical significant information to aid the reader in the life story of Rees Howells and the history of the Bible College of Wales.

In the same sentence Rees Howells could use the name "Holy Ghost" and "Holy Spirit" for the Third Person of the Trinity. For ease of continuity, I have replaced the name Holy Ghost with Holy Spirit.

Some of the stories may be familiar to readers of *Rees Howells Intercessor* by Norman Grubb (1952), a beloved friend of the College, and I have referenced where they can be found within that biography by use of footnotes. I have also added additional information which was passed on through BCW oral history, or from documentation. The stories may not read exactly as Grubb relayed them, because Rees Howells frequently repeated his experiences to each new batch of students and whilst the essence of each story is the same, the precise wording, or how it was transmuted could change. In the same way there were four Gospel writers but how Matthew, Mark, Luke and John captured the same event could vary slightly as each person had their own perspective and view of the same event for a different audience.

Mathew Backholer,
ByFaith Media

Left to right: Mathew Backholer, Samuel Rees Howells "Mr Samuel," Paul Backholer and Principal Richard Maton, 14 February 2000. The Prayer Room at Derwen Fawr Mansion on the fiftieth anniversary of Mr Samuel, as Director of BCW.

In the Vision

'Where there is no vision, the people perish: but he that keepeth the law, happy is he' (Proverbs 29:18, A.V.).

Jesus said, "Go into all the world and preach the Gospel to Every Creature. He who believes and is baptised will be saved; but he who does not believe will be condemned. And these signs will follow those who believe: In My name they will cast out demons; they will speak with new tongues; they will take up serpents; and if they drink anything deadly, it will by no means hurt them; they will lay hands on the sick, and they will recover" (Mark 16:15-18).

On 26 December 1934, Rees Howells at the Bible College of Wales (BCW) received the Every Creature Vision. This spiritual burden was interpreted as laying the responsibility on his team of intercessors to believe for Every Creature to be reached with the Gospel within three decades, but the time limitation was dropped under Samuel Howells' directorship.

The theology of the vision was based on Jesus words, "Go into all the world and preach the Gospel to Every Creature" (Mark 16:15) and, "This Gospel of the Kingdom will be preached in all the world as a witness to all nations, and then the end will come" (Matthew 24:14).

On 1 January 1935, Rees Howells shared this vision with the College body and the Every Creature Vision was central to their mission for the rest of their lives.

The *Twelfth Anniversary Booklet* (June 1936), stated that the 'fire of God fell on 29 March 1936' on the College, a time of revival and that one hundred and twenty students and staff were 'called out,' surrendering their mission calls to God. In addition, one hundred and seventy staff and *students (*three or four year courses) were praying and interceding three hours a day for the fulfilment of the Every Creature Commission.

Some staff members, who joined the College from the 1930s onwards would often entrust objects, items and oral history to younger staff members and senior students. The following is from the Bible College of Wales' *Twelfth Session 1936* annual report.

My copy of this booklet was entrusted to me when I was a staff member at BCW, for such a time as this.

"Without a Vision the People Perish"

The Holy Spirit has, in every generation, raised up a person or persons, through whom He has been able to reveal Himself as the Almighty God. That generation has been overwhelmed at the commission and their accomplishments of it has seemed entirely beyond the range of human powers. The very fact of their own sufficiency has induced them to look to God alone, and in the crisis of weakness, has God's strength been manifest, and His grace has proved sufficient. The record of these deliverances is a never failing inspiration to those who come after them.

During the last generation, the Lord raised up three men who were commissioned to do the impossible, and through each one of these the Holy Ghost made history in a life of faith and obedience.

1. General William Booth – who was commissioned to be the Apostle to the Down and Outs, the most persecuted man of his generation. He left a legacy of 17,000 Mission Halls, an army of 36,000 officers and 150,000 laymen. They are preaching the Gospel in 85 countries in 89 languages. He has outlived all his persecutors and will outlive them through the countless ages.

2. Dr. Hudson Taylor – who was commissioned to be the Apostle to the Chinese, to open every Province of Inland China, a task that a hundred missionaries could never accomplish unless they had the vision from God. Because Hudson Taylor believed it, he was called to glory from Honan, [now Henan] the last Province in China to be opened [in 1884]. He left nearly a thousand missionaries in that land, and truly, "A little one had become a thousand," and he has become the Father of Faith Missions.

In 1875, George Clark of the China Inland Mission (CIM) visited Honan to evangelise but was not permitted to reside there. In 1884, Henry Taylor of CIM and a Chinese evangelist called Yang were the first evangelical Christians to live in Honan.[1]

3. Mr George Müller – who was commissioned to raise an orphanage by faith, to prove that prayer and faith are effective

agents in the hands of the Holy Spirit to carry on God's work. He in reality became a millionaire on his knees, taking a million and a half [pounds/£1.5m] out of God's Treasury, [worth more than £90 million in 2022], without making a single appeal to man. He made history in a life of faith and his record has been a blessing to hundreds of thousands of people.

The Vision of the College

During this year the College has been brought face to face with the last Command of our Risen Lord, "Go ye into all the world and preach the Gospel to EVERY CREATURE." After nearly 2000 years, not one-third of the world has been evangelised, and over a hundred thousand souls are dying daily who have never heard of the Saviour, who made an atonement for their sin. The ministry of reconciliation was committed to the sons of men, but only one sect has made any real attempt to evangelise the world. This sect was the Moravian Church, and one out of every four of their members became a Foreign Missionary. These people always kept before them the Vision of the early church, of whom it was said "before thirty years had elapsed from the death of Christ, His followers spread from Palestine [Holy Land/Israel], through Syria, and all the districts of Asia Minor; through Greece and the Islands of the Aegean Sea, the coast of Africa, and even into Italy and Rome."

The College "Vision" is that in the next thirty years, the Lord will call 10,000 young people to serve Him in the foreign field. They will be able to have three years training in the School of Faith and prayer, which will teach them individually the way to take their personal needs out of God's Treasury, and to go forth taking nothing from the Gentiles, as the early Brethren did. They will be able to obey the Lord's commission in a most literal sense, "Carry neither purse nor script…because the labourer is worth his hire" [Luke 10:4, 7, and Matthew 10:10]. Men must learn through practical experience how to trust God for their temporal needs, and these lessons should be learnt before going to the Foreign Field, which is a real battle ground, not a training ground.

For the last few months the Lord has been daily unfolding His plan of campaign, and how He is going to reach EVERY CREATURE in the next THIRTY YEARS [a generation]:

1. By completing the vision given twelve years ago, by buying enough freehold land to build a College for 1,000 students; by giving Free Tuition, and Board and Residence for just half the actual cost, £10 a term (*£30 a session). [*Worth £2,260 in 2022].

2. By providing a Home and School for the children of Missionaries, so that not a child of a Foreign Missionary working on the Field is to be refused. These children are to receive Free Tuition and Board and Residence for less than half the actual cost, (for £25 a year or £30 a year including holidays).

3. By making a Missionary Home where Missionaries home on furlough can spend the first three months of their holiday in a spiritual atmosphere, and can be in touch with hundreds of students, and be near their children if they are at the Missionary School. This will also be given at half the actual cost, a guinea a week. [Old British money before decimalisation: in pounds, shillings and pence. There were 20 shillings to £1].

4. By building a large Hospital including Maternity Wards, where patients will be cared for by Christian Doctors and Nurses, instead of going to private Nursing Homes, where the expense is more than many can afford. The charge in this case will be the same as the Missionary Home, a guinea a week. [Before the NHS was founded with free British healthcare. A guinea was a gold coin worth £1 and one shilling. A guinea from 1936 is worth approximately £76 in 2022].

5. The College will get in touch with all the leaders of Faith Missions, those men who have had visions of evangelising their countries, and are opening up new territories, and are reaching new CREATURES. The College will supply them with Missionaries who have had the Vision of EVERY CREATURE, and have been trained in the College to live the life of Faith. The College will also give 25% of every donation over £100 to these Missions who are aiming at evangelising their respective countries. [£25 from 1936 is worth £1,880 in 2022].

END of 1936 BOOKLET

From an article in a local newspaper: 'There are rejoicings at the Bible College of Wales, Derwen Fawr, Swansea, that the College's first £10,000 gift, the coming of which was *predicted at the last Conference – has been paid into the College Bank Account.' (Swansea *Evening Post,* 22 July 1938).

*This appears to be a public prophecy at the Every Creature Conference of 1937. Rees Howells wrote about it in *God*

Challenges the Dictators (1939): '...That God would open His Treasury to finance the Vision – the first gift to be £10,000.' This was seen as a seal on the Vision. £10,000 from 1938 is worth approximately £717,000 in 2022!

From a newspaper article with a larger circulation: '£10,000 GIFT PROPHECY COMES TRUE. The Bible College of Wales, whose reliance on Faith to produce money to carry on its manifold activities is widely known, has just received its first gift of £10,000. This donation was predicted at a College Conference some time ago, and the Director, the Rev. Rees Howells, believes that it will be the first of many such gifts to be received.' (*Western Mail,* 23 July 1938).

THE BROADCASTER

ABOUT 65,000 Guides are now camping in this country.

AN unknown friend has given the Bible College of Wales at Swansea £10,000.

SEVENOAKS RURAL COUNCIL is buying 2000 acres of its countryside.

Newspaper clipping from July 1938, £10,000 gift given to the Bible College of Wales (centre), worth £717,000 in 2022

Rees Howells was not the first person to believe that the consummation of the age would be in "this generation" (thirty years), as other Christian workers had mentioned it from the 1860s onwards, including: J. Hudson Taylor (1832-1905), founder of the China Inland Mission, A. B. Simpson (1843-1919), founder of the Christian and Missionary Alliance and John R. Mott (1843-1919), missionary statesman.

In 1885, *The Evangelization of the World: A Threefold Appeal* by S. P. Smith, C. T. Studd and R. Radcliffe was published. In 1892, the Student Volunteer Missionary Union was inaugurated and in 1896 they adopted the watchword: 'The Evangelisation of this World in this Generation.' In 1910, the first International

Missionary Conference was held in Edinburgh, Scotland, its motto was: 'The Evangelisation of the World in this Generation.' In 1920, Jacob C. Kunzmann, President of the Pacific Theological Seminary and formerly Superintendent of Home Mission wrote *America and World Evangelization*.

The possibility of evangelising the world in our generation is nothing new, but the Vision Rees Howells received added great emphasis on individuals and Christian communities: personal responsibility in world evangelisation, a full surrender, total consecration and dependence on God. Going forth in power under the guidance of the Spirit to reconcile sinners back to God through the Saviour Jesus Christ, who is mighty to save.

Jesus said, "You shall receive power when the Holy Spirit has come upon you; and you shall be witnesses to Me in Jerusalem, and in all Judea and Samaria, and to the end of the earth" (Acts 1:8).

In 1920, Jacob C. Kunzmann wrote: 'This book was written at the call of the Home Mission forces of the General Council.... Its object is to set forth the claims and fundamental importance of Home Missions in America, not for the sake of the homeland, but for the most speedy evangelization of the world. ...The all-power of Jesus only accompanies men and means ordained and appointed by Him. Christ and Christianity are the only specifics for individual and world redemption.'[2]

'Oh, sing to the Lord a new song! Sing to the Lord, all the earth. Sing to the Lord, bless His name; proclaim the good news of His salvation from day to day. Declare His glory among the nations, His wonders among all peoples' (Psalm 96:1-3).

The Bible College of Wales (BCW) for around a decade under Rees Howells' leadership used some exclusive hymn books during their times of praise, worship and warfare. Rees Howells embraced worship as warfare and participated in it daily as did the staff and students at the College meetings. Visitors were introduced to this at the annual Every Creature Conference, held from one to two weeks at the end of July and into August.

The Holy Spirit taught Rees Howells the power of prophetic declarations. Many of the hymns, songs, choruses, poems and declarations were written by staff members of BCW, with one attributed to Rees Howells. These were originally typed sheets of paper and later in-house published hymn books. They encapsulate the promises God gave them as a centre of intercession at the College in prophetic praise and spiritual warfare, a powerhouse of faith during the critical war years from the late 1930s and into 1948. They were known as *Vision Hymns* (Volume 1, 1941 and Volume 2, 1943-1944), plus a *Jubilee Conference Hymn Book* (1948).

In 2021, under the direct revelation and commission by the Holy Spirit *Rees Howells, Vision Hymns of Spiritual Warfare, Intercessory Declarations* by Mathew Backholer was published.

Rees Howells along with many others believed the Devil himself had entered Hitler who was causing chaos across Europe and beyond. For those who were in the Vision, blood-bought and Spirit-taught saints, they believed the Every Creature Commission. They knew of the ultimate demise of the Devil who was defeated on the Cross of Calvary by Jesus Christ's sacrifice. Jesus died, was buried and rose again, because death could not hold Him!

The following spiritual song of eight short stanzas of four lines each, plus a chorus was written for the men and women at the Bible College of Wales. It is called 'Men and Women in the Vision.' Those who were interceding for God's will to be accomplished here on earth, as in Heaven (Matthew 6:10), and for the total demise and overthrow of the Third Reich which was hindering worldwide, the advance of the Gospel to Every Creature. The war was taking men and women away from the mission fields, as they were conscripted, drafted into the military, civil defence or other war related duties. Many future Christian leaders were cut down in the prime of their youth on the battlefields of Europe, North Africa, Africa, Asia or the Pacific Islands, etc. Others were injured during the many air-raids across Britain and other European countries. It was dangerous to travel abroad by sea due to u-boats (German submarines) and air, and more difficult to send money, gifts or supplies to those already labouring in different fields of harvest. Agricultural production ceased in some areas, crops were battle-damaged or destroyed by scorched earth policy, ill-equipped soldiers commandeered or stole animals, cereals and crops, whilst food prices increased and rationing ensued.

David Davies was a BCW student in the 1930s who was a missionary with the Worldwide Evangelisation Crusade in the Belgian Congo during World War Two. Speaking at the College more than fifty years later, he said that in Central Africa you did not know what was happening in the outside world because no news got through. After the war, he was able to travel to a Post Office depot, presumably on the East Coast of Africa, where an entire room contained mail and parcels for the missionaries, some of which had been sent years before, but they were undeliverable whilst the war raged.

'For our citizenship is in Heaven, from which we also eagerly wait for the Saviour, the Lord Jesus Christ, who will transform our lowly body that it may be conformed to His glorious body, according to the working by which He is able even to subdue all things to Himself' (Philippians 3:20-21).

Men and Women in the Vision

Men & women in the Vision take good heart today,
God has told us that the Devil shall not have his way
In the Vision he is bound, & this is what we say,
    His power at last is gone!

Chorus:
    His power at last is gone!
We are sure the victory's gained the battle won
He that had the power of death is conquered & un-done,
    His power at last is gone!

Lucifer accuser of the brethren is cast down,
O'er the Kingdoms of this world he never again will frown
God has intervened today & robbed him of his crown,
    His power at last is gone!

Tho' he has for ages been deceiving saints 'tis true,
God is only waiting all His judgments to accrue
Now his days are numbered & his end is well in view,
    His power at last is gone!

Hallelujah! He is but a poor defeated foe!
By the blessed Holy Spirit he is smitten so!
Boating his retreat his power is spent & very low,
    His power at last is gone!

Loving not our lives to death he cannot us withstand,
Neither can our word of testimony countermand
Now he's taken by the Holy Spirit well in hand,
    His power is at last is gone!

And we tell him in the Vision "Stop us if you can:"
Army of the overcomers we stand like one man
God thro' us is working out His purpose & His plan,
    His power at last is gone!

Calvary exposed him to a great & open shame,
And tho' Holy Ghost today is doing just the same
Often has He challenged him again & yet again,
    His power at last is gone!

As a "Dragon" great he has disguised himself today:
Over Continent & island he has held his sway
"War on him" our God declared and now he's held at bay,
    His power at last is gone![3]

'I trust in the Lord Jesus to send Timothy to you shortly, that I also may be encouraged when I know your state. For I have no one like-minded, who will sincerely care for your state. For all seek their own, not the things which are of Christ Jesus. But you know his proven character, that as a son with his father he served with me in the Gospel. Therefore I hope to send him at once, as soon as I see how it goes with me. But I trust in the Lord that I myself shall also come shortly. Yet I considered it necessary to send to you Epaphroditus, my brother, fellow worker, and fellow soldier, but your messenger and the one who ministered to my need; since he was longing for you all, and was distressed because you had heard that he was sick. For indeed he was sick almost unto death; but God had mercy on him, and not only on him but on me also, lest I should have sorrow upon sorrow. Therefore I sent him the more eagerly, that when you see him again you may rejoice, and I may be less sorrowful. Receive him therefore in the Lord with all gladness, and hold such men in esteem; because for the work of Christ he came close to death, not regarding his life, to supply what was lacking in your service toward me' (Philippians 2:19-30).

The original words of Rees Howells begin in chapter 1

Chapter 1

The Holy Spirit

Jesus said, "For everyone who asks receives, and he who seeks finds, and to him who knocks it will be opened. If a son asks for bread from any father among you, will he give him a stone? Or if he asks for a fish, will he give him a serpent instead of a fish? Or if he asks for an egg, will he offer him a scorpion? If you then, being evil, know how to give good gifts to your children, how much more will your Heavenly Father give the Holy Spirit to those who ask Him!" (Luke 11:10-13).

Jesus said, "If you love Me, keep My commandments. And I will pray the Father, and He will give you another Helper, that He may abide with you forever" (John 14:15-16).

Imagine yourself at a meeting and Rees Howells is speaking. These are the authentic words of Rees Howells...

One must be born again before the Holy Spirit offers Himself (Luke 11:11-13). All who are born again will receive the Holy Spirit as naturally as those who are sinners receive forgiveness of sins and eternal life.

Jesus said to Nicodemus, a ruler of the Jews, "Most assuredly, I say to you, unless one is born again, he cannot see the Kingdom of God." Nicodemus said to Him, "How can a man be born when he is old? Can he enter a second time into his mother's womb and be born?" Jesus answered, "Most assuredly, I say to you, unless one is born of water and the Spirit, he cannot enter the Kingdom of God. That which is born of the flesh is flesh, and that which is born of the Spirit is spirit. Do not marvel that I said to you, 'You must be born again.' The wind blows where it wishes, and you hear the sound of it, but cannot tell where it comes from and where it goes. So is everyone who is born of the Spirit" (John 3:3-8).

A captain on a ship guides it by a compass, but when he comes within about ten miles of the coast he is guided by a light. About five miles from the shore, a pilot who knows all the rocks and shoals comes on board and guides the ship into harbour. Now before I met the Saviour I guided my own life, but after I met Him I was guided by the Word of God. In keeping His laws, there was a very great glory, but when the Holy Spirit came in, He became a personal guide to me.

Llandrindod Wells, Pump Room.

Llandrindod Wells postcard, posted July 1909

In 1906, at the Llandrindod Wells Convention, on the second morning, in the little chapel, the preacher, the Rev. Evan Hopkins, spoke of the Holy Spirit as a Person, not an influence. The moment he did I saw Him, He stood before me. All that I had read about Him lit up to me.

As a Person, He has will, intelligence power and love. You think you know these things, but you do not, until they are revealed to you. The question came to me, "Can two persons with different wills live in the same body?" I answered the question myself. I said, "No, it is impossible." If He was to come in, I was to give way. I saw it and I left the meeting. I went out into a field and I thought I should have wept my eyes out. Unless you are near it, you do not see it. It was a sentence of death. He said, "I need a body I can speak through, intercede through, show the Saviour through." The Holy Spirit is not power, or an influence, but a Person. There is only One Witness of the Saviour and Calvary, and He is the Holy Spirit. The Holy Spirit is the only One who is in

Heaven and on earth and who can make God's will in any matter known to us. The Holy Spirit will be your Teacher, Guide and Intercessor. You will have to believe Him, and you will be tested in your obedience.

Llandrindod Wells Convention Tent, postcard 1909

The Holy Spirit is a Personal Guide, but He will never guide where self is. All that I need is that I should do nothing of myself. If I have not done it, He will look after it.

Although I may have brought arguments before Him, on the final decision I have never dictated to Him once. Anything He has told me to do has been done! If He has told you to do anything, do not go back on it. Say, "You died for me and the life I now live belongs to you" [Galatians 2:20 and 2 Corinthians 5:15]. If you give your word to Him, why do you touch it? You are a liar then! I only bowed my head once. I have been on the side of the Holy Spirit. I have no claim on myself, so I never did anything.

There was no mixture in me of what God had done and of what I had done. Be as clay in the hands of the Potter. All I tried to gain was to give my body to Him and let Him in. If I had tried to gain anything, a spiritual self would have come back. I became a prisoner to my Vision. Liability makes you a prisoner. Many have come and gone, but I have never been able to do it. You think you can take your will back if you are offended; you are free, you are not a prisoner. [A slave for Christ, 1 Corinthians 7:22].

'I beseech you therefore, brethren, by the mercies of God, that you present your bodies a living sacrifice, holy, acceptable to God, which is your reasonable service. And do not be conformed to this world, but be transformed by the renewing of your mind, that you may prove what is that good and acceptable and perfect will of God' (Romans 12:1-2).

Ask the Holy Spirit to reveal Himself to you (Joshua 5:13-15, the Commander of the Lord's Army. Joshua 10:12-14, the sun stood still over Gibeon and Moon in the Valley of Aijalon).

First God speaks, then you obey, and He reveals Himself only after you obey (Genesis 12, the call of Abram to leave his country to go to a land that God would show him).

Peter declared, "We are His witnesses to these things, and so also is the Holy Spirit whom God has given to those who obey Him" (Acts 5:32).

The Saviour and the Holy Spirit can dwell only in one who has been cleansed. 'The Lord said to Joshua, "This day I have rolled away the reproach of Egypt from you." Therefore the name of the place is called Gilgal to this day' (Joshua 5:9). Before the Holy Spirit will come in, you will have to agree not to tolerate self at a distance. He changes self-motives; you cannot.

The blessings are there to be claimed and it is only unbelief that stops a man from taking them. Unbelief is sin. God hates it. If ten people receive the Holy Spirit and ninety do not, the latter fail to accept Him through unbelief.

Jesus 'appeared to the eleven as they sat at the table and He rebuked their unbelief and hardness of heart, because they did not believe those who had seen Him after He had risen' (Mark 16:14).

Do not go after something which others have and which appears brighter and clearer than what you have. Do not think that your doubts are a sign of meekness or humility, or that you are very honest and sincere. You say you haven't the witness. How do you expect to have the witness when you do not believe? When the Holy Spirit offered me a position I always took it at once, but you are always slipping back to the same position.

Once you have the position you cease to be occupied with yourself, you leave that to Him and devote yourself entirely to His Kingdom. If you have made the surrender, take what He is offering. Not through more surrender, not through more sacrifice, but by accepting.

> 'I have been crucified with Christ; it is no longer I who live, but Christ lives in me; and the life which I now live in the flesh I live by faith in the Son of God, who loved me and gave Himself for me' (Galatians 2:20).

You need boldness to claim all these things against the Devil. Take your place in the Kingdom. Claim the fullness of the Holy Spirit. The three young men who went into the fire realised that they would have been dead had God not answered prayer at the time of the king's dream, so they did not attempt to save themselves, but yielded their bodies and the fire found in them nothing it could touch (Daniel 3).

The life that we now live belongs not to us, but to Him who died to redeem us (2 Corinthians 5:19-21). If we keep giving things to God, we show that we have not recognised this, for they belong to Him already. Also we cannot give our life away as we think best, for in so doing we give away the property of another.

If I sent you to town with ten shillings to buy me something, you might feel tempted to give away five shillings to someone on the road. [There were 20 shillings to £1]. But this would not be right; you would be giving away my money. Herein lies the difference between the man with the Holy Spirit and the man without Him; it is a difference as great as that between light and darkness. Unless you have seen this you will always be struggling and giving things. If you use this life for yourself, you are a thief, for it does not belong to you and God's Word says: "Thou shalt not steal" (Exodus 20:15), hands off. I never gave anything up. I knew that it belonged to Him already and I might not touch it.

> In the early days of the College a certain Mrs Williams was strongly impressed to bring £50 to the Director. [£50 in 1930 would be worth approximately £3,500 in 2022].
>
> On the way she met a friend who burst out that she was in need of that identical sum of £50 for something very pressing. But Mrs Williams stood to her guidance and brought the £50 to the College, where it was needed and they were praying for it.

Gifts Received, Receipt Number 316, 26 September 1925. The sum of £2-2-0 (pounds, shilling and pence, approximately £132 in 2022) from Mrs Williams of Penllergaer to the Bible College, written by Rees Howells, the Director, who in 1925 was the College Secretary.

'For the love of Christ compels us, because we judge thus: that if One died for all, then all died, and He died for all, that those who live should live no longer for themselves, but for Him who died for them and rose again. Therefore, from now on, we regard no one according to the flesh. Even though we have known Christ according to the flesh, yet now we know Him thus no longer. Therefore, if anyone is in Christ, he is a new creation; old things have passed away; behold, all things have become new' (2 Corinthians 5:14-17).

I always said I had one ambition in life and that was to do back for the Saviour what He did for me! [Give of himself whole-heartedly for the Kingdom of God as Christ had given of Himself].

Rhys Bevan "R. B." Jones was a minister who was used during the *Welsh Revival (1904-1905). *See Appendix A. In 1922, R. B. Jones (as he was known) spoke to Rees Howells about starting a Training College for the men and women who had been blessed under Rees' ministry, whilst on furlough for the South African General Mission (SAGM), and asked him to pray about it. It was then that the Lord said to Rees, "Be careful how you pray, I want to build a College through you."

In 1931, R. B. Jones wrote *Rent Heavens, the Revival of 1904*. Under the chapter Lasting Fruit he mentions 'Rees Howells and his wife who spent years in Africa,' and the founding in 1924 of 'The Bible College of Wales' as examples of 'some of the "lasting fruit" of the revival,' alongside his own 'Porth Training Institute,' founded in 1919, which changed its name by 1931 to 'The South Wales Bible Training Institute.'

R. B. Jones wrote: 'The main road between Cardiff and Swansea is a favourite one with many of the type referred to, "tramps" the workhouse casuals. A minister, in humble circumstances, whose church lay in a town on this road about midway between the two points named, felt moved of God to a special ministry to the "tramps." Every morning he would meet them as they tramped through the town, invite them to the school-room of his church, give them a meal, and – the Gospel. The repute of the work, as can easily be imagined, soon spread among this community concerned, with the result that, some mornings, he would have as many as forty or more guests! Gifts of money, in answer to prayer, to cover the cost of the breakfasts, came in, and also gifts of clothing – he knew not whence; only he knew that the Lord had prompted their being sent. Many were the conversions at these breakfasts, for this brother had received a most special gift for ministry to this class of men. Tramps, indeed, to speak but the literal truth, were his "speciality," and, quite as wonderful it was to note that, somehow, they too seemed to know it. In towns other than his own no tramp would pass this brother without some kind of mystical recognition and attraction. Frequently has he been seen kneeling on the roadside, in town and country, leading a tramp to the Saviour. Once, on a London street, this brother to his astonishment heard his name shouted from the dickey of a passing hansom [horse-drawn carriage for one passenger]. The cabman was one of the many converts at the "tramp" breakfasts at B—!' [Probably Bridgend].[1]

The Holy Spirit has feelings, a love beyond a mother's love; you must stretch a point in nature to love a man on the road [a tramp], and continue to love them. The Holy Spirit never talks lower than His level. He has no time for it. The Holy Spirit will not take a conversation on a lower level than His own.

All for all. If you think you can say, "Shall I do this or that?" You have another surrender to make. Why do you not receive the Holy Spirit in the same simple way as you received the Saviour at conversion? It is exactly the same for a man who is born again to receive the Holy Spirit as for a man who is not born again to receive the Saviour. He is given to those who obey (Acts 5:32). A full and complete surrender of the will.

"Behold, I stand at the door and knock: if any man...open the door, I will come in..." (Revelation 3:20). If you say that the door is open and that He does not come in, you say His Word is not true. Supposing you wanted to sell me some land, say a hundred acres, but you wanted to keep one acre in the middle of it. I might take you to law for walking over my land, but they would say, "If he has one acre in the middle, he must have a right of way to it." So to get to your acre you would spoil a number of acres of mine. If you withhold one acre of your life from the Holy Spirit the Devil will find, not one way of getting to it, but many. He is not respectable as a man; he runs all over the property.

In June 1923, Rees and Lizzie Howells resigned from the South Africa General Mission (SAGM) to build a Training College. One day they were walking along the promenade of Mumbles Road, Swansea, Wales, when they saw a Mansion set in large grounds. This estate was called Glyn Derwen at the end of the Derwen Fawr Lane (now Road), with an entrance also on the Mumbles Road, which led to the Halfway House public house. It was located at Blackpill (bordering Lower Sketty), Swansea. With trustees they agreed to purchase Glyn Derwen on 10 October 1923 by faith. The Bible College of Wales (BCW) was inaugurated and officially opened on 9 June 1924, Whit-Monday, Pentecost. The spelling of Glyn Derwen was later contracted to a single word Glynderwen.

In the subsequent years, Rees Howells purchased two more estates on the Derwen Fawr Road, Derwen Fawr Estate in 1929 and Sketty Isha (Isaf) Estate in 1932. They were opposite each other and were opened one year after purchase. Rees also bought farming and agricultural land; the largest plot was twenty acres, adjacent to Sketty towards Glynderwen. The Penllergaer Estate, vacant since 1927, in Penllergare, Swansea District, was purchased in September 1938 and opened the following year. Penllergaer is spelt differently than the Penllergare area. Glynderwen, Sketty Isaf (as it was then known, named after the Mansion) and Derwen Fawr consisted of 50 acres in total, plus 20 acres, whilst Penllergaer had 270 acres, including two lakes. Rees bought and sold plots of land as directed by the Holy Spirit and in total owned about 350 acres, though he was only the steward of God's properties. In January 1939, Rees Howells took ownership of a large property, Maison de l'Evangile (The Gospel House) in Bois-de-Boulogne, Paris, France, a Mission Hall with flats above. In December 1939, Rees Howells notes the four estates in Britain and wrote: 'Thus was founded the largest college of its kind in the country, with at one time, more than one hundred and forty students in residence.' Other properties abroad were also bought or ministries were established and their properties were absorbed into the BCW portfolio of mission advance working towards the fulfilment of the Great Commission. They also owned two chapels in Wales in other areas.

Maison de l'Evangile (The Gospel House) in Bois-de-Boulogne, Paris, France, c.1948. Originally known as the Wakefield Bible College after a previous owner. Muriel Todd began her studies at BCW in Swansea in January 1934, and was working at "Wakefield" in 1937, 'amongst a suffering people,' amongst 'the thousands of Russian' refugees in Paris. The Mission House cost Rees Howells the equivalent of £10,000 to buy in 1938, £717,000 in 2022, though the value of the property is considerably more. The College took ownership in January 1939, as part of the Bible College of Wales' European outreach. Rees Howells wrote: 'The College has already bought a freehold property in Paris where there is a large Mission Hall and room for students in residence. There we have opened a College, which is staffed by those who have spent three or four years in the Swansea College.'

Chapter 2

Hindering the Spirit

'Rejoice always, pray without ceasing, in everything give thanks; for this is the will of God in Christ Jesus for you. Do not quench the Spirit. Do not despise prophecies. Test all things; hold fast what is good. Abstain from every form of evil' (1 Thessalonians 5:16-22).

'Let no corrupt word proceed out of your mouth, but what is good for necessary edification, that it may impart grace to the hearers. And do not grieve the Holy Spirit of God, by whom you were sealed for the day of redemption' (Ephesians 4:29-30).

The Holy Spirit is always straight. Jacob showed up Laban's lies to his face. He said, "You would have sent me away empty" (Genesis 31:42). The Holy Spirit is more against you saying one thing and acting another than He is against anything. Tell a thing to Him that you are not; lie to Him and He will leave you in a second! You may not die a physical death, but you will die a spiritual death.

'What fruit did you have then in the things of which you are now ashamed? For the end of those things is death' (Romans 6:21). 'For to be carnally minded is death, but to be spiritually minded is life and peace' (Romans 8:6).

What you do is a hindrance to the Holy One of Israel. The sooner He puts you out of it the better. It is not your intelligence; your intelligence is that you do not believe this Book [the Bible].

It is not your strong reason; it is nothing of yours. When the Holy Spirit hears a man talking and saying he has done something great, He hates it.

Although there are times when you think you can do things. He comes in and shows you what a fool you have been. The Holy Spirit does not know doubt, misery, worry. These things are of self. You are like the Church in Laodicea, if the Holy Spirit is not in you (Revelation 3:14-22). If God has come in, is He very miserable? Does He try this and that?

A man with an unchanged nature consults people in a test. "Any port in a storm." [A proverb, seeking help from anyone and everywhere when in difficulty]. The man of the Holy Spirit never does it. There are no chances where God is.

'It is better to trust in the Lord than to put confidence in man. It is better to trust in the Lord than to put confidence in princes' (Psalm 118:8-9).

The Saviour came to make the atonement and the Holy Spirit came to reveal the victories of the Saviour. The Holy Spirit came to 'convict the world of sin' (John 16:8) because they believed not on the Lord Jesus. The only sin left is unbelief [Cf. John 20:27-29, Doubting Thomas], all the rest were put away at Calvary.

Impossibilities are opportunities to the Holy Spirit. The Holy Spirit did not come to give me a gift; He came to work *through me*. The life of faith is as easy and natural to the Holy Spirit as breathing is to the natural man.

The Holy Spirit brings conviction of sin, reveals genuine righteousness, guides into all truth, gives direction and instruction and glorifies Jesus Christ. The Holy Spirit can be 'resisted,' 'grieved' or 'quenched' all of which are forbidden in Scripture and we are commanded to be 'filled with the Spirit.' He is 'given to those who obey Him.'[1]

Any person who attributes the work of the Holy Spirit to the Devil blasphemes against the Holy Spirit. God is free to work, only when man has gone to his extremity. I long that the Holy Spirit may show Himself to the world without any mixture of man.

Jesus said, "Therefore I say to you, every sin and blasphemy will be forgiven men, but the blasphemy against the Spirit will not be forgiven men. Anyone who speaks a word against the Son of Man, it will be forgiven him; but whoever speaks against the Holy Spirit, it will not be forgiven him, either in this age or in the age to come" (Matthew 12:31-32).

People did not have anything to do with the sun rising this morning neither did the Nation [of Israel] have anything to do with the crossing of the Jordan. Cities at night, everybody as good as dead; nobody enjoying the moonlight; God carrying on alone. At seven o'clock, much bustling on the part of mortals. Now they think that *they* are the people who carry on.

Instead of doing your little things, come and see what God is doing. The difference between the believing of the Holy Spirit and that of man: If you see a need and try to supply it, God will bless you as far as He can lead you, but it is quite different when God says that He is coming down to evangelise a country. You say, "God told me, people under the influence of the Holy Spirit have done remarkable deeds, but they have never done this."

There will be nothing left of them but their preaching.

The Holy Spirit is watching you.

The Holy Spirit reasons with you.

The Holy Spirit lays bare hypocrisy.

It is not that you ask God to help you, but that He asks you to help Him [the Divine-human partnership, co-labouring with Him[2]]. Measure how far the Holy Spirit is working through you by what He is doing. He shows me what He is doing. I come into line with Him, and then He does it. I want to bring you into this. You do not believe a thing until it comes.

'To the intent that now the manifold wisdom of God might be made known by the Church to the principalities and powers in the heavenly places, according to the eternal purpose which He accomplished in Christ Jesus our Lord, in whom we have boldness and access with confidence through faith in Him' (Ephesians 3:10-12).

It is the Holy Spirit who has gained these positions of intercession. It is not you gaining them, but making room for the One who gained them.

The best work you can do is to come to know this Divine Person. In the early years, I came to know the Lord Jesus better than I knew anyone else. Hour after hour, minute after minute I was alone with Him. You could count on your hand the people with whom I had fellowship. In the first six years [1906-1911], I spent all my time with Him beyond the veil. I was not at home with people. He did not ask me to do anything except to come to know Him and to love Him. I wanted Him to use my body to gain positions of intercession, so that others should have the benefit.

- 40 -

He gave me plenty of time with Him before He gave me work to do, so that my attention should not be turned aside by it. My fellowship was with the Trinity.

We are apt to become active before we die. We think we must take this or that up. But this is not your life. Your life is the one which you live in fellowship with the Saviour. He has become nearer to me than the best and dearest friend on earth. I plead for you to be alone with God. If the Holy Spirit has taken you to the Presence of God, you have more fellowship with the other side than down here.

Ask yourself, "Do I live in such intimate communion with Him that I know Him and love Him better than my father?" He says, "I look to find a person whom I can love and who will rain love back on Me." When God calls you to His Presence He allows you to have fellowship with Him.

Jesus said, "If you love Me, keep My commandments. And I will pray the Father and He will give you another Helper, that He may abide with you forever – the Spirit of truth, whom the world cannot receive, because it neither sees Him nor knows Him; but you know Him, for He dwells with you and will be in you" (John 14:15-17).

Quit your activity; come back to God. Do you feel at home in the Presence? Or do you bring work with you? I never bring work in. You do not know Him; you have fellowship through doing something, but for years I did nothing [not at the Mission he founded or attending chapel meetings]. Do nothing until He tells you. Spend your time in fellowship with Him. When He gives you nothing to do, worship Him. [Rees did this often on the Black Mountains near where he lived]. You talk about everything, so He does not give you His confidence. 'The secret of the Lord is with those who fear Him and He will show them His covenant' (Psalm 25:14).

Jesus said, "I came to call sinners to repentance...to seek that which was lost" (Luke 5:32, Luke 19:10). [This is one of Rees Howells' compound Scriptures where he extracts the main point from two verses and cites it as one].

The moment you lose that, the Holy Spirit will have fellowship with somebody else. "There is joy among the angels of God over one sinner that repents" (Luke 15:7, 10).

One should not stretch a point when coming into His Presence. You need a Comforter, when there is a burden and the Devil tells it is unbelief or disobedience, the Holy Spirit knows it is only a burden and He tells me so.

Do you know that the least thing will disturb? Have dealings only with people who do not disturb. [Fellowship with men and women of God, not people of the world who have rejected Christ or Christians who are negative and defeated]. You say, "If I were alone, I could do a great work." Alone with whom? With the old man?

'Knowing this, that our old man was crucified with Him, that the body of sin might be done away with, that we should no longer be slaves of sin' (Romans 6:6). 'That you put off, concerning your former conduct, the old man which grows corrupt according to the deceitful lusts' (Ephesians 4:22).

If I were laid aside sometimes [not involved in an intercession or not taking meetings], the Lord used the time to give me a blessing. The trouble is that you use the time in the wrong way. Put the man of God where you like if God is there, it is Heaven upon earth. You know the man who is in the Presence of God. He is as fresh as the dawn.[3] When God is with you, you make everybody happy. His love is flowing through you.

Jesus said, "And behold, I send the promise of My Father upon you: but tarry in the city of Jerusalem until you be endued with *power* from on high…. And they worshipped Him, and returned to Jerusalem with great joy: and were continually in the temple, praising and blessing God" (Luke 24:49, 52-53).

Joy is not the sign that the Holy Spirit has come, nor are sorrow or testing proofs that He has not come. These people were rejoicing in the knowledge of eternal life and sins forgiven. "Until you be endued with power from on high" – not feelings. You need power for service.

It is as unreasonable for a missionary to go out without the power of the Holy Spirit, as it is for a minister to preach who is not born again. All that the Holy Spirit has gained for the Vision of giving the Gospel to Every Creature is offered to you as an inheritance.[4]

'Elijah said to Elisha, "Ask! What may I do for you, before I am taken away from you?" Elisha said, "Please let a double portion of your Spirit be upon me." So he said, "You have asked a hard thing. Nevertheless, if you see me when I am taken from you, it shall be so for you; but if not, it shall not be so." Then it happened, as they continued on and talked, that suddenly a chariot of fire appeared with horses of fire, and separated the two of them; and Elijah went up by a whirlwind into Heaven. And Elisha saw it, and he cried out, "My father, my father, the chariot of Israel and its horsemen!" So he saw him no more. And he took hold of his own clothes and tore them into two pieces. He also took up the mantle of Elijah that had fallen from him, and went back and stood by the bank of the Jordan. Then he took the mantle of Elijah that had fallen from him, and struck the water, and said, "Where is the Lord God of Elijah?" And when he also had struck the water, it was divided this way and that, and Elisha crossed over. Now when the sons of the prophets who were from Jericho saw him, they said, "The Spirit of Elijah rests on Elisha." And they came to meet him, and bowed to the ground before him' (2 Kings 2:9-15).

The new man is at first a babe handled by the adult old man. The Holy Spirit comes in to handle the old man, as the old man handled the new man. He operates on the old man as the new man grows; just as the new life of a tree pushes the old life off.

He came to dwell with the new man. Take care that the Holy Spirit has come in and that you do not interfere with Him while He is killing the old man. Be on His side.

The Holy Spirit would not live with the old man. He wanted my consent at the very first to losing my choice once and for eternity. Before He came in He told me everything He would do. There was no giving consent on any point afterwards; it was too late then. When you consent to an operation you finish with your choice there and then. If you have given your body to the Holy Spirit, He is coming in and He will deal with you.

You are exactly like a man yielding himself up to a surgeon. To separate you from yourself and link you up to God is as painful a process as a man dying from his family. The moment you hand yourself over to Him, He is coming in, that is all the mystery there is in it. There is no mystery at all. Do not try to make things for Him. Let Him speak to you. It is not you, it is the Holy Spirit.

While you are in authority, He is not there. I was to go to the cross and He was to come in. Don't live a shallow life; don't build a foundation all the time and then do away with it again. Do it once and forever. You lose your picking and choosing the moment He comes in.

All I ask you is: Be sure He is in. The way He comes in does not matter. Once He is in, He will do in a moment, more than He can in years while you are seeking. The Lord will not give you while this is not settled.

> During times of Heaven-sent revival many young converts will advance from milk to meat (Hebrews 5:12) in a short space of time, as if being fast-tracked by God in a greenhouse environment of accelerated growth (Joel 2:25a). The biblical principles that have taken us years or decades to learn, they may learn in as little as a few weeks or months.

Fight well. Go against yourselves. Be steady. Sign it. Say, "I will die before I disobey His command." Face it like a man. Don't be shallow. Put it that you die the moment that you withdraw. But see that it is properly done. You may have given up your money, your home, your other things, but what about yourself, your will? What you need is a surrendered will, a yielded body and a broken and contrite spirit. The moment you lose your will you can do nothing [but God can work in and through you for His glory].

> Jesus said, "I can of Myself do nothing. As I hear, I judge; and My judgment is righteous, because I do not seek My own will but the will of the Father who sent Me" (John 5:30).

When you have given your life up entirely, you have no right to take it back, to make a kick. You will have no more claim on your body than another person has. When your life has been completely given to God, you take everything from God, whether it seems to be for you or against you.

> 'And it came to pass, when Joshua was by Jericho, that he lifted his eyes and looked, and behold, a Man stood opposite him with His sword drawn in His hand. And Joshua went to Him and said to Him, "Are You for us or for our adversaries?" So He said, "No, but as Commander of the Army of the Lord I have now come." And Joshua fell on his face to the earth and worshipped, and said to Him, "What does my Lord say to His servant?" Then the Commander of the Lord's Army said to Joshua, "Take your sandal off your foot, for the place where you stand is holy." And Joshua did so' (Joshua 5:13-15).

No surrender appears anything when in the light of Calvary. I never made a second surrender. I never touched what I gave Him. I am certain that the surrender must have been real and that there must have been cleansing. There has never been a moment in my life when I could have taken another course.

There was a certain squire who owned the whole of a village, except for one small cottage and this bothered him a good deal. So one day he offered to buy this cottage from the old man who owned it. The old man said, "On condition that you cover my kitchen table with gold pieces." "Done!" cried the gentleman greatly delighted with his bargain. The next day he brought down with him his bag of gold. The table was cleared and with a smile he began laying them flat one by one on the table. "Stop, sir, please," called the poor man, "that's not the way I meant! You must stand them all up on edge." The gentleman said, "Why, the cottage and the garden are not worth it." "That's my bargain," was the reply of the old man, "take it or leave it." "Then I will leave it," answered the gentleman, white with rage, as he hastily put the coins back into his bag. He then strode out of the house. The last thing he heard from the old man, as he passed through the gate, was, "Good day sir, and remember that this village belongs to me and to thee."

The lesson of this story: Is there a little corner of your life where Satan has a hold and which enables him to say to Christ, "This heart belongs to me and to Thee."

The Holy Spirit knew that if I kept my word as a believer and a born again man, I would keep it in this [aspect of full surrender]. Once His word was given, He never dealt with me about eternal life, so I have kept my word to Him. The moment He asked you to make a surrender He took it.

Once He deals with you and says, "That is settled now," don't touch it again. Why do you not praise Him all the time?[5]

Why do you look inwards for feelings? Say, "Lord, I have handed over the property [my body and will] to You. If You do not take it, I am not going to touch it, but just leave it lying there."

As Jesus and His followers journeyed on the road, someone said to Him, "Lord, I will follow You wherever You go." And Jesus said to him, "Foxes have holes and birds of the air have nests, but the Son of Man has nowhere to lay His head." Then He said to another, "Follow Me." But he said, "Lord, let me first go and bury my father." Jesus said to him, "Let the dead bury their own dead, but you go and preach the Kingdom of God." And another also said, "Lord, I will follow You, but let me first go and bid them farewell who are at my house." But Jesus said to him, "No one, having put his hand to the plow, and looking back, is fit for the Kingdom of God" (Luke 9:57-62). This echoed the call of Elisha who was ploughing with twelve yoke of oxen when called by Elijah (1 Kings 19:19-21).

The Lord wants to call you and make you, but you go on searching if there is anything more to give up. You have put your body on the altar; believe that it is there. Do not analyse this blessing. Whether there is much or little to be burnt is God's concern, not yours. Once you have proved that you have given your life, you are not tested on that again. [It is a decision, a choice; you must make the surrender, so Jesus is Lord of all].

You made your surrender at the crisis; you do not need to prove it on little things, but march on and build up a definite work. As the Lord says, "Advance, come and do it now." The moment you fail He will take you no further. I would not allow my time to be taken by things that are less than what I have given up. The proof that the Holy Spirit has come to you is that you have lost your own will [and you now live for Him].

If we resist what the Holy Spirit is doing then we are carnal rebels and rebellion is as the sin of witchcraft (1 Samuel 15:23). We are commanded not to 'quench' nor 'grieve' the Holy Spirit (1 Thessalonians 5:19 and Ephesians 4:30) and 'resisting' Him is just as sinful (Acts 7:51), and if we do, then how can we call Jesus our Lord? As the saying goes: 'Either He is Lord of all (your life) or He is not Lord at all.' Cf. Matthew 7:21.

To quench the Holy Spirit is like putting water on a fire, sticking to a routine of religion, our traditions and not allowing Him to do what He wants to. To grieve the Holy Spirit, is to go into the flesh, to sin, or *to attribute something which is of God as being from the evil one or to stop what the Holy Spirit is doing in a meeting. To quench or grieve the Holy Spirit both displace His rightful place within a meeting therefore disenabling Him to glorify Jesus. *This is the unpardonable sin which Jesus warned of, blaspheming the Holy Spirit (Matthew 12:24-31), when His anointing was attributed to Beelzebub, the ruler of demons. To resist the Holy Spirit is being stiff-necked, rejecting Him and resisting what He wants to do in either our lives or the life of the Church; in effect we are saying, "We know better than God and our judgment is superior!"[6]

Chapter 3

Dependence on God

'Unto You I lift up my eyes, O You who dwell in the Heavens. Behold, as the eyes of servants look to the hand of their masters, as the eyes of a maid to the hand of her mistress, so our eyes look to the Lord our God...' (Psalm 123:1-2).

'Trust in the Lord with all your heart, and lean not on your own understanding; in all your ways acknowledge Him, and He shall direct your paths' (Proverbs 3:5-6).

The moment you hand over your life you lose your choice, but He is responsible. It is like joining the Army. There is no choice, only discipline. We are in a great war; 1.5 billion souls are in darkness. He will train, discipline and send you. [There are approximately 7.9 billion people in the world in 2022, with an estimated 2.6 billion adherents to Christianity].

Anything you give to God, He is able to keep. I do not pray to God to keep Samuel [Samuel Rees Howells, 1912-2004]. I never did in Africa [arrived in 1915 with his wife, see Appendix B]. There is no need to pray to Him to protect His own property.[1]

> Hannah said to Eli the priest, ' "O my lord! As your soul lives, my lord, I am the woman who stood by you here, praying to the Lord. For this child I prayed and the Lord has granted me my petition which I asked of Him. Therefore I also have lent him to the Lord; as long as he lives he shall be lent to the Lord." So they worshipped the Lord there' (1 Samuel 1:26-28).

A gift of £30 to the Bible College of Wales, April 1924 from Mrs Phillips, received by Rees Howells, worth £1,950 in 2022

1913 Studio portrait of Mrs Lizzie Hannah Howells, Rev. Rees Howells and their baby son, Samuel, born 31 August 1912. Lizzie was also known as "Elizabeth" though not on official documentation such as her birth certificate or passport. It appears that Rees Howells addressed her by her middle name "Hannah," though later addressed her as "Elizabeth." Cf. Genesis 17:15.

In this life you do not apologise for your weak points, for your weak points are strong points and your strong points are weak points. If you think you can do anything of yourself, it is there that you fail. 'Therefore I take pleasure in infirmities, in reproaches, in needs, in persecutions, in distresses, for Christ's sake. For when I am weak, then I am strong' (2 Corinthians 12:10).

The man to whom the Holy Spirit has revealed Himself knows that he can do nothing. Just as it is more difficult for a good-living, religious person to see his need of salvation than for a drunkard or harlot, so it is more difficult for a man who has been used by God in his converted days to see his need of the Holy Spirit. But when you receive Him you know it and others know it.

If we feel we are too weak to do what He says, it is then that He can help us. If you try to do in your own strength what is beyond you, God will show you that you cannot do it. Say, "I cannot do this, therefore do it through me." While you try, you show that you have not seen it.

'I can do all things through Christ who strengthens me' (Philippians 4:13).

The first thing He said He was going to do through me was to bind the Devil.[2] How could I do that? You are not able to do it, but He is able. You say that you cannot do it, but the point is, do you believe that He can do it? Do you realise that He is a Person different from you and like the Saviour? That He speaks and does things like Him? Or do you make a mixture and say that He comes on you, and works with you, and you are not able to distinguish between His working and yours?

You are not sick, but you have infirmities and your health will give way too when you go to the tropics. "I will glory in my infirmities" (2 Corinthians 12:9), why? Because they were taken away. There is a position where the Holy Spirit comes in and quickens you. Jesus said to him, "I will come and heal him" (Matthew 8:17).

The life of a person with the Holy Spirit is that of a child [complete dependency]. The man of the Holy Spirit has not one thing to do with his guidance or popularity.

The prophet Elijah had no strength of his own. The Lord weakened him down to get him out of the way. People said, "What a coward!" and God had the glory for the miracles (1 Kings chapters 18-19, Elijah on Mount Carmel against the prophets of

Baal, the fire of God fell! Then Elijah fled before Jezebel). There was nothing in Jeremiah outwardly; I believe he was a weak man. But it is a weak man that God wants!

It is not you, it is God. It is not teaching about the Holy Spirit, but He Himself living in you. Do not preach about the Holy Spirit, let Him demonstrate Himself. Haven't you seen that it is this Person who is to do things and not you? The Holy Spirit put me to die and every death brought the hundredfold back to Him.

The world will see the Holy Spirit only in the bodies of men and women. The Holy Spirit told me, "Of all that the Father hath given Me to do, see that you lose nothing" (John 6:39). When God is working through human beings, it is not He that fails, but that you fail Him. Where you fail is that you try things out of your reach. You have not let the Holy Spirit bring you up to it. He never tries anything out of your reach. It gives people cause to criticise, and they put doubt in you. But they can never put doubt in the Holy Spirit.

A man can never go beyond what he thinks ['For as he thinks in his heart, so is he...' Proverbs 23:7]. If God is in you, He does not look to man and He can do it. After all your surrender, you will be offended if you fail to move God. But if you have the Holy Spirit in you, you will never be offended.

Do not look for chances. When the Holy Spirit sees you are ready, He will bring them in your way and work through you.

The Saviour proved what the Devil tested Him on when His Father told Him to do it.

Jesus, being filled with the Holy Spirit, returned from the Jordan and was led by the Spirit into the wilderness, being tempted for forty days by the Devil. And in those days He ate nothing, and afterward, when they had ended, He was hungry. And the Devil said to Him, "If You are the Son of God, command this stone to become bread." But Jesus answered him, saying, "It is written, 'Man shall not live by bread alone, but by every word of God' " (Luke 4:1-4). Feeding of the five thousand, multiplication of bread (Matthew 14:16-21 and Matthew 16:9).

Have you seen the Holy Spirit taking every opportunity? Not that you go rushing after people, but that He commissions you and really brings the people through. I heard the Holy Spirit praying *through me first for the man in the Tin Mill. I found Him loving that person more than anyone else I know. [*Romans 8:26].

He sent me among drunkards and harlots, and I had more fellowship with these converted souls than with any other Christians. I would not allow a single person to suffer [to go hungry, unclothed, no coal, or no money for rent]. The second year, I left Llandrindod [annual Convention] after a week to go back to these people and I said I would not leave them again. I changed altogether. I had joy in being the first sufferer.[3]

Without the Holy Spirit you cannot carry a burden that does not touch you personally. Only the Holy Spirit can groan for people suffering at a distance (Romans 8:26-27).

One day when I was traveling by train in Africa, I began to be affected by the heat, the Holy Spirit said to me, "Supposing you were the man on the footplate?" [Shoveling the coal into the fire to heat the water in the boiler for the steam train]. So I praised the Lord for the rest of the journey. Only men of the Holy Spirit will stand the test of death (Jeremiah chapter 1, the call of Jeremiah. Jeremiah chapter 26, the threat of death. Jeremiah chapter 45, the message to Baruch the scribe).

Rees and Lizzie Howells trekking in Portuguese East Africa (PEA) c.1918, as part of their annual evangelistic outreach to PEA

Keep to the thing the Holy Spirit is doing. Do not give your life for anything less than the Kingdom – anything less than that for which the Saviour used His own.

HERBERT GOODFELLOW
Heart of africa 1934

ALBERT COOK
(Heart of Africa)

MR. JOHN HARBESON,
COLOMBIA.

Sailed for Colombia. S. america
in Dec. 1934.

Miss RACHAEL GOODFELLOW
(Colombia)

Jan 1935
Mrs W. Harbeson

BCW graduates, missionaries to South America and central Africa in 1934 and 1935. Students studied three or four years under Rees Howells, learning the life of faith, mission principles, medical etc. Herbert Goodfellow and Rachel Goodfellow (later Mrs Harbeson) were brother and sister, with callings to different continents.[4]

Do I mean that the God who said, "Let there be light" (Genesis 1:3) is dwelling in me? That is why I do not spend my time doing petty things that a man can do. There is an atmosphere about the person who spends much time alone with God.

The Holy Spirit is the only Person who can keep me steady, so that the suggestions the Devil gives me do not disturb me. The Holy Spirit was always on my side in a test. He never looked on me with a judge's eyes but as a friend.

The Holy Spirit would never show a position if one could not come up to it. If He sends you to a difficult place, is that because He is against you? No, He sends you because you are needed. Happier I could not be [to see you become missionaries]. All I want is for Him to give enough to carry His own work on [in Swansea]. When He came in, He brought everything in with Him. I do not want anything more. If you have the Holy Spirit you have perfect satisfaction.

The life of the Holy Spirit is always attractive. This seeing self all the time is not of the Holy Spirit. So many of you have no joy; your faces show it; your religion would not attract anybody.

'…For the joy of the Lord is your strength' (Nehemiah 8:10).

'Let all those rejoice who put their trust in You; let them ever shout for joy, because You defend them; let those also who love Your name be joyful in You' (Psalm 5:11).

'You will show me the path of life; in Your presence is fullness of joy; at Your right hand are pleasures forevermore' (Psalm 16:11).

'Now to Him who is able to keep you from stumbling and to present you faultless before the presence of His glory with exceeding joy' (Jude 1:24).

People saw God in me. I made this life attractive. The very best would follow this [even mature leaders]. There is nothing worse than men who say they have this, yet people find faults in them and the faults should *not* be there! If the Holy Spirit is in you, do people see Him, and does He make everything you do prosper?

Joseph: 'And his master saw that the Lord was with him and that the Lord made all he did to prosper in his hand' (Genesis 39:3).

The keeper of the prison did not look into anything that was under Joseph's authority, because the Lord was with him and whatever he did, the Lord made it prosper' (Genesis 39:23).

Joseph's rise to power in Egypt (Genesis 41:38-45).

How can people see God in you, if you are worried about yourself or your family? This life is as free as it is great – running like a river. The realisation that He was in me was so great that it affected everyone I met. I hated self as I hated the Devil. Every time the Holy Spirit was fighting I was there, but at other times I was perfectly natural all day. I have never been afraid of the Devil from the moment the Holy Spirit came in. He said, "I am going to attack the Devil and put him to an open shame." I am on the offensive all the time.

'Having disarmed principalities and powers, He made a public spectacle of them, triumphing over them in it' (Colossians 2:15).

Measure this blessing by the power which you have. If He is the same God as in the time of Moses, let Him begin in you now. No one can stop you where God is. You do more by the Holy Spirit believing through you than by any effort. I saw the position: fighting down from a position gained, not fighting to gain a position.*

*This refers to an incident in the Second Boer War (1899-1902) which Rees Howells described. The Black Watch attempted to climb Mount Majuba before the dawn broke. The Boer soldiers had a superior position on higher ground and were able to repel them. It is very similar to what happened in the First Boer War on 27 February 1881 at the Battle of Majuba Hill, at the same location where the Boers had a decisive victory over the British.

The disciples saw the things that the Lord did and believed them. When the Holy Spirit came on them they did the things they had seen done. You try to give a proof in words that the Holy Spirit has come in. There is no need to give a single proof.

You are trying to do things and everything is great to you, but to the Holy Spirit everything is small. He is never in a panic. I tell you these things to show you that you are living, because you make everything big. If it is only power you have, there comes a time when you cannot use it, but the Holy Spirit uses it through you. Everything in this life is simple. It is as natural as breathing. There is no mystery in it. You do not struggle. As long as we remain within bounds there is no mystery in finance.

'My God shall supply all your need according to His riches in glory by Christ Jesus' (Philippians 4:19).

I would talk about £10,000 more simply than you would talk about £10. It is because you have not walked it. Life is so pleasant, so natural when the Holy Spirit takes it.

In a waiting time between two things I am just like any other person. Without the Holy Spirit you can do nothing, with Him you can do all things.

Jesus said, "You shall receive power when the Holy Spirit has come upon you; and you shall be witnesses to Me in Jerusalem, and in all Judea and Samaria, and to the end of the earth" (Acts 1:8).

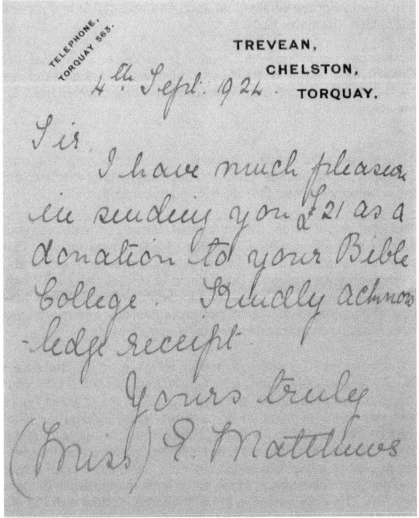

September 1924, donation of £21 to the Bible College, worth £1,360 in 2022. 'Kindly acknowledge receipt,' from Miss L Matthews

Chapter 4

Dying that you May Live

'I beseech you therefore, brethren, by the mercies of God, that you present your bodies a living sacrifice, holy, acceptable to God, which is your reasonable service. And do not be conformed to this world, but be transformed by the renewing of your mind, that you may prove what is that good and acceptable and perfect will of God' (Romans 12:1-2).

'I have been crucified with Christ; it is no longer I who live, but Christ lives in me; and the life which I now live in the flesh I live by faith in the Son of God, who loved me and gave Himself for me' (Galatians 2:20).

The surrender of outward things is only the beginning. You may give up a million pounds, but if you have anything of the flesh left, the adversary (1 Peter 5:8) will get you every time.

The Lord said, "Simon, Simon! Indeed, Satan has asked for you, that he may sift you as wheat. But I have prayed for you, that your faith should not fail, and when you have returned to Me, strengthen your brethren." But he said to Him, "Lord, I am ready to go with You, both to prison and to death." Then He said, "I tell you, Peter, the rooster shall not crow this day before you will deny three times that you know Me" (Luke 22:31-34).

You must give up self, not merely things outside. The surest proof that the Holy Spirit is in you is that He deals with your thoughts every second of the day. I used to spend three hours with Him every evening [in Brynamman, after handing the local mission he founded to his friend, his future brother-in-law], and if ever I allowed myself to think any evil thought for a few minutes, He would bring it up and say, "Confess it." The other proof is that you get your deliverances to the exact time and the exact amount [money]. The Lord comes in to be in charge, to deal with the old man when He wants to, not when I want.

I came in only when there was a clash. The first clash was when He told me to pray only the prayers He gave me. He would make known to me what He wanted to do and I would take it back to Him. So all I had to do was to worship Him, not with a worship that I made.[1]

> Great multitudes went with Jesus and He turned and said to them, "If anyone comes to Me and does not hate his father and mother, wife and children, brothers and sisters, yes, and his own life also, he cannot be My disciple. And whoever does not bear his cross and come after Me cannot be My disciple. For which of you, intending to build a tower, does not sit down first and count the cost, whether he has enough to finish it – lest, after he has laid the foundation, and is not able to finish, all who see it begin to mock him, saying, 'This man began to build and was not able to finish.' So likewise, whoever of you does not forsake all that he has cannot be My disciple" (Luke 14:25-30, 33).

When a man is born again, there is still another nature beside the new nature and this gives rise to a conflict. You see that in the seventh chapter of Romans. The new nature is stronger than the old nature and overcomes it, but in a very great test like that of Job, the old nature may come up and take the lead. However, in a very good test the new nature is stronger.

When you are quiet before God He shows this self to you. He has to get it out of you. When the Holy Spirit comes in, He shows you yourself as He sees you and for the first time you begin to hate yourself. [The apostle Paul: 'O wretched man that I am' Romans 7:24, and the 'chief of sinners,' 1 Timothy 1:15].

There was not a single person who told me about this old man and how the Lord had to deal with it every day [never heard it preached]. I can go into a public house without being tempted to drink, because the bad habit has not had dominion over me. But a drunkard cannot do it, so it is with those who go to tropical countries, [heat has an oppressive power which can damage health and upset the mind, plus many tropical diseases, with no complete treatment in Rees' day]. If they have not been worked out of themselves they find everything there that tests and pulls them down. Your old man is your reason. Your old man is the understanding God told you not to trust.

'Trust in the Lord with all your heart and lean not on your own understanding; in all your ways acknowledge Him, and He shall direct your paths' (Proverbs 3:5-6).

FRONT VIEW OF COLLEGE

Glyn Derwen Mansion, from the 1924 Bible College of Wales Prospectus; 500 were printed. The front, south facing view of the College with views over Swansea Bay (and towards Mumbles) as the land dropped away in three tiers. The rooms on the second floor facing Swansea Bay were named "Millionaires' View."

SIDE VIEW OF COLLEGE

Glyn Derwen was later contracted to Glynderwen, the end, west facing view. There were three entrances to this property. The ivy and foliage were removed from this building within a few years.

Do not take pride in your old man. It is the old man that is the big man. The old man doubts God. The new man believes Him.

The people who had seen the miracles in Egypt were those who failed to believe, whereas their children who had not seen them believed Joshua every time. The old man always says that God has not spoken. Do you live with desires not fulfilled? The Lord gave you a promise that He would supply all your need (Philippians 4:19), and the old man hinders you from believing.

You cannot do what you desire to do until this body of sin is destroyed.

'For if we have been united together in the likeness of His death, certainly we also shall be in the likeness of His resurrection, knowing this, that our old man was crucified with Him, that the body of sin might be done away with, that we should no longer be slaves of sin. For he who has died has been freed from sin' (Romans 6:5-7).

After God shows you self, He cleanses you (Isaiah chapter 6, the prophet Isaiah's vision and commission from the God).

You are one hundred percent self. The Holy Spirit comes in to make you one hundred percent Divine Nature, but before He comes in, you agree not to tolerate self at a distance. Every self motive, every self thought has to be changed. *You cannot change them.*

The reason why you find yourself back in the same position is that self has not been crucified. You are like a man to whom they are going to give a major operation and who runs away after a preliminary minor operation. If this old man is not put out completely, you are not going to be a success in this life. Your old self, every bit of it, is to go. It does not matter whether you are anointed or not; if your nature has not been changed you will be a failure (1 Samuel chapter 15, God rejects King Saul).

If there is anything in you in which the enemy has a hold, you cannot fight (Ephesians 6:10-18, put on the full armour of God, defend yourself and pray). Your nature must be changed on every point. This is the simplest life. It is God taking your place.

What I want is for you to become something outside of your ordinary work. Be alone with God and walk steadily. Once you begin it you are safe. When the Holy Spirit comes in He begins to put the old nature out and once He has dealt with you on a point, a temptation of that kind cannot overcome you again ('...greater is He that is in you, than he that is in the world' 1 John 4:4). When He has *fully* changed you, you can reach to the pattern of the Saviour, who said, "The Prince of this world cometh and hath nothing in me" (John 14:30). Unless God will work you out of yourselves you will never attain to a higher position than that of Joshua. God will not magnify a man until self has been dealt with.

'The Lord said to Joshua, "This day I will begin to exalt you in the sight of all Israel, that they may know that, as I was with Moses, so I will be with you" (Joshua 3:7).

If you are to be leaders, you must have the Saviour living this life through you, without stretching a point. Before the Holy Spirit has cleared you out of yourselves, you live in a very small world. Have you obtained an inheritance [of sanctification, Acts 20:32, Acts 26:18], in addition to forgiveness of sins? I do want you to begin this life. I should spend all my time with God; you have no time for things down here. Would you like to be changed? Would you like to pay the price now and begin with the Lord for eternity?

If you could believe that the King is coming back and that the Holy Spirit has come to prepare you to meet Him, would not that be cause for rejoicing all day? Let Him in and let Him deal with you.

'The Lord Himself will descend from Heaven with a shout, with the voice of an archangel, and with the trumpet of God. And the dead in Christ will rise first. Then we who are alive and remain shall be caught up together with them in the clouds to meet the Lord in the air. And thus we shall always be with the Lord' (1 Thessalonians 4:16-17).

It is far better to fall into the hands of God than into the hands of man (1 Chronicles 21:13, King David knew this). All that God wants to do is to change you, not for you to make sacrifices. You try to deal with self. I never tried to deal with it. Do not deal with yourselves. Do not be like these people in the fifty-eighth chapter of Isaiah or like Buddha. Do not afflict your body it will be a good friend to you. Self watching self. Leave self in His hands. The Devil will keep you going all day. That does not come into this realm. Oh, you try to suppress this lust, but it is you and you have to go to the cross! [To suppress is to hide, to surrender is to give over]. He can disappoint you until He kills you completely, and you are happier in the killing than you ever were before. It is your doing it. Suppose you gave up things and the Devil brings some of them back. Would the Holy Spirit busy Himself with anything like this while 1.5 billion souls are going down to Hell?

The trouble is that you do not die. You merely become passive and revive again as soon as you get a chance. What I try to do all the time is to stop you from coming alive and trying to do things.

The fullest possible consent while He deals. He doesn't bow down to you for one second! All the Lord needs to do is to break you once.

> Jesus said, "Whoever falls on this stone will be broken; but on whomever it falls, it will grind him to powder" (Matthew 21:44).
> '...Present your bodies a living sacrifice, holy, acceptable to God, which is your reasonable service' (Romans 12:1).

When He tells you not to do a thing, try to break through that and you will soon know whether you have a Master living in you! So many people haven't a Master living in them. They are so free; they can do this and that. [They live for self, not for the Kingdom].

The Holy Spirit has come to deliver us from self. I am always on His side. When He said He was going to take my money, I let Him take it. When He touched my food I let Him; it was His body. Then He touched my health, I let Him take it; it belonged to Him Then I let Him take all.

> 'For the love of Christ compels us, because we judge thus: that if One died for all, then all died; and He died for all, that those who live should live no longer for themselves, but for Him who died for them and rose again. Therefore, from now on, we regard no one according to the flesh. Even though we have known Christ according to the flesh, yet now we know Him thus no longer. Therefore, if anyone is in Christ, he is a new creation; old things have passed away; behold, all things have become new' (2 Corinthians 5:14-17).

See if the Lord disappoints you, how it affects you! That is the proof that self is there. Sometimes I would insist on something that was quite right, but He would not be moved, so I came to His side and said He was quite right to put self out. Didn't I rejoice when He found me out every time?

The Holy Spirit must strip you. He has not asked you to neglect essentials, but He asks you never to give time to non-essentials instead of allowing Him to deal with you. That is why I started to pray in the evenings instead of going to the Mission.[2] I was never to allow thoughts to come to me. I was never to allow people to walk with me. I was never to make a call [to visit someone].[3]

Derwen Fawr Mansion c.1932, with extension (left)

In the beginning God dealt with Moses alone. After the rolling away of the reproach He dealt with the people personally (Joshua chapter 7). He is dealing with you and you have no time to deal with other people. Do not lean one on another; God does not prune two people alike at the same time. God will never deal with others through you until He has finished dealing with you.

> Jesus said, "I am the true Vine, and My Father is the Vinedresser. Every branch in Me that does not bear fruit He takes away; and every branch that bears fruit He prunes, that it may bear more fruit" (John 15:1-2).

If the Holy Spirit is in you, He is dealing with you every second. An ordinary man can use his own thoughts, his own imagination, but in this life you cannot. The Holy Spirit said, "Do not come before Me again until you have obeyed Me on the point which I have revealed to you." He never allowed me to escape once. If ever I had a thought against anyone without a cause, He compelled me to go to that person.[4]

> 'He who covers his sins will not prosper, but whoever confesses and forsakes them will have mercy' (Proverbs 28:13).

It is strange that the very pulling down that puts doubt in the man of flesh confirms to the man with the Holy Spirit that He has come in. Joseph went to the throne through the prison (Genesis chapters 40-41). When a man's life is wholly given to God, every trial brings out what is in his heart, that God may take it away (Deuteronomy 8:2-5, testings for forty years in the wilderness and provision of food, whilst clothing did not wear out).

The owner of an old cottage in New York sold his little property. Before leaving it he painted it in order to make it look respectable for the new owner. When the buyer saw what had been done he laughed and said, "It was the site I wanted. The cottage will be pulled down." It is like that with this corrupt nature and you must have nothing to do with it [do not paint it, deal with it]. You do not struggle with it. The Holy Spirit comes in and does what He likes without consulting you. He comes in to pull you right to the ground.

Once God would speak to me, He would cure me on that point forever. When I did a thing once I did it perfectly, it did not have to be done again. The moment you are above in a thing and God cannot test you any further in it, there is no need for God to keep you there any longer. The Lord has never called me to have a place to go to another except from the peak of success.

This is what God is at, to work you out of yourself until you do nothing according to your own understanding, and that is what you are doing now all the time.

Jesus said, "Not everyone who says to Me, 'Lord, Lord,' shall enter the Kingdom of Heaven, but he who does the will of My Father in Heaven" (Matthew 7:21).

John the Baptist declared, "He must increase, but I must decrease" (John 3:30).

'For the law of the Spirit of life in Christ Jesus has made me free from the law of sin and death' (Romans 8:2).

'For to be carnally minded is death, but to be spiritually minded is life and peace' (Romans 8:6).

'For if you live according to the flesh you will die; but if by the Spirit you put to death the deeds of the body, you will live' (Romans 8:13).

Chapter 5

Stop Struggling

'For we know that the law is spiritual, but I am carnal, sold under sin. For what I am doing, I do not understand. For what I will to do, that I do not practice; but what I hate, that I do. If then I do what I will not to do, I agree with the law that it is good. But now, it is no longer I who do it, but sin that dwells in me. For I know that in me (that is, in my flesh) nothing good dwells; for to will is present with me, but how to perform what is good I do not find. For the good that I will to do, I do not do; but the evil I will not to do, that I practice' (Romans 7:14-19).

'For I delight in the law of God according to the inward man. But I see another law in my members, warring against the law of my mind, and bringing me into captivity to the law of sin which is in my members. O wretched man that I am! Who will deliver me from this body of death?' (Romans 7:22-24).

Your reason is very feeble where God is. Cease your struggling. You cannot do anything unless your reason helps you – and your reason cannot help you here. Do not trust your understanding. Do not bring anything from your fallen reason that you had before into this realm. You will always do it until the Lord works it out of you. You always pray for the wrong thing or at the wrong time, and you do not know that you lack guidance.

Missionary to China J. Hudson Taylor founded the China Inland Mission in June 1865. Rees Howells was inspired by his life of faith, surrender to the will of God and his zeal for the every creature commission to reach China for Christ.

To a friend who needed guidance, J. Hudson Taylor wrote: 'Light we no doubt be given you. Do not forget, however, in seeking more, the importance of walking according to the light you have. If you feel called to the work, do not be anxious about the time and way. He will make it plain...I desire increasingly to leave all my affairs in the hands of God, who alone can and who

It was not when compared with other people that I appeared ugly. For three and a half years I never saw self once. The moment the Third Person of the Godhead came in, He showed it up. I never saw before that the "good" self and the "bad" self were one. I was corrupt as sin could make me. When you have seen this self once, you will not be offended when He touches it. If you bemoan this or that in you, you have never seen that you are all corrupt. Every thought, every imagination is evil continually. That is what God thinks of you.

'The Lord saw that the wickedness of man was great in the earth, and that every intent of the thoughts of his heart was only evil continually. And the Lord was sorry that He had made man on the earth, and He was grieved in His heart' (Genesis 6:5-6).

"The heart is deceitful above all things and desperately wicked; who can know it? I, the Lord, search the heart, I test the mind, even to give every man according to his ways, according to the fruit of his doings" (Jeremiah 17:9-10).

The seed potato dies as the new plant develops. You do not know how the Holy Spirit looks on you when you take anything you gain from Him directly and yet refuse anything for which you have to die first. This life is not great, it is small. The Holy Spirit has not come in to make a display. When you have a death you say, "I haven't got the blessing," and the Devil knocks the foundation away. No, it is quite simple, it is death. Have you been immersed into death, so that you cannot use that old man, so that you cannot do what an ordinary believer does?

'For the death that He died, He died to sin once for all; but the life that He lives, He lives to God. Likewise you also, reckon yourselves to be dead indeed to sin, but alive to God in Christ Jesus our Lord. Therefore do not let sin reign in your mortal body, that you should obey it in its lusts' (Romans 6:10-12).

If you have died to your will, why do you exercise your will to do things which are not in this? Actual death leaves no excuse for 'flaring up,' it never allows us to insert our own will, and it comes to us through other people.

You say you want to die – then take death. If you ever think you can use this body, or hinder or disturb the Holy Spirit, you have not done it. Jesus said, "Most assuredly, I say to you, unless a grain of wheat falls into the ground and dies, it remains alone; but if it dies, it produces much grain. He who loves his life will lose it, and he who hates his life in this world will keep it for eternal life" (John 12:24-25).

In the life of every man of God there is a final crisis (Genesis 22, Abraham and the sacrifice of Isaac). Not an atom of this flesh will go beyond the veil, for the veil is the grave. Until you die completely you cannot reap the hundredfold. Supposing there were no food and I had a sack of potatoes. If I were foolish I should eat it, but if I put it in the ground, in two or three months I should have the hundredfold. The Lord says, "Whatever you have given up for My sake or the Gospel's, you will have back on the hundredfold" (Matthew 19:29). The hundredfold – nothing of it before you die, all of it after.

'There is therefore now no condemnation to those who are in Christ Jesus, who do not walk according to the flesh, but according to the Spirit. For the law of the Spirit of life in Christ Jesus has made me free from the law of sin and death. For what the law could not do in that it was weak through the flesh, God did by sending His own Son in the likeness of sinful flesh, on account of sin: He condemned sin in the flesh, that the righteous requirement of the law might be fulfilled in us who do not walk according to the flesh, but according to the Spirit. For those who live according to the flesh set their minds on the things of the flesh, but those who live according to the Spirit, the things of the Spirit. For to be carnally minded is death, but to be spiritually minded is life and peace. Because the carnal mind is enmity against God; for it is not subject to the law of God, nor indeed can be. So then, those who are in the flesh cannot please God. But you are not in the flesh but in the Spirit, if indeed the Spirit of God dwells in you. Now if anyone does not have the Spirit of Christ, he is not His. And if Christ is in you, the body is dead because of sin, but the Spirit is life because of righteousness. But if the Spirit of Him who raised Jesus from the dead dwells in you, He who raised Christ from the dead will also give life to your mortal bodies through His Spirit who dwells in you' (Romans 8:1-11).

September 1965, David 'Dai' Rees using a rotavator, to turn the earth on the top field of Glynderwen Estate, a field that was often used for planting potatoes and other vegetables especially cabbages. Dai (as he was known, David in Welsh) was a student from the late 1930s and later became a respected staff member. He was one of four pallbearers who had the honour of carrying Rees Howells' coffin to the Conference Hall on the Derwen Fawr Estate where the funeral of "the Director" was held in February 1950. Tommy Howells (of Brynamman and no relation to Rees) and Toby Bergin were also pallbearers. Glynderwen Mansion (out of view) was to the left and back. Three buildings in far background are classrooms of Glynderwen Grammar School. Rees Howells followed James' instruction of active faith being expressed through works. Whilst he prayed in millions of pounds in current coin, his team worked the land, sowed seed and reaped a harvest. It was cheaper to grow your own food than to buy it and during the war (1939-1945), the Dig for Victory campaign demanded it.

- 68 -

When you are dead to everything of nature, the Devil cannot lodge his fiery darts. Unless you die you are not living in the Kingdom. Do you really go down to the grave and rise again in newness of life? That is why I could spend twenty-three months alone with this old Book [the Bible]. Every word was like a pearl.[2] If you die in a voluntary way, the Devil can never kill you until God has finished His work through you.

Charles and Lettie Cowman founded the Oriental Missionary Society in 1901. Mr Cowman was promoted to glory in 1924, the year that the Bible College of Wales (BCW) officially opened. As a widow, Mrs Lettie Cowman (the author, Mrs Charles E. Cowman) came to the Bible College in 1936 for one month, but stayed for more than one year. Mrs Howells and Mrs Cowman travelled together from December 1936 to May 1937 visiting mission related sites and preaching. They visited a number of Middle Eastern countries including Egypt, Syria and the Holy Land, as well as Turkey and travelled through a number of European countries: France, Belgium, Austria and Switzerland, plus the Island of Malta in the central Mediterranean. Mrs Cowman was one of the speakers at BCW's Every Creature Conference 1937. In 1949, Mrs Cowman founded World Gospel Crusades. She passed into glory on Easter Sunday 1960. Written in a leaf of her Bible were the following words: 'If we want to know God, we must give ourselves entirely up to the study of God's Word. Man was made to know and to love God.'[3]

I lost my will and had nothing to do with it. You are miserable and blind (Revelation 3:17, church of Laodicea), because He has not come in to deal with it. The Divine Person has come in to make you less than the least. It is never equal joy to take either course as long as self remains. If you have no personal interest you will always act rightly; God can sway you as He wishes (1 Samuel 16:1-13, the shepherd boy David anointed King of Israel). If your will is not a hundred percent gone and you are not dead, you are sure to be swayed in the wrong way, and the Holy Spirit will never be able to use you.

'I have been crucified with Christ; it is no longer I who live, but Christ lives in me; and the life which I now live in the flesh I live by faith in the Son of God, who loved me and gave Himself for me' (Galatians 2:20).

If you are a hundred percent in God's will, you are sure to be guided by Him without putting a hand to touch it. If it is God's will you are doing, you are completely out of it (Joshua chapters 1 and 3). A man who has been prepared by God is never disappointed (Genesis chapters 39 and 40, Joseph). Let God build you up again after the stripping. Do not try to do it yourself.

In an operation for cancer there is the greatest pain, half starvation, twelve months in bed, but at the end – life! It is a painful process, but what is at the end of it![4]

My mother had a fear of sea-sickness, so much so that she would never go to Ilfracombe [in North Devon, England] by steamer, but when I was ill in America she wanted to come out to nurse me. Her love took the fear away.

MARTINS FERRY, OHIO BIRD'S-EYE VIEW.   Ernest K. Hose

Postcard of Martin's Ferry c.1902, a city in Belmont County, Ohio, America, where Rees Howells lived and worked for less than one year. Martin's Ferry is approximately sixty miles from Pittsburgh, Pennsylvania. This postcard is a photograph; however the buildings in the background (top left) to the bridge (far right) have been drawn. The distant images were either out of focus or an earlier photograph was used and to save costs, new buildings etc. were added by hand. This postcard was printed in Germany (as were the majority of Christmas cards) due to the country's superior printing processes.

Rees Howells lived and worked in Martin's Ferry for around eight months. It was here that he caught typhoid fever, alone in his lodgings he cried out to the Lord asking Him not to allow him to die. Rees said, "Give me one more chance and I will give my life to You!" For five months he was searching for God until he moved to Connellsville, Pennsylvania, where he met the Saviour under the evangelist Maurice Reuben, a converted Jew.

While the Lord is using us He is changing our nature; it is an all round blessing. When He has finished with you, the change will be as great as that which He made in the Twelve Apostles.

'Recall the former days in which, after you were illuminated, you endured a great struggle with sufferings: partly while you were made a spectacle both by reproaches and tribulations and partly while you became companions of those who were so treated; for you had compassion on me in my chains, and joyfully accepted the plundering of your goods, knowing that you have a better and an enduring possession for yourselves in Heaven. Therefore do not cast away your confidence, which has great reward. For you have need of endurance, so that after you have done the will of God, you may receive the promise: "For yet a little while and He who is coming will come and will not tarry. Now the just shall live by faith; but if anyone draws back, My soul has no pleasure in him." But we are not of those who draw back to perdition, but of those who believe to the saving of the soul' (Hebrews 1:32-39).

'If you endure chastening, God deals with you as with sons; for what son is there whom a father does not chasten? But if you are without chastening, of which all have become partakers, then you are illegitimate and not sons. Furthermore, we have had human fathers who corrected us, and we paid them respect. Shall we not much more readily be in subjection to the Father of spirits and live? For they indeed for a few days chastened us as seemed best to them, but He for our profit, that we may be partakers of His holiness. Now no chastening seems to be joyful for the present, but painful; nevertheless, afterward it yields the peaceable fruit of righteousness to those who have been trained by it' (Hebrews 12:7-11).

'My brethren, count it all joy when you fall into various trials, knowing that the testing of your faith produces patience. But let patience have its perfect work, that you may be perfect and complete, lacking nothing' (James 1:2-4).

Chapter 6

Abiding in the Vine

Jesus said, "Abide in Me and I in you. As the branch cannot bear fruit of itself, unless it abides in the vine, neither can you, unless you abide in Me. I am the vine, you are the branches. He who abides in Me and I in him, bears much fruit; for without Me you can do nothing. If you abide in Me and My words abide in you, you will ask what you desire and it shall be done for you. By this My Father is glorified, that you bear much fruit; so you will be My disciples. As the Father loved Me, I also have loved you; abide in My love" (John 15:4-5, 7-9).

'…If we love one another, God abides in us and His love has been perfected in us. By this we know that we abide in Him and He in us, because He has given us of His Spirit' (1 John 4:12-13).

Abiding means allowing the Holy Spirit to do through you what the Saviour would have done when He was on earth. Abiding is the primary thing.

There are three great heads in the Bible: Facts, commandments and promises. We have to accept the first, obey the second, and believe the third. Abiding means doing all three and abiding will produce the life of faith. Then if we are not getting through for our needs [what we are praying for, and for the students and staff Rees Howells was addressing, it was often financial needs], we should go back to the Lord and see why.

You are always tested on the individual point. It is not being kind on this point and failure on another. It is a whole life, like the life of the Master. Your weakest point is your breaking point, on that you are tested. It is His life which flows through me, although it took Him a long time to get self out of the way. He always took it out on the lowest. The first person I helped was one of the lowest.[1] [This was Jim Stakes]. I walked every inch of it and now life is flowing through me. The Holy Spirit is looking through my eyes on a lost world. He can search me through and through without finding a trace of self. This is the abiding against us which the Devil cannot throw his fiery darts.

Whenever I had an object to gain there was an abiding to be done. You can gain any position on John 15:7: "If ye abide in Me and My words abide in you, ye shall ask what ye will, and it shall be done for you." If you come to the place of abiding, you can claim your deliverance. "Charity [Christian love]...seeketh not her own" (1 Corinthians 13:4-5) – that is the secret.

The Lord said, "In Divine healing do not deal with others any further than you have dealt with your wife."[2] [When Lizzie Howells was close to death after childbirth, they were to trust wholly in God, not in medicine or doctors. This was a test to trust the Lord, for when they would be far from any hospital in Southern Africa].

I changed in such a way that I will never take the popularity of the world more than I have taken its criticism.

1919 Rees & Lizzie Howells at their home, Rusitu, Gazaland, from a Magic Lantern Slide. These were shown when on deputation work around Britain from 1921 to June 1923, on behalf of the SAGM.

You cannot tell the millionth part of what I am going through and you will never know until you reach the plane [position] I am in.

Do I abide? I certainly do, every moment, to the full. It is a steady work, bearing fruit every day, a steady flow (John 15).

The only value of ordinances and sacrifices was that they were means by which God tested men's attitudes to Him. Do you give God the best of your time, your things, your everything? Do I? You do not know that your actions, your attitudes are being continually weighed. When Abraham refused to take the spoil from the King of Sodom (Genesis 14:21-24), he set up a standard for future generations.

"Be ye therefore perfect, even as your Father which is in Heaven is perfect" (Matthew 5:48). Only the Saviour in you can live this standard. You cannot live this life with your corrupt nature; but with the Saviour living in you, you cannot live anything else, [Matthew 5-6 and Luke 6, the Sermon on the Mount].

Jesus said, "Blessed are the poor in spirit, for theirs is the Kingdom of Heaven. Blessed are those who mourn, for they shall be comforted. Blessed are the meek, for they shall inherit the earth. Blessed are those who hunger and thirst for righteousness, for they shall be filled. Blessed are the merciful, for they shall obtain mercy. Blessed are the pure in heart, for they shall see God. Blessed are the peacemakers, for they shall be called sons of God. Blessed are those who are persecuted for righteousness' sake, for theirs is the Kingdom of Heaven. Blessed are you when they revile and persecute you, and say all kinds of evil against you falsely for My sake" (Matthew 5:3-11).

If He bore my sin and was in me, there was no need for me to sin. "If ye abide..." (John 15:7), not if you break it and begin to abide again. God is not coming down to help your disobedience. Lie low before God. Be natural, do your work well and give time to God.

It is by obedience, by abiding that we shall have the "faith of God" (Mark 11:22, "Have faith in God"). It is important that you keep abiding every second. Once He told me a thing, I never dared to break it. If you break a thing He has told you, you will not pick that up. It was not until Jacob had put away the strange gods and had gone back to Bethel that God made the Covenant (Genesis 35:1-15, God blesses and renames Jacob).

One becomes faithful by obeying God in the thing that He tells one and it would be foolish to add to it.

2011, Sketty Isaf Mansion on the Sketty Isha Estate. The Estate was bought in 1932, as a Home and School for Missionary children and was later known as Sketty Isaf, then just Sketty. The four-storeys on the left (including a garage with maintenance pit, out of view) was an extension commissioned by Rees Howells.

Trying to live laws brings one to an extremity in which the law is written on the heart (Jeremiah 31:33). Thus, 'All things work together for good' (Romans 8:28), while we are obedient. Your finances depend on your obedience to God [when praying in money]. The life of faith is ninety percent giving and ten percent guidance. The secret of power is obedience to the Lord's commands (Luke 9:1-6, Jesus sends out the Twelve Apostles).

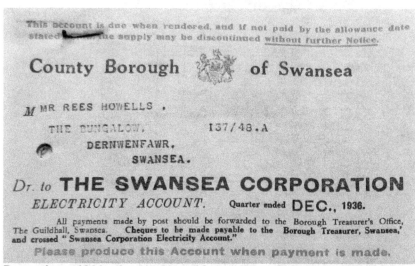

This account is due when rendered, and if not paid by the allowance date stated the supply may be discontinued without further Notice.

County Borough of Swansea

M MR REES HOWELLS .

THE BUNGALOW,   137/48.A
⟋   DERNWENFAWR,
          SWANSEA.

Dr. to THE SWANSEA CORPORATION
ELECTRICITY ACCOUNT.   Quarter ended DEC., 1936.

All payments made by post should be forwarded to the Borough Treasurer's Office, The Guildhall, Swansea.   Cheques to be made payable to the Borough Treasurer, Swansea,' and crossed " Swansea Corporation Electricity Account."

Please produce this Account when payment is made.

December 1936, local rates from The Swansea Corporation (Council) for Electricity to the Bungalow (near the Hospital) on the Derwen Fawr Estate. Bills for electricity for each quarter on the same estate were required for the Hospital, Men's Hostel, Derwen Fawr Mansion, Bungalow, Chapel and Conference Hall.

At one time Rees Howells had to pay £40 rates. £40 in 1936 is worth £3,050 in 2022. Rates were charged quarterly for each Estate owned by the Bible College, whilst some rates were chargeable for different buildings on one site. Rees had £7 (£534 in 2022) towards this amount, but the Lord told him that a friend of his was also in need of money to pay his rates and that the £7 (which was not enough for the rates of the College), would be enough for his friend. Rees Howells took the £7 to him and found the whole family on their knees, praying for the rates. When Rees returned to the College, he found that a gift of £40 had been received. The principles of sowing and reaping, and first call, first need, played out as the Spirit led him.

It was the responsibility of some staff members in the 1930s to pray in the money for different buildings, e.g. the male staff member in charge of the Men's Hostel. There were also water rates, local taxes and income tax on property and land owned by Rees Howells, including income from Derwen Fawr Lodge, a small cottage that was rented out. It was located off Ashleigh Road, at the bottom of Derwen Fawr Estate, near Mumbles Road. Rates and Taxes were also due from all the Estates under Rees Howells' stewardship. Without financial partners, Rees and his team had to trust God for their daily bread, with weekly financial deadlines. As the structure of the College community grew, so did the liability and responsibility, as everything was subsidised by fifty percent, the Bible College students and boarders at the School, therefore the balance had to be prayed in. The Penllergaer Estate with 270 acres was bought at the end of 1938 for £20,000 (£1,434,000 in 2022). However, after major renovations the insurance company in 1939, valued the Mansion on its own for £30,000 (£2,237,000 in 2022) and Rees had to pay those premiums. Then there was Glynderwen, Sketty, Derwen Fawr and Maison de l'Evangile in Paris, France.

In July 1938, the College began to benefit from some form of charitable status to reduce Rees Howells' huge tax bill as a landowner with many properties. All the properties were vested in a 'Charity Trust.' This was solidified in the mid-1950s under Samuel Rees Howells.

In this abiding you wait before God. Supposing a thought against some person comes to you, He says, "The next time that thought comes to you, I will have you go to that person."[3] Well, you must take very good care that it does not happen again. You must die to this.

Do not run after everyone [to confess] with that corrupt nature of yours. Let the Lord change you first. I had to confess because of the high position I had. If you have sinned against someone you should confess to that person as well as to God alone. Go to God and He will tell you whether to confess openly or not. The Holy

Spirit has never allowed me to take confessions from people. If a matter is between God and you, confess it only to God. One should never intrude into the inner secrets of a man's soul.

J. Edwin Orr visited the Bible College of Wales (BCW) in 1934 as part of his tour of Britain. He went on to be used in many localised revivals in the mid-1930s in Eastern Europe, America, Africa and Australia. Two years on from visiting BCW, Edwin Orr wrote: 'If you sin secretly, confess secretly, admitting publicly that you need the victory, but keeping the details to yourself. If you sin openly, confess openly to remove stumbling-blocks from those whom you have hindered. If you have sinned spiritually (prayerlessness, lovelessness, and unbelief as well as their offspring, criticism, etc.) then confess to the church that you have been a hindrance. The Devil is ever ready to take advantage of distress of heart, but the Holy Spirit can give the last word in wisdom.'[4]

The Saviour has cleared the past and He gives victory in the present. He not only forgives, but He cleanses all the time, continually from all sin (1 John 1:5-10). If you have fallen short, ask the Holy Spirit to overlook it, then leave it (Joshua 9:3-27, the Gibeonite deception. Joshua 10:1-15, the sun stands still).

'For sin shall not have dominion over you, for you are not under law but under grace' (Romans 6:14).
'Their sins and their lawless deeds I will remember no more' (Hebrews 10:17).
'He who covers his sins will not prosper, but whoever confesses and forsakes them will have mercy' (Proverbs 28:13).

Do not lose your attitude of praise [towards God, for], you have a great cause for it. You have not seen the value of things, [your salvation, answers to prayers, of provision etc.], if you had you would be praising from morning to night. Do not be afraid to give praise lest people take advantage [and you become downcast].

'A Psalm. Oh, sing to the Lord a new song! For He has done marvellous things; His right hand and His holy arm have gained Him the victory. The Lord has made known His salvation; His righteousness He has revealed in the sight of the nations' (Psalm 98:1-2).

'Praise the Lord! I will praise the Lord with my whole heart, in the assembly of the upright and in the congregation. The works of the Lord are great, studied by all who have pleasure in them. His work is honourable and glorious and His righteousness endures forever. He has made His wonderful works to be remembered; the Lord is gracious and full of compassion' (Psalm 111:1-4).

'Praise the Lord! Praise God in His sanctuary; praise Him in His mighty firmament! Praise Him for His mighty acts; praise Him according to His excellent greatness! Let everything that has breath praise the Lord. Praise the Lord!' (Psalm 150:1-2, 6).

REES HOWELLS

Vision Hymns

of Spiritual Warfare
Intercessory Declarations

A section of the front cover of *Rees Howells, Vision Hymns*

Rees Howells embraced worship as warfare and participated in it daily. The Holy Spirit taught him the power of prophetic praise and declarations. In the College meetings, Rees led his team of intercessors through the Bible in prayer and found guidance for spiritual warfare in worship, praise and celebration. As a unique powerhouse of faith, intercession and prophetic praise, Rees Howells and his intercessors composed and compiled a selection of songs, hymns, declarations and poems. These were brought to light in 2021 in *Rees Howells, Vision Hymns of Spiritual Warfare, Intercessory Declarations* by Mathew Backholer.

'Let the high praises of God be in their mouth and a two-edged sword in their hand. To execute vengeance on the nations, and punishments on the peoples; to bind their kings with chains, and their nobles with fetters of iron; to execute on them the written judgment – this honour have all His saints. Praise the Lord!' (Psalm 149:6-9).

The joy of giving is greater than the joy of receiving. [However, when you are tested and in much need], the joy of receiving £10,000 when you have *not given* is a selfish joy, you are proud of doing a big thing. Never defend a weakness, but make it strong.

Keep trusting in God, even when the religious critics mock you and say, "You have missed God's will!" They will criticise you regardless of whether you do a great thing with God or a little thing for God. The critics will never be silent as they espouse their low spiritual state by attempting to discredit and destroy others. Like Nehemiah, I am doing a great work and will not be distracted from what God has called me to do (Nehemiah 6).

The Holy Spirit said, "Do not defend yourself; if you do, I will not defend you."

'But I, like a deaf man, do not hear; and I am like a mute who does not open his mouth. Thus I am like a man who does not hear, and in whose mouth is no response. For in You, O Lord, I hope; You will hear, O Lord my God' (Psalm 38:13-15).

'He was oppressed and He was afflicted, yet He opened not His mouth; He was led as a lamb to the slaughter, and as a sheep before its shearers is silent, so He opened not His mouth' (Isaiah 53:7).

Chapter 7

Preaching, Faith and Temptation

Jesus began to preach and to say, "Repent, for the Kingdom of Heaven is at hand" (Matthew 4:17). Jesus said to His disciples, "And as you go, preach, saying, 'The Kingdom of Heaven is at hand' " (Matthew 10:7).

A man came to Jesus and said, "Lord, have mercy on my son, for he is an epileptic and suffers severely; for he often falls into the fire and often into the water. So I brought him to Your disciples, but they could not cure him." Jesus rebuked the demon and it came out of him. Jesus said to His disciples, "This kind does not go out except by prayer and fasting" (Matthew 17:14-16, 21).

I have never tried to explain anything in a way in which it is not explained in the Word. If you can prove through the Word what you preach and unfold it from experience, I do not believe that you will find a child of God, attacking that. When a man preaches, it is like throwing an [ammunition] cartridge at somebody; when the Holy Spirit preaches, it is like firing from a gun [on target and it hits its mark]. We often preach things we have no authority to preach, and because of that, we cannot convince people; the Holy Spirit will never use power through us to convince others on a higher grade than what we have gained ourselves, and certainly we cannot have the power of intercession.

You cannot abide with any known sin, unjudged and unconfessed. You cannot abide with unbelief; you cannot abide unless you are willing to obey to the hilt (John chapter 15, abiding). Self cannot abide; all of you is rotten (Jeremiah 17:9, the heart is deceitful), you cannot abide with a trace of self. You may come to a position of abiding, but that is only abiding in part. You must be very much at fault if others can see faults in you. I never judge by what I hear. I do not want to hear things. Gossip is sin. 'Where there is no talebearer, the strife ceaseth' (Proverbs 26:20). Jesus said, "...That every idle word that men shall speak, they shall give account thereof in the Day of Judgment" (Matthew 12:36).

> 'An ungodly man digs up evil and it is on his lips like a burning fire. A perverse man sows strife and a whisperer separates the best of friends' (Proverbs 16:27-28).

The Lord will always test you on one soul before he gives you many. I am always patient with a man who is slow in coming up to it. Will you work in unity, each one esteeming the other better than himself? (Philippians 2:3). Live a life without regrets. Would the prophet Samuel pray that King Saul be used as much as himself? (1 Samuel 8:1-22). That is a very high position.

In preaching you should not go beyond what you have actually put into practice. Get a solid life of faith and some facts to put before the people. I know immediately when a man not in victory preaches that he is 'more than a conqueror' (Romans 8:37). He's like a blind man carrying a lantern to prevent others from knocking against him. Do not preach the Kingdom until you are sure that the Lord has given you a place in it. The Holy Spirit asks you not to.

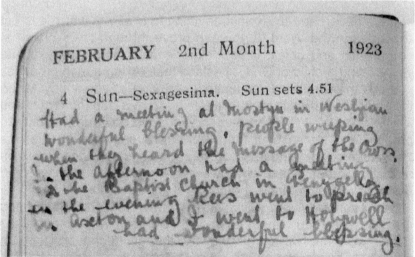

February 1923, from Lizzie Howells' Pocket Diary: 'Had a meeting at Mostyn [North Wales] in Wesleyan [Chapel] wonderful blessing, people weeping when they heard the message of the cross. In the afternoon, had a meeting in the Baptist Church in Penygelli. In the evening Rees went to preach in Aseton and I went to Holywell had wonderful blessing.' These diary entries from Mrs Howells' hand were written during Rees and Lizzie's South Africa General Mission (SAGM) deputation work. To fulfil more engagements, they often separated and spoke in different towns, to reunite, generally, within a day or two.

> 'Jesus said to His followers, "Let us go into the next towns that I may preach there also, because for this purpose I have come forth." 'And He was preaching in their synagogues throughout all Galilee, and casting out demons' (Mark 1:38-39).
>
> Jesus 'appointed twelve, that they might be with Him and that He might send them out to preach' (Mark 3:14).
>
> Jesus said, "Go into all the world and preach the Gospel to Every Creature" (Mark 16:15).

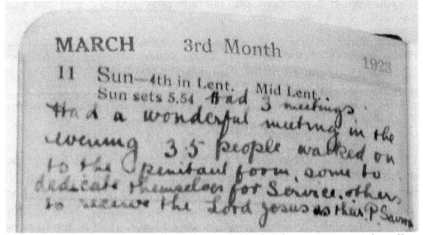

March 1923, Lizzie Howells at Ashton-Under-Lyne, a town six miles from Manchester, England: 'Had 3 meetings. Had a wonderful meeting in the evening 35 people walked on to the penitent form [altar at front], some to dedicate themselves for service, others to receive the Lord Jesus as their P[ersonal] Saviour.'

The Holy Spirit warned me, "Don't preach anything higher than what you have proved or I will compel you to walk it back." And several times He compelled me to walk it back.[1]

All the time we try to do things that God has not given us to do. If there is anything to do He will tell me quicker than anything. He is God and will do things far better than I can. Never do anything unless God tells you. You will have enough to do with what He gives you. Give all your attention to it.

Life is serious. You have given your bodies to the Holy Spirit. You have no right to entertain yourself by talking to people. Tact: Say only what is essential. Be alone with God. Do not allow thoughts to come to you. I never searched for a thing to satisfy my curiosity if God had not disclosed it.

"This is the Father's will which hath sent Me, that of all which He hath given Me I should lose nothing..." (John 6:39).

When the Lord made me to abide for a soul, I did nothing else. If, after the Holy Spirit said to me, "Build Me a College," [in 1922] I did everything else, but failed to build a College, I should be condemned. It was a College I had to build. The one thing He gives me to do is the one thing that I do. Anything else I do not count. All of me in this Vision [the Every Creature Vision/Commission].[2]

Look to God only. Ask men for nothing. If you rely on anything of yourself and not on God, He will pick you out and put you aside.

Rees Howells' principle was: Don't make appeals for money: '...Taking nothing from the Gentiles' (3 John 1:17), but appeal only to God, to provide for your needs and if called to, those of others. If you trust in your ability to influence people you may build the Tower of Babel and call it God's work.

Don't watch another person and imitate him. Can't you stand alone with the Holy Spirit? To imitate others is the most devilish thing you can do. Everything has been copied and the Devil has used it to the full. He is an imitator and an infiltrator.[3] The enemy has been coming in and using phrases I have used and positions I have gained [probably other preachers], all on a low level. It is not trying to get victory. It is having it without effort, I have never forced religion down people's throats, but my work gives me the opportunity to speak of God [to the postman, milkman, solicitor, agent, bank manager etc.]. I am not willing to do all this insulting: asking people if they are saved and so on. No, I ask nobody to believe anything unless I can prove it (Daniel 1:8-16, Daniel purposed in his heart that he would not defile himself with the portion of the king's delicacies and asked the steward to test him and his friends for ten days, eating only vegetables and drinking water. At the end of ten days their features appeared better than all the young men who ate the portion of the king's delicacies).

I would always be tested and come to the place that I could not do it myself. Then I would ask the Holy Spirit to do it through me. When I was called to build a College, it was only natural that I should receive thousands of pounds. The Lord saw the danger. He caused me to leave the Mission [SAGM in June 1923] and shut myself up in my room [in Brynamman] away from people. For ten months I went through the Bible, spending from 6am to

5pm, in my room, and having only one meal a day. [This was ten hours a day reading the Bible and in prayer (around one hour break, but not lunch, as Rees ate at 5pm) for more than 300 days. From late October 1923 into 1924, Mrs Howells was furnishing Glynderwen, buying rugs, drapes and linen etc.].

Abiding is not always doing things such as fasting and giving away clothes, but being in the Lord's Presence all the time. It may not show outwardly, but you know it inwardly. I never throw my life or my health away. [Fasting for too many days when inexperienced or giving away your only coat in winter to the detriment of yourself]. I never neglect my health.

When Elijah found that the woman was making her last meal, he did not sacrifice his meal and consider himself the meekest man on the face of the earth (1 Kings 17:8-16).

I have never done anything foolish in the sight of the people. If the wisdom of God is in you, you will not do such things. You might think Samuel was not being straight when he anointed David in secret, not at all; you are not bound to tell all your plans to the Devil (1 Samuel 16:1-13). [Learn to keep secrets in the Kingdom, do not publish abroad your intent, unless the Holy Spirit has told you to, e.g. Rees Howells buying the Derwen Fawr Estate, which was a step of faith].

Do not try to do God's part; do your own. All the time you try to make your own *deliverance [by hinting or trying to influence others to give. *An answer to prayer, often financial], instead of allowing God to do His part. It is your part to abide and seek the Kingdom, it is His part to move people to deliver you.

Jesus said, "If you abide in Me, and My words abide in you, you will ask what you desire, and it shall be done for you" (John 15:7).

Jesus said, "But seek first the Kingdom of God and His righteousness, and all these things shall be added to you. Therefore do not worry about tomorrow, for tomorrow will worry about its own things. Sufficient for the day is its own trouble" (Matthew 6:33-34). Hanani the seer said, "For the eyes of the Lord run to and fro throughout the whole earth, to show Himself strong in the behalf of them whose heart is perfect towards him..." (2 Chronicles 16:9).

We continually try to do God's part. Our part is to see that our heart is perfect towards Him, and to trust Him for everything else. The Lord wants you to come to your extremity and see that you cannot do it. All you have to do is your part, not God's. I have always known my part and God's part. The difficulty is not to do, but to remain quiet. All the time there is this trying. It is not that. Is it God's work or is it man's work? If it is God's work, I am like a child. All I have to do is to abide, to refrain from iniquity, to keep quiet, until He tells me to do something. If it is man's work I am to do it like an ordinary man. He does not throw me out altogether. [We must walk in the wisdom that He has given us; use our commonsense and be faithful stewards in all that is entrusted to us]. If I want to know what colour to paint the new laboratory, I do not go to God about it. He would say, "Paint it any colour you like. Any colour you choose will be very nice." But in anything He gives me, I am very steady.

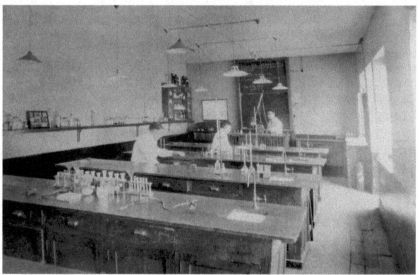

School Science Laboratory 1949, located on the Glynderwen Estate, from the Bible College School Prospectus, May 1950

The Bible College School became Emmanuel Grammar School in April 1949, but the Prospectus for May 1950 had not been updated, possibly due to Emmanuel Preparatory School (located on Sketty and Derwen Fawr Estates), sharing a Prospectus. The teacher at the front is John Rocha. In January 1940, aged twelve John became a boarder at the School in Swansea. His dad was of Jewish ancestry, a medical missionary in Brazil and later associated with the Mildmay Mission to the Jews. John became a student-teacher at the school in 1948, whilst training at Trinity College, Carmarthen, and then worked full-time at Emmanuel Grammar School from September 1949, teaching General

Science and Bible Knowledge. He spent two months in Israel in 1976 and emigrated to Israel in 1977. However, he returned to Swansea at the request of Samuel Rees Howells and Dr. Kingsley Priddy to help out for a few terms until a full-time teacher could be found. His mortal remains were buried in Haifa, Israel, in April 2013.

When you come to this position you do not lose your head over a little work you do. It is the relationship which is the thing. A man promoted to be a General would not stay on the field when there ceased to be a need for him there. When I work for God, my mind is right on it for the time, but afterwards I go home (John 17:17-26, part of Jesus' High Priestly prayer).

Have no ambition to do what a man can do. 'But without faith it is impossible to please Him, for he who comes to God must believe that He is, and that He is a rewarder of those who diligently seek Him' (Hebrews 11:6).

People will work for God, but not for you. If it is God's work, people will work. This work is too sacred for you to touch it. We are all after work [labouring like Martha] and not after giving our time to become like the Master [as Mary sat at His feet]. In anything spiritual you do not bring your natural activity in. Your effort is a hindrance where God is. This is a thing of itself and it does not prevent you from doing your other work to perfection.

If you want the Devil to give you work, do nothing. If you have nothing to do in the morning, the Devil will suggest something for you to do, and you will do it. Then in the evening you will wonder if you did the wrong thing – and you did.

While Moses was on the Mount, the Devil was getting at the people, when the Master was in the Garden of Gethsemane he was getting at the disciples. Mind that he does not get at you. Hide in the cleft of the rock. 'All seek their own' (Philippians 2:21). You do not know what you will do if you go back.

I know how rough a man is by the thoughts that the Devil throws against me. Thoughts, suggestions and temptations are not sin. Thank God they are not sin! Temptation is not sin, but yielding is sin. The Devil did not get me to yield. Take care that the Devil does not put temptation in your way to turn your attention from this Vision to reach Every Creature.

'Blessed is the man who endures temptation; for when he has been approved, he will receive the crown of life which the Lord has promised to those who love Him. Let no one say when he is tempted, "I am tempted by God," for God cannot be tempted by evil, nor does He Himself tempt anyone. But each one is tempted when he is drawn away by his own desires and enticed. Then, when desire has conceived, it gives birth to sin; and sin, when it is full-grown, brings forth death' (James 1:12-15).

People without the Holy Spirit are always doing things when there is a test. Are you bothered with non-essentials? Don't allow any triflings to touch you. Don't miss this. Don't live in a small world at this time. This dressing up of the old man is a devilish thing, when it is done with an emphasis that is not on souls.

Tiredness is of the enemy. A person with the Holy Spirit living in him is full of life.

'It is vain for you to rise up early, to sit up late, to eat the bread of sorrows; for so He gives His beloved sleep' (Psalm 127:2).

Jesus in the Garden of Gethsemane found His disciples sleeping. He said to Peter, "What! Could you not watch with Me one hour? Watch and pray, lest you enter into temptation. The spirit indeed is willing, but the flesh is weak" (Matthew 26:40-41).

A. J. Russell was a famous London Fleet Street journalist who interviewed Prime Ministers, Heads of State, European Royalty, nobility, politicians, prohibitionists, pioneering aviators, authors, celebrities, musicians, murderers on death row, bishops, as well as leaders, including Gandhi and General William Booth. He later became a newspaper editor and then worked freelance.

In 1939, A. J. Russell was Rees Howells' editor on *God Challenges the Dictators* (1939) and Literary Agent into 1940. Russell got right with God in the same year that Rees Howells opened the Bible College of Wales in 1924. However, it was not until 1931 with Russell's introduction to the Oxford Group, which was ten years old, that there began a real work of sanctification in his life. This included forsaking and confession of sin, restitution and a serious concern for the advancement of the Kingdom of God. He became a Life-Changer, the name given to people connected with the Oxford Group, who in 1931 had more than one thousand groups across the world including: Canada, USA, Europe, South America, Australia, South Africa, Egypt and China.

A. J. Russell in his first Christian book *For Sinners Only* (1932) wrote: 'If a man's life is thoroughly integrated in God, he finds a dominant purpose in which everything fits. It does not mean rigidity, but being so flexible as to be responsive to unexpected opportunities giving further opportunities to serve God, whose ways are not men's way, as Paul found when he was going his roundabout way to Rome.'

The leader of the Oxford Group was referred to only as "Frank," he lived by faith for more than a decade and was middle-aged. A. J. Russell wrote: 'Through his constant practice of losing his life daily he has come to find himself. He awakes in the morning with the idea that today is not his day, but God's day. Losing his life, he finds it all the time. The result of his discipline is abounding energy – which he is confident comes from the Holy Spirit. This discipline at the heart of the movement means complete freedom.'[4]

Even what you think is essential talk is nothing. [Jesus said, "For every idle word men may speak, they will give account of it in the day of judgment. For by your words you will be justified, and by your words you will be condemned" Matthew 12:36-37]. I was never unwise. I never went around offending people. I did what He told me. The thing of itself became a conflict. [The Holy Spirit in Rees was stronger than the unbelief in religious critics].

You carry something with you [and bear the burden of criticism], so that people do not insult the Holy Spirit. You may test anybody but your own people, and the Holy Spirit does not take it.

When Jesus 'had come to His own country, He taught them in their synagogue, so that they were astonished and said, "Where did this Man get this wisdom and these mighty works? Is this not the carpenter's son? Is not His mother called Mary? And His brothers James, Joses, Simon, and Judas? And His sisters, are they not all with us? Where then did this Man get all these things?" So they were offended at Him. But Jesus said to them, "A prophet is not without honour except in his own country and in his own house." Now He did not do many mighty works there because of their unbelief' (Matthew 13:54-58).

I would not take a place at home as a son that they would not give to the Saviour. It was only during the clash that I proved to them that I was willing to take any place at home as a son, but not at the cost of preferring them to the Saviour. [Rees welcomed the tramps at the family home but some members disapproved, yet the Saviour welcomed all. This was the test, to love the unlovable even when family resisted]. It was only while there was a conflict with the Holy Spirit that I was against them.[5]

1911 Carmarthen Theological College students and staff. Rees Howells is standing, second row from top, third from the right

I wrote every week when I was in America [1902-1904]. I wrote every Friday when I was in the College [at Carmarthen]. I have always been on the best terms with my family from the moment they acknowledged the claims of the Holy Spirit.

In around February 1911, Rees Howells visited America with a friend for three months and began to preach again. Back at Brynamman, Wales, with his wife they attended Gibea Congregational Church where a move of the Spirit broke out and Rees was called into the ministry by the Lord.

When Rees Howells was a ministerial student, he was sent to various local chapels during the weekends to preach. On one occasion, the students were watching a list of preaching engagements being put up on a board, when one of them nudged Rees Howells and whispered to him not to take a certain chapel because they gave only ten shillings (10s in 1912 is worth £61 in 2022), but to go to another, where they gave fourteen shillings (£85.40 in 2022). As a married man, Rees had to pay twenty-eight shillings (£170.80 in 2022) rent on the following Monday. Apart from receiving it from a chapel, there seemed no likelihood from a natural standpoint of the money arriving in time for collection on Monday. The Holy Spirit taught him never to "run-on the spoil," (to take advantage), so it did not take him a moment to decide on the chapel; the one that gave the least money.

On the Saturday, Rees set out on the long walk across the fields to the chapel and on arriving sought out the home of a believer who was to give him hospitality. (Because some preaching appointments were difficult to get to, often preachers would arrive on Saturday evening, have a meal, a bed for the night, breakfast and then take the morning service, followed by lunch. The preacher could take an afternoon or evening service and then depart for home, whilst some hosts provided food before the evening service). While Rees was at his host's home, he was told of a tragedy that had just occurred. A man with three small children had been bereaved of his wife.

On Sunday, Rees Howells went early to the chapel, as was his custom (the host accompanied him), and waited there so that the Holy Spirit would "change the atmosphere" before he began to preach. Whilst there, the widower also arrived early and sat down in one of the front seats and the host pointed out the man. Rees Howells looked at him and the Holy Spirit asked him if he would give the man the money he would receive for preaching, instead of putting it towards his rent. Rees Howells decided to give the man the money and trust the Lord to supply the rent in full. The moment he made the decision he came into great liberty, the Presence of God was felt in the chapel, and when he began to preach it was with such power that a deep impression was made on the congregation.

After the morning service, Rees Howells learnt further facts about the unfortunate widower: he was well-to-do and owned several houses. Rees Howells then saw that the Holy Spirit had been merely testing his willingness to give and he no longer felt constrained to do so. He continued in the same liberty for the rest of the day. The people were so stirred during the evening service that at the close, a deacon rose to his feet and said, "We have often had special speakers here, but we have never heard preaching like this before. I feel we cannot let this young man go with a gift of only ten shillings." Rees Howells rose to protest. The Deacon raised his hand authoritatively, "Sit down young man," he said, "This is our business." Rees Howells complied and the chapel took-up a special collection. At that time in Wales, it was unusual for people to carry much money with them to chapel; it seemed out-of-keeping with the Lord's Day. The collection consisted of a large quantity of pennies, halfpennies and farthings. It was not until Rees was about to retire for the night that he found an opportunity to count the money. It was twenty-eight shillings to the farthing, the exact amount for the rent! Rees was afraid to blow the candle out (no electricity) as the angels seemed so near!

Chapter 8

Fasting in the Kingdom

Jesus said, "When you fast do not be like the hypocrites, with a sad countenance. For they disfigure their faces that they may appear before men to be fasting. But you, when you fast anoint your head and wash your face, so that you do not appear to men to be fasting, but to your Father who is in the secret place, and your Father who sees in secret will reward you openly" (Matthew 6:16-18).

The disciples of John came to Jesus and said, "Why do we and the Pharisees fast often, but Your disciples do not fast?" Jesus replied, "Can the friends of the bridegroom mourn as long as the bridegroom is with them? But the days will come when the bridegroom will be taken away from them, and then they will fast" (Matthew 9:14-15).

In beginning to build a life of faith or a ministry, do not build on anything but abiding. Faith is the outcome of the walk with God. Real obedience gives faith. All my deliverances have come through my obedience.

I nearly always carrying a burden – and I am better with it. "Rejoice in the Lord always and again I say, Rejoice" (Philippians 4:4). This is the consequence. You do rejoice when you come to a place of abiding. If you come to it the other things will be added to you.

If you want to fast during Lent, fast in this way: let the Holy Spirit love others through you as the Lord Jesus loved you. Do not allow a single thought to come against another. If you give up food *with* this, that is alright, but it is of no use without it. The other way is alright if the Lord calls a man to it. When I did it He made me give my food away to help others.[1]

Fasting is not necessarily just abstaining from food, but to walk in the statutes of God and to uphold justice and mercy. See Isaiah 1:12-17, Isaiah chapters 58-59 and Matthew chapters 5-7. Jesus said, "Woe to you, scribes and Pharisees, hypocrites! For you pay tithe of mint and anise and cummin, and have neglected the weightier matters of the law: justice and mercy and faith. These you ought to have done, without leaving the others undone" (Matthew 23:23).

James wrote: 'Pure and undefiled religion before God and the Father is this: to visit orphans and widows in their trouble and to keep oneself unspotted from the world' (James 1:27).

The biggest fasting you can do is to keep to this abiding: to 'esteem others better than yourself' (Philippians 2:3), and to pray for others to be delivered (Cf. Philippians 2:4, the interests of others), and then He will deliver you. Don't rush into foolish things and then go back to worse than you have left. Giving up food is not essential. Along with this spend time to allow the Lord to speak to you, and to think on what He did for you on Good Friday. I remember the first Lent I spent with the Master. I had such fellowship with Him that I did not go back to ordinary life for two and a half years.[2]

Some Evangelical Churches do not follow Lent, but Rees Howells and the Bible College used this period to reflect upon the Saviour's sacrifice for mankind.

The period of Lent is forty days leading up to Easter, remembering the death and resurrection of Jesus Christ. It begins on Shrove Tuesday (Pancake Day) and is a period of prayer and fasting, giving something up, especially sweet foods that we enjoy to focus more on Jesus. It reminds us of Jesus' forty days in the wilderness, where He fasted and was tempted by the Devil (Matthew 4:1-11, Mark 1:12-13 and Luke 4:1-13). After this, Jesus' ministry began.

Easter does not have a fixed date. For the Western Church it is celebrated in March or April, whilst for the Eastern Church it can be as much as five weeks apart or on the same day. The difference began with the change from the Julian Calendar to the Gregorian Calendar in 1752 in England and its colonies. New Year's Day which was formerly on 25 March, was moved to 1 January. In September 1752, eleven days were skipped to bring the new calendar into alignment.[3]

If you wish to know what the Master suffered for you, let the Holy Spirit take you through this experience in the next six weeks and make it real to you. Nothing could take the Master's attention. Allow the Holy Spirit to give you a chance to walk exactly as the

Master walked, for He knows exactly what the Master suffered. He became sin for you.

> 'For He made Him who knew no sin to be sin for us, that we might become the righteousness of God in Him' (2 Corinthians 5:21).

There is nothing in the world that will make you men and women except understanding what you deserve for your sins and what the Master took for you. [Christ loved you when you were unlovable in the eyes of the world and you deserved Hell because 'the wages of sin is death, but the gift of God is eternal life in Jesus Christ our Lord']. You do not have to try to love one another. Say to the Holy Spirit, "I am going to give all my attention to You. Let me go through some of the things the Master went through." You will never have the faintest idea of what the Master went through until the Holy Spirit makes it real to you. After two or three Lents you may walk it.

When God requires us to do anything, He makes Himself responsible for the consequences. For example, take the fasting in the first chapter of Daniel. Can you imagine that God would require a man to do anything that would impair his health? The young men were to be tested. The Holy Spirit is always fair and considers others. He will never guide you to do a thing which will impair your health and make you less useful in the future. There is a guidance in this life, 'A highway…the wayfaring, men, though fools, shall not err therein' (Isaiah 35:8).

God never does away with natural law and our bodies would never allow us to do things by leaps and bounds, or we should have to pay the penalty.

> This is what happened to Evan Roberts during the *Welsh Revival (1904-1905). He neglected times of rest and food, which led to several breakdowns. Later on Rees Howells was on good terms with Evan and called him a friend. For a period of time Evan would come to the Bible College and Rees and Evan would pray together.[4] See Appendix A.

In fasting one is worked up gradually, to overcome habits and lusts, and it is only the Holy Spirit bringing in the Divine Nature and replacing the self-craving nature of ours that will enable us to allow our bodies to be subject to the Spirit.

As a miner, Rees Howells was used to having four good meals a day. God did not call him immediately to have one meal every three days as his place of abiding and God never called him to a two week fast whilst down the mines as it would have been impossible without supernatural intervention. God gradually led Rees into not eating one meal a day, then only having two meals a day, then fasting an entire day, then having one meal every other day until he enjoyed his one meal every third day more than his previous four meals a day.

God knows your life and your responsibilities that you have with your family or at work, and if He calls you to intercession then He will give you a place of abiding that He knows you can cope with. God may not call you to fast, but God may tell you that your place of abiding is to pray in your tea break or to read certain books of the Bible. You may be called to give up certain drinks (perhaps sugary soft drinks or caffeine) or sweet foods or any combination. Often an abiding is something that has a hold over you so that during your intercession you are also helped to break an addiction, unhealthy lifestyle or to help you die to self, as in the abiding of a Nazirite (Numbers 6), not shaving or cutting your hair! You may be called to eat only simple foods, like Daniel (Daniel 1:8-16) or to only eat certain types of food, e.g. one bowl of rice a day as you identify with the person or people you are interceding for. Your abiding may mean not going to a certain place (a place which is not sinful) which you are accustomed to attend. You may be called to read your Bible in your lunch break, or not to weigh yourself during your fast, or any combination of abiding – whatever the Holy Spirit says. Experience has taught intercessors that God starts off small and gradually increases responsibility as you climb the ladder of intercession. Whatever you are called to do, be obedient.[5]

When the Holy Spirit comes in, He will point out scores of things to us that we have taken to be harmless and essential to life, as nothing but habits and lusts of the flesh. The Lord Himself said to the imperfect disciples when they asked Him why they could not cast the devil out, "This kind cometh forth, but by prayer and fasting." [Deliverance/exorcism was not unknown to Rees Howells as the strong man was bound (Mark 3:27), his goods were plundered and those under his sway were set free and delivered from evil and oppressing spirits].

We often wonder why in this generation we cannot cast out devils. The answer is simple, that we have left out of our lives this very important thing – fasting! Moffatt's translation is: "Nothing can make this kind come out but prayer and fasting." Some people have been comforting themselves because two of the best manuscripts omit "and fasting," and if any one is glad it is omitted it is the Devil himself, because it is the missing link to cast him out.[6]

> A man spoke to Jesus about his mute son, because His disciples could not cast the demon out. He said, "Wherever it seizes him, it throws him down; he foams at the mouth, gnashes his teeth and becomes rigid." The boy was brought to Jesus and the evil spirit convulsed him and he fell on the ground, foaming at the mouth. The man said, "If You can do anything, have compassion on us and help us." Jesus replied, "If you can believe, all things are possible to him who believes." The father cried out and said with tears, "Lord, I believe; help my unbelief!" Jesus rebuked the unclean spirit, "Deaf and dumb spirit, I command you, come out of him and enter him no more!" The spirit cried out, convulsed him greatly and came out. Jesus took him by the hand and lifted him up. The disciples asked Jesus privately, "Why could we not cast it out?" He said, "This kind can come out by nothing but prayer and fasting" (Mark 9:17-29). Notice that the boy did not need prayer for healing, but prayer for deliverance, to be set free from an oppressing spirit, a demon, and then he was healed.

The motive the Lord had in calling me to fasting was to make the body subject to the Spirit. I fasted to give my food to the hungry, not to afflict my soul (Isaiah 58:5-7, to give bread to the hungry). I was working hard at the time. I was a spiritually minded man. I never had a headache or indigestion. On the way over to the Mission, I was in the Presence of God. I was like light from Heaven when I went in. I never afflicted myself. Do not fast unless the Lord tells you to do it for a purpose. Many have done it and have said that nothing has come of it.

> Before Rees Howells went to Africa in 1915, he stayed with a farmer who would never allow anyone to speak to him on spiritual matters. In order to prepare himself for the mission field, Rees waited on the Lord for several days in prayer and fasting. The farmer became very subdued. Every time he came into the house he asked his wife, "Is he still there?"
> The Holy Spirit in Rees brought in an atmosphere of the Presence of God. The same as when Rees Howells was to

speak at chapel, church or mission hall; he would turn up early to pray and allow the atmosphere to be changed by the Holy Spirit (as referenced in chapter 7). This made it easier to preach, and for a response to the claims of Calvary, full surrender and the importance of the Great Commission with fields that are 'white unto harvest' (John 4:35), but 'few labourers' (Matthew 9:37).

We are inclined to imitate Daniel and his companions in what they did in regard to food [water and vegetables only]. We should not follow them in what they did outwardly, but in their stand for God and their refusal to compromise to obtain this world's advantages. It is not the food; that is where the Devil comes in; it is man giving obedience to God and being trained. The greatest fasting is where the Holy Spirit deals with your thoughts and motives. When I became a minister, the Lord told me to put away fasting so that others would not imitate me, and yet not be changed, like Buddha.

'Two things I request of You (deprive me not before I die). Remove falsehood and lies far from me; give me neither poverty nor riches – feed me with the food allotted to me; lest I be full and deny You, and say, "Who is the Lord?" Or lest I be poor and steal, and profane the name of my God' (Proverbs 30:7-9).

"Is it a fast that I have chosen, a day for a man to afflict his soul? Is it to bow down his head like a bulrush [a tall waterside plant], and to spread out sackcloth and ashes? Would you call this a fast, and an acceptable day to the Lord? Is this not the fast that I have chosen: To loose the bonds of wickedness, to undo the heavy burdens, to let the oppressed go free, and that you break every yoke? Is it not to share your bread with the hungry, and that you bring to your house the poor who are cast out; when you see the naked, that you cover him, and not hide yourself from your own flesh? Then your light shall break forth like the morning, your healing shall spring forth speedily, and your righteousness shall go before you; the glory of the Lord shall be your rear guard."

"If you extend your soul to the hungry and satisfy the afflicted soul, then your light shall dawn in the darkness, and your darkness shall be as the noonday. The Lord will guide you continually, and satisfy your soul in drought, and strengthen your bones; you shall be like a watered garden, and like a spring of water, whose waters do not fail" (Isaiah 58:5-8, 10-11).

Chapter 9

The Prayers of Faith

Jesus said, "In this manner, therefore, pray, 'Our Father in Heaven, hallowed be Your name. Your Kingdom come. Your will be done on earth as it is in Heaven. Give us this day our daily bread. And forgive us our debts, as we forgive our debtors. And do not lead us into temptation, but deliver us from the evil one. For Yours is the Kingdom and the power and the glory forever. Amen' " (Matthew 6:9-13).

Jesus said, "I say to you, whatever things you ask when you pray, believe that you receive them, and you will have them. And whenever you stand praying, if you have anything against anyone, forgive him that your Father in Heaven may also forgive you your trespasses. But if you do not forgive, neither will your Father in Heaven forgive your trespasses" (Mark 11:24-26).

When you intercede in the prayers of the Holy Spirit your supplications will never be for self or self-advancement. We pray His will to be done on earth as it is in Heaven.

What you pray you are not running headlong without knowing where you are. You have to start right at the bottom like babes. All you need to do is to cry for your needs as a baby cries. There are two kinds of prayer:
1. The need causing us to pray. When we see a need, if we are impressed by it, we take it to the Lord in prayer. We have a perfect right to do that, but we do not always take it in the Lord's time.

Is it God's time to meet this need or is there a deeper truth God is trying to reveal by holding back the answer? Moses had to be broken in the wilderness, to die to self, and Egypt taken out of him. All this had to happen *before* he could be led by God and lead the Israelites out of Egypt. Remember that "no" is also an answer, though may not be the one we want to hear. The answer of silence, no response, is often a period to reflect and wait.

Joseph was sold as a slave by his brothers, falsely accused in Potiphar's household, thrown into prison for at least a decade, but was raised up in a day, as the Prime Minster of Egypt, second only to Pharaoh. At least thirteen years elapsed from when Joseph's brothers sold him into slavery until he was raised up as Prime Minister of Egypt (Genesis 37:2 and Genesis 41:46). It is believed that he spent from 10-12 years in prison. It was around twenty years before he saw his brothers again, based on the seven good years, followed by seven years of famine.

2. The Holy Spirit revealing God's will in prayer. The great principles here are to bring about those things which it is God's will to do and that we should lose nothing.

'Now He who searches the hearts knows what the mind of the Spirit is, because He makes intercession for the saints according to the will of God' (Romans 8:27).

Jesus said, "For I have come down from Heaven, not to do My own will, but the will of Him who sent Me. This is the will of the Father who sent Me, that of all He has given Me I should lose nothing, but should raise it up at the last day" (John 6:38-39).

If you are in need, you ought to be alone with God. When you are alone with God, be on your knees [Rees is talking to young men and women who can get back up from their knees]. Remember that you are a sinful man that the Lord cannot come near you until He has cleared you out of yourselves. It is not a struggle, but as though you had an afternoon to spend with your parents after a long time away. You would not allow anyone to disturb you. Don't allow anyone or anything to disturb you. Not once, not one thing.

Being in the attitude of prayer keeps people away, but keeping people at arms length in the flesh is no good.

Get out of yourselves. See that it is God you are asking and He the Creator. Is He a real Person to you? Do you speak to Him as though He is really there? Do you know that in all this the Holy Spirit will not allow a single doubt in me? See that you are speaking to the Creator.

'That which we have seen and heard we declare to you, that you also may have fellowship with us; and truly our fellowship is with the Father and with His Son Jesus Christ. And these things we write to you that your joy may be full' (1 John 1:3-4).

You must know exactly what God has told you to do. Do not make your own prayers. Go before God and find out what He wants you to pray for. Where you fail, and all fail who have not the Holy Spirit, it's because you make your own prayers. [You prayed your own thoughts, ideas and feelings. The Twelve Apostles would have made Jesus the King of Israel if it was their will be done. God's will was to make Him King of kings through His death and resurrection]. You cannot fail unless you undertake a prayer that God has not given you.

I am not at sea [aimlessly floating around] while I refrain from praying, a thing that the Lord has not told me. You do not come into this and the reason is that the Lord has not worked you out of yourself.

The Lord told me:

1. "You are not to do anything."

2. "Do not pray a single prayer except those I give you. Leave all your own prayers."

3. "I will make you responsible for every prayer that you pray."[1]

So I had nothing to do but have fellowship with Him and be made like the Son of God.

> Jesus said, "For if you love those who love you, what reward have you? Do not even the tax collectors do the same? And if you greet your brethren only, what do you do more than others? Do not even the tax collectors do so? Therefore you shall be perfect, just as your Father in Heaven is perfect" (Matthew 5:46-48).

Leave all other prayers and pray the essential prayers. Pray prayers in which you must be delivered. What you 'need' is deliverance where you are. If it is health you need, pray for that.

Where to move Him? On your essentials. If you are in need because you stepped out, go back and get that need supplied. The Lord told His disciples to go out taking nothing and that the labourer is worthy of his hire (Matthew 10:9-10).

> Jesus 'called the twelve to Himself and began to send them out two by two, and gave them power over unclean spirits. He commanded them to take nothing for the journey except a staff – no bag, no bread, no copper in their money belts – but to wear sandals, and not to put on two tunics. So they went out and preached that people should repent. And they cast out many

demons, and anointed with oil many who were sick, and healed them (Mark 6:7-9, 12-13).

You remain undelivered as though it was pleasing God! I want you to move God in every meeting. There is one thing you must have, and that is victory where you are.

You must succeed in getting your personal prayers – your needs met – before you join in the Holy Spirit's great prayers. As a soldier, learn to win one-on-one battles in training before you can be promoted to a Major or a General. Rees Howells told many prospective students to pray in their first term's fees of £10 as a sign, "a seal" that they were meant to be at the Bible College. It was the same with visitors who wanted to attend the Every Creature Conference, but could not afford the reduced cost. They were told, as it was already subsidised (by fifty percent), they should pray for the money. If God wanted them to attend, He would provide for their needs.

Isaiah and Jeremiah had different messages in conditions that appeared similar. In the second siege, men in the flesh would pray like Isaiah. Men in the flesh always copy (2 Kings chapter 19, Isaiah reassures Hezekiah over the King of Assyria's threats to invade. Jeremiah chapter 37, Jeremiah warns King Zedekiah over the invading Babylonians).

For Isaiah, during the reign of King Hezekiah it was God's will to deliver the people from the enemy. For Jeremiah, during King Zedekiah's reign, it was God's will to punish the rebellious people. The people of Israel wanted to be delivered on both occasions, but it was the godly prophets who knew God's will, and for Jeremiah it was a time of captivity, not deliverance, regardless of what was prayed. At other times you may be forbidden to pray: "Do not pray for this people" (Jeremiah 7:16-17, Jeremiah 11:14-15, Jeremiah 14:11-12). There is also a point of no return, when God has resolutely decided on His judgment because sin has run its course. These are times when no prayers can prevail. God said to Ezekiel, "Son of man, when a land sins against Me by persistent unfaithfulness, I will stretch out My hand against it; I will cut off its supply of bread, send famine on it, and cut off man and beast from it. Even if these three men, Noah, Daniel, and Job, were in it, they would deliver only themselves by their righteousness" (Ezekiel 14:13-14).

God said to Jeremiah, "Even if Moses and Samuel stood before Me, My mind would not be favourable toward this people. Cast them out of My sight, and let them go forth. And it shall be, if they say to you, 'Where should we go?' then you shall tell them, 'Thus says the Lord: "Such as are for death, to death; and such as are for the sword, to the sword; and such as are for the famine, to the famine; and such as are for the captivity, to the captivity" (Jeremiah 15:1-2).

If you fight the battles of the Holy Spirit, He will help you when you are in need on the mission field.

'To the intent that now the manifold wisdom of God might be made known by the Church to the principalities and powers in the heavenly places, according to the eternal purpose which He accomplished in Christ Jesus our Lord' (Ephesians 3:10-11).
'For we do not wrestle against flesh and blood, but against principalities, against powers, against the rulers of the darkness of this age, against spiritual hosts of wickedness in the heavenly places' (Ephesians 6:12).

There is a quietness over the College between four and five o'clock in the morning; I pray and the Lord shows me what to do (Lent, 1938).[2]

Believe continually and pray when the need comes. I am going to be tested Monday or Tuesday. I am not doubting now. Would I pray if I was doubting? Oh no! Fancy praying when you are doubting!

Not a need, but only a prompting of the Holy Spirit should inspire a prayer. There is no fear in the prompting of the Holy Spirit, which should inspire a prayer. There is no fear in the life of faith. It is sane and intelligent.

It appears to be a very simple truth that every prayer can be answered. Dr. Andrew Murray used to say, "The meaning of prayer is answer." [Perhaps the answer is "no." What is the will of the Lord? Do not confuse this with wishful thinking, one's own desires or preferences].

"If ye shall ask anything in My Name, I will do it" (John 14:14).

"If you abide in Me and My words abide in you, you will ask what you desire, and it shall be done for you" (John 15:7).

'By this we know that we abide in Him and He in us, because He has given us of His Spirit' (1 John 4:13).

In Africa, I was on my knees at a quarter to five in the morning, and I let everyone of the people pass before me. [Rees was visualising the people and thus praying for them as they passed before his mind. He was not praying in public like the Pharisees, to be seen by men]. At six o'clock we rang the bell. The moment there is to be a change; He calls me to His Presence at four o'clock in the morning [woken up by God to pray]. If not, He does not call me. When He has given me a message I come free.[3]

1918 Rees Howells teaching in Evangelism Class to local evangelists and Christian workers, Rusitu, Gazaland

In experience, we so often prove that the meaning of prayer is not answer, simply because our prayers are not given to us by the Holy Spirit, and they are not according to God's will. He does not listen to the prayers of the old man. Prayer to the old man is like music, but there's no outcome to it.

Do not rush into prayer; the Holy Spirit will not allow you to play with the Word of God. If you leave unanswered any prayer that has been given to you, you disobey the Holy Spirit. (Exodus 10:24-29, Pharaoh told Moses to go and serve God, but let your flocks and livestock stay behind, which was contrary to what God wanted, so Moses refused).

> Jesus said, "All that the Father gives Me will come to Me, and the one who comes to Me I will by no means cast out. For I have come down from Heaven, not to do My own will, but the will of Him who sent Me. This is the will of the Father who sent Me, that of all He has given Me I should lose nothing, but should raise it up at the last day" (John 6:37-39).

When you have a need at a certain time, you are not to let that prayer go until the need is met. People cry when something touches them personally, but they do not cry for souls like that. [Never pray for another person to give, if you can give it yourself, that is, when you can answer your own prayer]. Be awake to these responsibilities. Do not nurse unbelief and failure. The Holy Spirit is not a failure. [The flesh fails every time because the flesh is of the world. The flesh can build the Tower of Babel, but God builds the New Jerusalem that will come down from Heaven].

> Rev. Jacob Christoph Kunzmann was the President of the Pacific Theological Seminary and formerly Superintendent of Home Mission. In *America and World Evangelization* (1920) he wrote: 'A farmer, pious after the fashion of many professors, lived at the edge of a town in which the mills and factories were closed and many were in need. More pious than others, he gathered his family morning and evening for worship. As he prayed, he prayed that God would have mercy upon the hungry and send them help. But, not pious enough, he gave them nothing. One morning his son said, "Father, give me the wheat in the wheat-bin." "Why, my son?" "I want to answer your prayer." It was no prayer. It was simply a mumbling of words. Prayer which will not send us in the way of fulfilment, with all our power and resources, is hypocrisy. God has no wheat fields or flour mills in Heaven. They are on earth, in the possession of His creatures, in order to feed its population. God blessed the labours of the farmer and gave him more than enough, in order that he might help the needy. The failure is at the distribution point, at the human end. So it is with the work of salvation. On God's part all has been done that can be done. Christ tasted death for every man. In the days of His flesh, the oxen and the fatlings had been killed and all was ready for the marriage, the consummation of redemption. Why must the chariots of God still wait? Simply because we have not gone out into the highways and hedges of the country or into the streets and lanes of the city, and by the constraining power of love compelled them to come in. The all-power of Jesus is ready to

Do not tell me you have this Divine Person dwelling in you if your prayers are not answered. The Holy Spirit made me responsible for my prayers. Before that I had the liberty to pray just what I liked and it did not matter whether the answer would come or not. If it was not answered I would put it down that it was not God's will. The question was, why did I pray it if it was not according to God's will? Until that time, I had never realised how I had been slighting God and His promises by not finding out why it was that my prayers were not answered.

The promise was: "If ye shall ask anything in My Name, I will do it, if ye abide in Me" (John 14:14, John 15:7).

We are dishonouring the words of our Lord if we continue to repeat prayers that are not answered. People may never come to know of it, but it weakens one's faith. Although the Lord is dealing with you and training you to be intercessors, that does not prevent Him from answering you on the way. When God lifts a burden He has put on you, you know prayer is answered.

The Holy Spirit never allowed me to pray more than one prayer at a time. It would be a very good lesson for you to learn this before you go out to these countries, so that you may get your prayers from the Holy Spirit and not be beating the air all the time. The way to have liberty in your prayers is to pray the prayers of the Spirit. You can be side-tracked in a second.

If you are in need and ought to be delivered [especially financially], you have not the right to bring in other prayers. In this I see the Devil very clearly: you do anything, and he lets you pray anything, except to be delivered. Would I pray anything else if I were not delivered? You do anything except go back to God.

Never pray another prayer until the previous one is answered. God requires you to carry this burden of the Kingdom and *no other*. You cannot carry the burden of the Kingdom and one of your own (Numbers chapter 11, the people complained against God and Moses in the wilderness; elders were appointed to help judge and thus ease Moses' burdens).

Jesus looked around and said, "How hard it is for those who have riches to enter the Kingdom of God!" (Mark 10:23).

Jesus said to them, "I must preach the Kingdom of God to the other cities also, because for this purpose I have been sent" (Luke 4:43).

Chapter 10

Praying For Provisions

Jesus said, "In this manner, therefore, pray: Our Father in Heaven, hallowed be Your name. Your Kingdom come. Your will be done on earth as it is in Heaven. Give us this day our daily bread. And forgive us our debts, as we forgive our debtors" (Matthew 6:9-10).

'My God shall supply all your need according to His riches in glory by Christ Jesus' (Philippians 4:19).

Why do you pray for anything else when you are not delivered for your needs? If you pray for China, how do you know if your prayers are answered? You would be foolish to pray prayers which are not in line with your work, to which there is no outcome.

You are not going to have these victories for nothing. Zacharias and Elizabeth were blameless before God, yet it seemed that those who ought to have had a son would be without one (Luke 1:6-7). He is a Sovereign God: you cannot force His hand. We are inclined to drop a prayer when it has not been answered after a long time (Luke chapter 1, the birth of John the Baptist, the forerunner, and the Messiah foretold to Mary).

If the Lord sees you let a prayer go, He will let it go. You go into the Presence of God, you come out – and it is just as good as if you had never been there.[1]

During the ten months spent by Rees Howells in praying for the large sums necessary to complete the purchase of Glyn Derwen, the first estate of the Bible College of Wales, he used to spend his days in prayer in his little upstairs bedroom in his mother's home at Brynamman, alone with God and His Word from 6am to 5pm, before he took his first meal. In the evenings, Rees continued in prayer with his newly found prayer partner, Tommy Howells. At that time Rees' mother was suffering from the illness which eventually caused her death. When she had a severe attack one morning, Rees went down to see her. Just then a neighbour came in (a culture of open-doors for neighbours) and spoke to him about Africa. There was nothing sinful in anything she said, but it drew his attention away from the subject of his prayer. When he returned to his room, he found that he could not get back into the Presence of God all day.

You say that you have given Him your bodies. Then surely He will not let you suffer, will He? If you have asked Him for an essential thing within the scope of your obedience, don't go astray until you get it. He says, "Go back to ask for a certain thing and if you do not at first get it, keep on going back until you are delivered."

You do not pray before a need arises, if you are up to it (Hebrews 11:1, faith is substance).

27 April 1938, the Bible College of Wales, Bankbook Statement, from Westminster Bank, Swansea. The signature of Rees Howells is not 'live ink' (by hand), but is from a rubber ink stamp for efficiency; sometimes it is upside down or double-stamped.

I have needed a sum of money for a time, but the Lord has given me other things to do. I continue to wait and believe, and on the day He will tell me, "Someone is going to give you that money. Pray for him now and help him." Then I pray and in about half an hour the whole thing is settled. There is no effort because He told me. [These sums of money were often delivered in person with a story behind it, or left anonymously inside the porch. Glynderwen and Derwen Fawr had no letterboxes].

Jesus said to His disciples, "Therefore I say to you, do not worry about your life, what you will eat; nor about the body, what you will put on. Life is more than food and the body is more than clothing. Consider the ravens, for they neither sow nor reap, which have neither storehouse nor barn; and God feeds them. Of how much more value are you than the birds? And which of you by worrying can add one cubit to his stature? If you then are not able to do the least, why are you anxious for the rest?" (Luke 12:22-26).

In the first place you must have faith; then you must have knowledge of God's will. If I went on praying and the donor had been moved, I should have lost my guidance. If on the other hand I left off praying and the donor had not been moved, my guidance would be equally wrong.[2] What we have to face is this: "Has the donor been moved or not?" We do not want any guesswork here. You must find this out every time. The Lord brings you to prayer, then to a place where you do nothing and He questions you. 'The angel of the Lord encamps all around those who fear Him and delivers them' (Psalm 34:7).

Do not pray until you are abiding (John chapter 15). It is not worth praying if you break one commandment.

When Abram was ninety-nine years old, the Lord appeared to Abram and said to him, "I am Almighty God; walk before Me and be blameless" (Genesis 17:1).

Jesus said, "Most assuredly, I say to you, he who believes in Me, the works that I do he will do also; and greater works than these he will do, because I go to My Father. And whatever you ask in My name, that I will do, that the Father may be glorified in the Son. If you ask anything in My name, I will do it. If you love Me, keep My commandments" (John 14:12-15).

For Rees Howells and his staff members, they had given up everything for the Kingdom and were part of the College community in the life of faith. Because of this they had a claim on God's Heavenly Treasury because they had forsaken all to follow

Him. They had made deposits and were therefore able to make withdrawals. If they had lived for self, they would have no claim as sons, but because they lived for Him and the Every Creature Commission, they had a claim on God's provision.

There is a struggle in this. It is alright to labour in prayer, but do not labour in unbelief; there must be obedience. It is hard to distinguish between labouring and struggling; you sweat in both, you know. [This reveals the intensity of some of Rees Howells' prayers and intercessions. Jesus in Gethsemane: 'And being in agony, He prayed more earnestly. Then His sweat became like great drops of blood falling down to the ground' (Luke 22:44)].

It is not that you have not been asking; the trouble is here: 'It is no more I that do it, but sin that dwelleth in me...the body of this death' (Romans 7:17, 24). [Another of Rees Howells' compound Scriptures]. When I pray that people may give to the Lord, it is easier than if I pray that they will give to me, for this is His work.

Whenever I needed anything, He told me *never* to go to the 'agent,' [asking a person, solicitation] but to come directly to Him, the Owner. Are you asking God, or are you doubting it? If you are in need because you stepped out in faith, ask God to do it. If you say man is a failure, let someone come in who can do it. It is not your struggling, it is asking. It is not that you are worthy; it is that you move the Creator.

A man cannot pray; the Holy Spirit can, God knows that you do not know how to pray as you ought. Why do you not allow the Holy Spirit to pray His prayers through you?

'Likewise the Spirit also helps in our weaknesses. For we do not know what we should pray for as we ought, but the Spirit Himself makes intercession for us with groanings which cannot be uttered. Now He who searches the hearts knows what the mind of the Spirit is, because He makes intercession for the saints according to the will of God' (Romans 8:26-27).

During one of the evening meetings at the Bible College, Rees Howells suddenly announced that the Lord told him to leave the subject of prayer and pray for Jack Wilson because his life was in danger. He was a former student from the late 1920s, early 1930s, a missionary to the Arabs and Bedouins. The events of the meeting were relayed to Jack. Sometime afterwards a letter came from Jack Wilson saying that at that very hour, two Arabs had been lurking outside his tent with the intent to kill him, but without any outward change in circumstances, they had changed their minds and gone away! The power of prayer, but more importantly, being led of the Spirit and acting in obedience. What if Rees Howells and the College had not stopped and prayed?

BEDOUINS OF THE SINAI PENINSULA MET BY MR. WILSON.

A BEDOUIN TENT IN THE DESERT, VISITED BY MR. JACK WILSON.

Jack Wilson, whose calling was to Arabia, 1933. The Arabian Peninsula now includes: Kuwait, Oman, Qatar, Saudi Arabia, the United Arab Emirates and Yemen, plus the southern portions of Iraq and Jordan. Top photo, Jack Wilson is far right with a family of Bedouins of the Sinai Peninsula, in Egypt. Below is a Bedouin tent which Jack Wilson visited to share the Good News and received nomadic hospitality of food, drink and shade.

BARCLAYS BANK (DOMINION, COLONIAL AND OVERSEAS)
(INCORPORATED IN THE UNITED KINGDOM WITH LIMITED LIABILITY)

JERUSALEM, 30th Septe., 193 7.
PALESTINE

EXCHANGE/Jb

The Bible College of Wales,
        Derwen Fawr,
              Swansea.

Dear Sirs,

        We thank you for your letter of the 24th instant,
enclosing cheque for £5.- for account of Mr. Jack Wilson of
Ajlun, Transjordan.

        Please note that this cheques was passed to the
credit of the Rev. John Wilson of Ajloun, Transjordan, and
we shall be glad if you will confirm our action.

                        Yours faithfully,

                        MANAGER.

Money from Rees Howells of the Bible College of Wales sent to a former student Jack Wilson of Ajloun, Transjordan, September 1937. £5 in 1937 is worth £370 in 2022. The Cheque was credited to Rev. John Wilson of Ajloun, who would forward the money to Jack. The man may have been related or it is a clerical error. Ajloun can also be spelled Ajlun and is a hilly town in present-day north Jordan. The distance by road from Ajloun to Jerusalem, Israel, is less than 80 miles.

I love Moses especially, because he came to the place where he could move God and prevail on Him to change His mind.

The Israelites made a Golden Calf and began to worship it when Moses was on the mountain, and the people were unrestrained. When Moses returned the following day, he said to the people, "You have committed a great sin. So now I will go up to the Lord; perhaps I can make atonement for your sin." Moses returned to the Lord and said, "Oh, these people have committed a great sin, and have made for themselves a god of gold! Yet now, if You will forgive their sin – but if not, I pray, blot me out of Your book which You have written" (Exodus 32:30-32).

Coal Mining Colliers at work from a from a South Wales postcard c.1910. Rees Howells was miner for many years and emigrated to America where the pay was superior. Rees' first mining job was at the local Tin Mill age twelve. As he was one year younger than legal requirements, his name was not on the payroll. He would wake up at 6am and not return home until nearly 6pm. A routine he kept up for ten years before sailing to America aged twenty-two, where men from his village sent a good report. One years wage in America was the same as five years wages in Wales! After Rees' conversion he no longer lived for money and pleasure, but for the will of God and Kingdom advancement.

I always pray through the Word. I never use my own thoughts, even in prayer. I have never read my Bible sitting down, but always on my knees.[3]

At the pulpit, Rees Howells stood to read the Word of God, but here he is talking of private devotions. As a former miner, he often worked on his knees at the tin and coalface and kneeling for prolonged periods of time as a young man did not affect him. Whilst there were chairs at the College meetings, most people who were able, got down on their knees when praying. If the meeting was tightly packed it would be easier to kneel facing away from the pulpit so the people could hold onto their wooden chairs, or rest their elbows on the seat, otherwise your forehead would be on the back-rest in front of you. As the decades passed and the young staff became elderly this practice was discontinued. You may be able to kneel, but can you get back up?

When you are in need why do you not plead with God through the Word? (Luke 18:1-8, the parable of the persistent widow). If there was a prayer to be answered the Holy Spirit would not let me do anything else but spend time on my knees with the Bible till it was answered. You are never to bring worldly thoughts, that is, thoughts, on a low level, into the Presence of God. You are to occupy yourself with some matter, which is worthy of the fellowship of God, something to do with the Kingdom. Say, "Lord, what will Thou have me to do?" Go through the Bible on your knees. You pick a few verses here and there in the Bible, but you need to know it, and you will know it only as you come up to it in experience. You tend to interpret God's Word in the light of your own experience and so limit Him.

It would be well for you if, instead of reading here and there without blessing in it, you followed the lives of these men in the Bible and asked God to bring your experience up to the level of theirs.[4]

Speak to God. Ask God to do it. Ask the Holy Spirit to pray through you. Let the Holy Spirit appeal through you to the Throne. The Holy Spirit said to me, "I shall never pray a prayer through you for other people if I can answer it through you." He did not consult me. He only told me what He was doing.[5]

If you pray, you must be prepared to pay [£, $, €]. I do not ask the Lord to do anything that I have not allowed Him to do through me. The Holy Spirit said, "Do not pray for anybody else to give money when I am able to answer the prayer by giving yours. When you go to your extremity, you can come back to Me." There was a test in giving up the last pound.[6]

There is a golden rule in the life of faith that the Christian can never prevail upon God to move others to give larger sums of money towards God's work, than he himself has either given, or proved that he would be willing to give, if it were in his power to do so.[7]

You can never move God to feel more through your prayers than you feel yourself (Esther chapters 4-6).

Sometimes you need to wrestle with God in prayer. He smiles on your willingness to fight. And Jacob was left alone, and there wrestled a man with him until the breaking of the day (Genesis 32:24). Have you wrestled with God like this? Can you get near God? Your position counts as nothing; you are all the same before God. What counts is that you are all to come before God and prevail. Do not allow yourself to worry or be disappointed by things that do not concern the Kingdom.

The Spirit said to me, "Let Me wash you in the Blood, and do not allow thoughts of things that have happened, or words that people have said, to come to My Presence."

It is not the length of *time* you spend on your knees, but the *stillness* to which the Holy Spirit brings you, which takes you to the Presence of God. Difficulties vanish when you come into the Lord's Presence. [Rees Howells taught that you should live in an attitude of prayer, perpetual abiding].

I never failed to get an audience with the King of course, I cannot force myself in there, but my needs are so great that I can go back to Him. I talk to Him all the time. I try to picture other people's lives, rushing into His Presence and out again – Oh, I have never done that!

You need to keep in touch with God. Walking over to the Mission I used every minute to pray. Have you entered in so that you remain in all the time?

All should pray in the meetings. You may say, "Oh! I have never been delivered before." Daniel and his companions had never been delivered before. Do they look down on us and say, "Their prayer meeting is a tame affair? They are not much concerned about it. Afterwards they will go away and eat their supper, look at the moon, and think no more about it." What kind of appeal did Daniel make to the Throne? Their lives would go in a day or two if they were not delivered. They could not make an excuse. Their lives were at stake!

Do not allow the Devil to shut your mouths. Individual failure should not be confessed in the meetings as it hinders faith. How many of you go together to pray? Do not do it as a formality. The old man is so low, so vile; so rotten that he does not want to go to the Presence of God. I want to hear God's voice. I want Him to pray through me.

Rees Howells' Passport issued in Jersey, 3 September 1928. It may have been an emergency replacement passport as it was not issued in London. The passport lists his birth as 10 October 1880, which was a clerical error as Rees was born in 1879. Rees and Lizzie Howells had friends and supporters in Jersey and Guernsey, and visited these British islands near France at least once.

Scriptures to Claim when Praying His Will

Jesus said, "Whatever you ask in My name that will I do, that the Father may be glorified in the Son. If you ask anything in My name, I will do it" (John 14:13-14).

Jesus said, "I say to you, ask, and it will be given to you; seek and you will find; knock, and it will be opened to you" (Luke 11:9).

And: '...I will call upon God...' (Psalm 55:16).

Jesus said, "If you abide in Me and My Words abide in you, you will ask what you desire and it shall be done for you" (John 15:7).

Jesus said, "In that day you will ask Me nothing. Most assuredly, I say to you, whatever you ask the Father in My name He will give you. Until now you have asked nothing in My name. Ask and you will receive, that your joy may be full" (John 16:23-24).

Jesus said, "I say to you that if two or three of you on earth agree concerning anything that they ask it will be done for them by My Father in Heaven. For where two or three are gathered together in My name, I am there in the midst of them" (Matthew 18:19-20).

When we pray asking in His name, it means in His will, for His glory. The flesh cannot pray in His name, it prays for itself – comfort, self and desires. When you abide in the Vine, your desires are God's desires and you pray His will. Therefore, the prayer is answered because it is His will, not your feelings or desires that you pray. When two or three agree to pray in His name, as Rees Howells and the College did, it means to pray Kingdom prayers. God will not give your flesh its desires. Those desires are harmful and can destroy your walk with the Spirit. This is another world altogether. The flesh lusts against the Spirit and the Spirit against the flesh. You misquote Jesus when you claim your flesh can pray for anything and receive, because the answer will be, "No!" When the prayer is from the Spirit, it is God's will and you will receive a positive answer.

Key Scriptural Principles for Answered Prayer
Confess and forsake sin (Psalm 66:18 and Proverbs 28:13).
What is our motive in praying for ——? (James 4:3).
Does the prayer glorify God? (John 14:13-14 and John 16:23).
Is it a need or a want? (Matthew 6:9-13, 33).
Is it God's will? (1 John 5:14).
Ask in Jesus' name (John 16:23).
Believe and have faith (Mark 11:24).
We must have good relationships (Matthew 5:23-24), but especially between a husband and wife (1 Peter 3:7).
There needs to be unity based on the Holy Spirit's anointing but not compromise (Psalm 133, John chapters 13 and 15).
Be persistent in your prayers (Luke 11:5-10 and Luke 18:1).[8]

Chapter 11

Intercession

'To the intent that now the manifold wisdom of God might be made known by the Church to the principalities and powers in the heavenly places, according to the eternal purpose which He accomplished in Christ Jesus our Lord, in whom we have boldness and access with confidence through faith in Him' (Ephesians 3:10-12).

'The Spirit also helps in our weaknesses. For we do not know what we should pray for as we ought, but the Spirit Himself makes intercession for us with groanings which cannot be uttered. Now He who searches the heart knows what the mind of the Spirit is, because He makes intercession for the saints according to the will of God' (Romans 8:26-27).

A man is so simple when you come to intercession. The very people who think they know most about the Creation are those who try to prove that there is no Saviour. A man who discovers what God has done thinks he has great understanding.

Intercession means taking the place of another; just that and nothing else. Do not think that you can intercede until the Holy Spirit has killed you completely [death to self]. One sinner cannot intercede for another. Until you have come to your extremity, to the end of yourself, you will never work intercession.

Intercession is prayer, but it's not praying for the things we want or desire, but praying the will of God as revealed by the Holy Spirit. Sometimes we want God's will, i.e. souls to be saved, but in intercession it is God who gives us the burden and shows us what and how to pray, so that the prayer will be answered. Often there is an obedience to be followed, a place of abiding and if we step outside of this abiding then the intercession will fail. There can also be identification and at times agony (travail), groanings in the Spirit. You can stand in the gap on behalf of a person or a town etc. and plead for its people, e.g. Abraham and Lot from Sodom, and Jonah at Nineveh.

> 'When they cast you down and you say, 'Exaltation will come!' Then He will save the *humble person. He will even deliver one who is not innocent; yes he will be delivered by the purity of your hands' (Job 22:30). See Psalm 15, Psalm 24:1-6 and *Micah 6:8.
>
> 'If anyone sees his brother sinning a sin which does not lead to death, he will ask and He will give him life for those who commit sin not leading to death. There is sin leading to death. I do not say that he should pray about that' (1 John 5:16).

You will never touch intercession until the Lord has finished with you. You have to become perfectly satisfied with what God has given you before you can become an intercessor for other people.

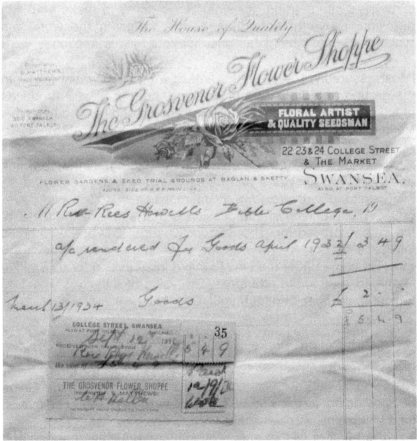

April 1932, seed order invoice from The Grosvenor Flower Shoppe, Swansea, paid in Sept. 1932. It was common in the 1920s and 30s to have business accounts from one to six months with no interest. During the war years businesses preferred to settle bills quickly.

Intercession is like sowing seeds, they have to die first or be buried before they will sprout and bloom. Sometimes God gives a seed of intercession and it dies before bearing fruit. At other times He makes you responsible for the flowering intercession of another, you must tend what another has birthed. Cf. John 4:37.

We sent for a box of seeds from the Continent and they cost forty-five shillings. [45 shillings or £2-5-0 (pounds, shillings & pence) from 1932 is worth £168 in 2022]. If we had bought a similar sized box in Swansea it would have cost about five shillings [£18.67 in 2022]. Why did we pay extra? Because it was the flowers we were buying and not the seeds. Christ completed the work for your wretched self. We minister in the power of His completed intercession, for what He is going to make you. So, one soul is worth more than all the things in the world put together. He paid the higher price for your full redemption.

'Most assuredly, I say to you, unless a grain of wheat falls into the ground and dies, it remains alone; but if it dies, it produces much grain. He who loves his life will lose it and he who hates his life in this world will keep it for eternal life' (John 12:24-25).

What I am trying to make clear to you is that until the Lord has dealt with you for years and years, you are not going to be an intercessor. There are laws in intercession that God can never break. The meaning of intercession is that you take the place of the person prayed for. The Saviour was the only one who could intercede for sin, for He was the only one who was above the Law. He came under the Law to make intercession for us and He is able to save to the uttermost. The value of a thing is what you pay for it. If Christ died for a soul, Christ is the value of it.

God said, "Son of man, I have made you a watchman for the house of Israel [your country or town]; therefore hear a word from My mouth, and give them warning from Me" (Ezekiel 3:17).
'Praying always with all prayer and supplication in the Spirit, being watchful to this end with all perseverance and supplication for all the saints' (Ephesians 6:18).
'I exhort first of all that supplications, prayers, intercessions and giving of thanks be made for all men, for kings and all who are in authority, that we may lead a quiet and peaceable life in all godliness and reverence. For this is good and acceptable in the

sight of God our Saviour who desires all men to be saved and to come to the knowledge of the truth' (1 Timothy 2:1-4).

I used to say that if the Saviour, who was perfect, was made sin for me, I should be sorry throughout eternity if He did more for me [helping people, sharing the Gospel, intercession etc.] than I would allow the Holy Spirit to do through me for others.

'We are ambassadors for Christ, as though God were pleading through us: we implore you on Christ's behalf, be reconciled to God. For He made Him who knew no sin to be sin for us, that we might become the righteousness of God in Him' (2 Corinthians 5:20-21).

The Holy Spirit showed me a village where they were all down-and-outs, drunkards, and suchlike. He said, "I want to prove My love to these people, you be the first sufferer." I became the first sufferer. I longed to come to my extremity, so that I could begin on God's resources.[1]

c.1908, Village Ministry fellow workers, friends and family members. Probably taken at Brynamman on the edge of the Black Mountains. At least three of the men in this photo plus Rees Howells were key workers in the Mission, which over time, worked out of three locations. Rees Howells is sitting, middle row, third from left. Lizzie Hannah Jones (later Mrs Howells) is on the back row fifth from left.

For children I have both natural love and intercession. God said to me concerning the natives in Africa, "Your preaching, your kindness will never prevail, but your intercession will!" Six Gospel hardened men came to work on the house, and five out of the six came through to Christ.[2]

Emmanuel boarders with a rocking-horse on the Glynderwen Estate outside the south end of El-Shaddai, c.1947. A small porch was later built at the end. The girl wearing glasses is Ruth Bavington, her parents were originally missionaries in Little Tibet, now known as Ladakh, a union territory in Northern India.

The College had a Nursery with three full-time female staff members. One was Ivy Impey; she had a large heart for Israel and was incredibly modest about her nursery work during the war years. In *Rees Howells Intercessor* (1952), the first photo is Rees Howells holding baby Ruth Mathilde Bavington. She was born on 2 May 1933 in Zurich, Switzerland, whilst her parents, Reginald

"Rex" and Julie (married in July 1928) were on furlough from India. Mr and Mrs Bavington handed baby Ruth into the care of Rees and Lizzie Howells whilst her siblings, twins, John and Helene, born in Peshawar in April 1930, went with relatives to Watford, England. Mr and Mrs Bavington returned to India in late 1933 or early 1934 whilst their children were left in Britain. On Rees Howells' fifty-fifth birthday, 10 October 1934, Daniel Bavington was born in Shigar, Baltistan, Kashmir State.

A year after Daniel's birth the Bavingtons left the Worldwide Evangelisation Crusade (WEC) and went to work on the North-West Frontier Province, in India, now known as Khyber Pakhtunkhwa in Pakistan. In 1935, Reginald began training for the Anglican Church in Calcutta, India, whilst Julie took their son Daniel to England, where she was united with John, Helene and Ruth, so Ruth, now a toddler, left Swansea in 1935.

In a College meeting, Rees spoke about the pain he felt when baby Ruth Bavington was taken from the College, as they had raised her as their own. He went on to say that it was more painful to see her leave than when they gave up Samuel (to his relatives) because they had an attachment with her. Rees told the Lord, the pain was unbearable and if this is what it would be like for each child coming to the Home and School for Missionary Children then it would be better if no more came.

Mrs Julie Bavington and her four children returned to India in 1935 or 1936. They lived in Srinagar, the capital of Kashmir, where Reginald Bavington worked for the Church Mission Society (CMS) School run by the veteran missionary, Canon Cecil Tyndale-Biscoe. After Reginald was ordained in c.1939, the family moved to Lahore, in the Punjab, where Rev. Bavington was in charge of St. Oswald's Church. During that time the twins were sent to a boarding school in Murree, Punjab, India, (now in Pakistan). When Rev. Bavington was posted as a chaplain in the British Army on the Frontier, about 1941, Julie Bavington took Ruth and Daniel to live in Murree, to attend the school, Lawrence College, as 'day children.'

In 1946, Daniel aged twelve was sent back to England, to stay with the relatives in Watford. Ruth returned to England with the rest of the family in 1947, aged thirteen, just before Indian Independence, as Rev. Bavington's job with the British Army was coming to an end. The Bavington's had no family home in England and in autumn 1947, Ruth and Daniel became boarders at Rees Howells' Bible College School, Swansea, (known in late 1949 as Emmanuel Grammar School). Ruth left school in 1950 and Daniel left in 1951. Ruth lived in Switzerland (Lausanne area) for a year or two at a 'House Training School.' Later, whilst doing "Nurse Aid" training, she lived with her brother Daniel and his wife (also called Ruth) in Croydon, England, as her health problems (asthma etc.) prevented her from doing the full nurses' training. Ruth Mathilde Bavington later returned to the Swansea area to work. Daniel (and his family) went to Pakistan in 1961 as a civil engineer. In the mid-70s, Daniel learned of Ruth's serous illness and visited her several times in Kings College Hospital, London, England, where she had been taken, in a coma, with severe hepatitis. Daniel saw Ruth a couple of times, but she never recovered. She was promoted to glory on 10 March 1976. Daniel attended her funeral at a graveyard above Sketty, Swansea.[3]

It was on Barabbas that the Master made intercession for souls (Matthew 27:15-26). Jesus took his place as He took ours. Supposing I were gaining a position of intercession in Divine healing and went to pray with this person and that one, and my test prayer was not answered? Would answers to the other prayers show that I had gained the position? No! If I failed in my test case I should fail altogether.

It was on the tramps that I gained intercession and I am using it for the missionaries [intercession for consumption and practical support]. I allowed God to give the body I gave Him for the sake of others. All I had to do with it was let Him do it. So that was how it became an intercession. It was not I who did it.[4]

That is intercession that you have had victory over something and the Holy Spirit brings it back to you, and you walk it again for other people.

Note: When cholera swept Egypt in 1947 it threatened to stop Jewish immigration into Israel, but the victory Rees Howells had gained over the influenza epidemic in Africa enabled him to pray against the cholera. A gained position or intercession can be applied as the Holy Spirit directs; in other cases without deep travail, the price has been paid. As with African children, so with the children of missionaries, as with influenza, so with cholera. For Rees Howells in Africa see Appendix B.

Mary Morrison of The Faith Mission, Scotland, was one of four female evangelists who saw the North Uist Revival (1957-1958). In 1913, Mrs Lizzie Howells spent a year at The Faith Mission in preparation for the mission field. Four decades later, Mary

Morrison was a speaker at the Bible College of Wales (as was Duncan Campbell); she later married Rev. Dr. Colin N. Peckham, Principal of The Faith Mission, Edinburgh. Dr. Peckham wrote: 'God uses those who are available and useable. He uses those who are cleansed and filled with His Holy Spirit. He uses those who are prepared to pay the price of soul-travail. Burdened, broken, bold praying is the nerve-centre of revival...intercession costs...true intercession is sacrifice. Because of the demands and price of intercessory prayer, many do not enter its portals and consequently do not gain its benefits....'[5]

Travail: Very few people will be responsible for souls. I see a man as shallow as he can be. All these places, four estates in Swansea, have been bought because I carried a burden. By choice I would not lose this travail of soul. [Rees Howells wrestled with God for provision and He provided for his daily needs, from when he was called out of wage-earning].

'Yet it pleased the Lord to bruise Him; He has put Him to grief. When You make His soul an offering for sin, He shall see His seed, He shall prolong His days, and the pleasure of the Lord shall prosper in His hand. He shall see the travail of His soul and be satisfied. By His knowledge My righteous Servant shall justify many, for He shall bear their iniquities' (Isaiah 53:10-11).

Intercession once gained works from an extremity. A spiritual law can never come down to take the place of a lower one. In Divine healing there was nothing in it except that I was in a position to believe it. You cannot see spiritual things except from a position. If an assistant prays and believes with a doctor who has gained a position of intercession, he must not assume that his believing will be adequate in a similar case if the doctor is not there to deal with it. [The Spirit must be present and it must be God's will to minister the gained position of intercession. The intercessor is a vessel, a steward of His will and not the Master].

I was walking along one day and I met a man who had lost both his arms [probably a soldier from one of the World Wars]. The Devil said to me, "Rush after him! Give him both his arms back! If you don't, you will commit a terrible sin against God!" The Devil knew that I had not gained the position [in creative miracles]. In intercession, you do not put yourself in a position [to take responsibility without God's guidance. Beware of the sin of presumption].

If there is anything that I believe strongly I have, it is Divine healing, but I never step into it, unless God steps into it.

Swansea, Bible College of Wales Hospital postcard 1939. In the foreground (left) is the Bungalow, a former Kindergarten. The original Hospital was the two-storey building at the end with six sets of windows at the front. The middle section was an extension from 1936; the architect's drawing is in chapter 18.

The second floor of the middle section of the Hospital was an extension from 1936, whilst the first floor was used as classrooms and accommodation. The Hospital accommodated fifty patients, some with private rooms (maternity or isolation). Over the years most of the College buildings were used for multiple purposes depending on the need and how many students were in residence. In December 1937, there were four medical staff that lived at the College alongside six nurses. By March 1938, there were five nurses in residence. Dr. Margaret FitzHerbert was the first female doctor to arrive in 1935; she looked after the women students and was known as the Medical Officer. Dr. Robert Brien cared for the men students, whilst his wife Dr. Brien oversaw the women staff. Dr. Kingsley Priddy was responsible for the men staff. Dr. John Howells (Rees Howells' cousin) was a local practitioner who taught healthcare to BCW students, as did some of the other doctors already mentioned. Lectures included First Aid, Nursing and Tropical Medicine. (Three other relatives of Rees Howells were also doctors; Dr. Wilfred V. Howells was teaching at BCW in 1932). Dr. Kenneth Symonds "Symbo" later joined the College, whilst Dr. W. Hughes (a woman) joined in late 1940s or early 1950s. She stayed for a few years before serving the Lord in Ramallah, north of Jerusalem, in a Girl's School associated with the College.

Yesterday (September 1937), I was in the dark concerning the selling of the fields, now He is beginning to throw light on it. When the moment comes, I shall know exactly what to do. He plays on you, reveals a thing here, stops you there and brings you right through. I am impartial; it is equal joy to take either course.

For fourteen years I could not sell the unwanted land in Glyn Derwen [at the bottom entrance by the Mumbles Road which included the Half Way Public House, which in 1924 was converted into a Men's Hostel for the students], but when the Lord arranged it, I sold a part to the garage.

Looking towards Swansea Bay, c.1947. Photo taken from El-Shaddai (building) on the Glynderwen Estate. Notice the decrease in elevation of the land (which was in three tiers). The two-storey building (front left) was classrooms. The unwanted land is where the buildings on the right are, and the garage (in white) on the left.

Previous photo: Notice the boys playing on the Emmanuel School field. The fields to the left extended to Ashleigh Road in a rectangular strip. The single-storey white building (background left) is the garage, next to other homes. The plain middle building is the general location of the former Men's Hostel, which had been the Half Way Public House. Between the Public House and the garage was (and still is) a private access entrance from Mumbles Road onto the fields. Other buildings on the right were newly built homes, formerly College owned land.

It was some years after Rees Howells' promotion to glory that the name Glyn Derwen was contracted to Glynderwen. The difficulty with the land was that it was 'liable to flooding' as marked on old Ordinance Survey maps. This is due to the unnamed stream, its small outlet into the sea and high tides where, on occasions, the water would flow backwards and overflow its banks. In the late 1960s, Samuel Howells spent a fortune removing 200 tons of silt and debris from the river, having pipe laid for one fork of the river and multiple tons of concrete for the banks.

Rees and Samuel Howells, whilst best known as intercessors, as part of their ministry at the Bible College of Wales were also engaged in the practical realities of managing large estates and the oversight of hundreds of people. This included the Bible College, Schools, Hospital etc., work and ministry abroad, liaising with the Council, allaying neighbors' concerns (noise, mature trees, boundaries, naughty school students, invasive Japanese knotweed and entry and exits points), lectures, interviews, pastoral care, College meetings and Sunday services, accounts, paperwork and much daily correspondence. Rees had three secretaries. Thankfully, there was a large body of skillful staff members with multiple giftings and talents who could step in at a moments notice to fill any gap. The medical doctors used to preach, as well as the mechanics and gardeners. Most staff had multiple job functions and roles.

As Director, Rees and then Samuel had to know what went on in each department and to keep the organisation as pure and holy as possible, for God to continually bless the work.

The first-fruits go to the altar; they belong to God. [As in the case with the woman with consumption (T.B.), the woman from the village ministry who had burnt her bread on the Sabbath and Rees Howells reimbursed her for her loss. And the death of Lord Radstock's eldest daughter].[6]

Cartle Postale (Postcard) from Lord Radstock to Rees Howells, 19 February 1910, from Nice, Grimaldi, France to Llandeilo Road Brynamman, nr (near) Swansea, Angleterre [England].

The reverse of the postcard to Rees Howells: 'Hotel Grimaldi, Nice. 19-2-10. There is a great battle here, many thousands of visitors from different countries come for comfort and pleasure. Few X [Christians] & these not working together. Pray for blessing Sunday. Inte[rcession] for & meeting of pastors in neighborhood, Monday 28th. He is all. Lord Radstock.'

Now it came to pass after these things that God tested Abraham, and said to him, "Abraham!" And he said, "Here I am." Then He said, "Take now your son, your only son Isaac, whom you love, and go to the land of Moriah, and offer him there as a burnt offering on one of the mountains of which I shall tell you."

'Abraham stretched out his hand and took the knife to slay his son. But the Angel of the Lord called to him from Heaven and said, "Abraham, Abraham!" So he said, "Here I am." And He said, "Do not lay your hand on the lad, or do anything to him; for now I know that you fear God, since you have not withheld your son, your only son, from Me" (Genesis 22:1-2, 10-12).

'The first-fruits of your grain and your new wine and your oil, and the first of the fleece of your sheep, you shall give Him' (Deuteronomy 18:4).

A covenant is entirely on God's side. Therefore, He makes it only with a man who is entirely in His hands and who has come up to the position of the man with whom He made it first.

Abraham laid all on the altar, just as Rees Howells and his staff members did in the twentieth century. You cannot claim the hundredfold until *all* is on the altar. You have to sow first, before you can reap. Be faithful with the little you have now, so later, you can be entrusted with true riches. Some have tried to make a claim on the hundredfold, but have not met the legal conditions, whilst others have claimed to have 'sold all' and yet kept back part of the price. All must be surrendered on the altar.

The Holy Spirit will not use these positions through you if there is anything doubtful or anything of which He would disapprove in your life.

Your surrender must be as real as that of the one through whom the positions were gained. You may think when people give freely to the Vision [of themselves or financially] that they will give to you. Not a bit of it; but they will give to God. The Holy Spirit has gained all the positions of intercession; there is no need for you to gain them. He can deal with you quickly, in two or three years probably. He will never allow self-indulgence in any form. If you do not get through yourself, you will be just the same as if the intercession over finance had not been gained. You can do more through intercession before you go out to the mission field than you will accomplish by working when you go out to your field of labour and harvest.

Chapter 12

Faith is Substance

'Now faith is the substance of things hoped for, the evidence of things not seen. For by it the elders obtained a good testimony' (Hebrews 11:1-2).

'Thus also faith by itself, if it does not have works, is dead. But someone will say, "You have faith, and I have works." Show me your faith without your works, and I will show you my faith by my works' (James 2:17-18).

The entrance fee to a life of faith is a full and complete surrender. "...I am thine and all that I have" (1 Kings 20:4). If you want to know what a full surrender is, it is this. You have made the same surrender as Elisha [who left everything, to serve and be trained by Elijah]. Do not be slow to claim on your surrender (1 Kings 19:19-21). Only one thing you know: God has told you to do it and He will inspire faith in you.

Faith works when you are in a test by choice, not when you cannot get out of it (Exodus 14, crossing the Red Sea). I had money when the Holy Spirit came to take my life and with my body I handed my money over to Him. He said, "When we finish your money we will begin on the unlimited resources of God." As really as I believed there was forgiveness of sins and eternal life in the atonement, I believed in the hundredfold. For fifteen years I had not been without money and the Holy Ghost was running me to my extremity. It took Him nearly twelve months to give it away. I was watching where that change would come in from a man's extremity to the unbounded resources of God. I remember the night when I knew a change was going to be made in me. I had come to the last pound; that night I gave it away and touched bottom. I remember the Spirit coming on me as He does when He gives a revelation. He said, "Cut the ropes [your security] and take the promise" [of God's provision]. From the moment He said it, the promises became equal to me to money in the bank.[1]

It came just naturally as breathing. If I needed £7-10 (£7 and ten shillings) and had £5, I prayed for £2-10. I never expected this to fail. I never doubted. He took my money away in order to take my limitations away. [There were 20 shillings to £1 in old English money. If Rees Howells needed £7-10 in 1911, when he was called out from wage-earning this is worth £942 in 2022].

The Holy Spirit said, "If you want Me to lead and guide you, you can come out on faith." When He called me I had only one penny. He made me hold up my hand as a sign on that small bridge that I would not take a meal at home unless I paid for it. It was settled that I was to pay at the end of the month. I did nothing for a month, and He delivered me the moment I was in need. On the day that I had to pay my mother I was delivered on the spot.[2]

Rees Howells on the bridge c.1939, on the Black Mountains, where he made his vow before God in the summer of 1911 to trust Him for his needs and not in man. This meant no financial appeals to man, no solicitation and no dropping hints of one's need. These photos were also printed in portrait mode. I have come across many of these images; most are inside a card holder with a protective flap. As many staff members owned copies, they may have been given to those present at Rees Howells' funeral in February 1950. Rees and Samuel Howells were regular visitors to this footbridge (since removed), as were groups of students.

Whatever else you do is not great. You do not like to come out into the open. Be very careful about stopping simple sources of provision. I stopped home supplies for a time, but when the Lord told me to go back I went and from that time was never without a home. What applies to one person does not apply to another.

Never let your parents know your need. Do not refuse money from home unless definitely guided to do so. [God can use strangers as well as co-workers, friends and relatives]. Have that simplicity; trust in your Heavenly Father that since He called you out of wage-earning into His service, He will supply your personal needs. But He will never deliver you while you are not abiding. He will deliver you every time while you are abiding [in God's good, pleasing and perfect will].

The Howells' semi-detached cottage styled home (right-hand side), 1950. Rees Howells was born here on 10 October 1879. It was occupied by his parents and their eleven children! This is the back of the house and not the side seen from Llandeilo Road, Brynamman. The room (top right window) was where Rees Howells prayed from 6am to 5pm for ten months for the Bible College from June/July 1923. The house has undergone extensive renovations since the last Howells family member lived at 'Waunhelygen' which is now numbered as 26. 'Waun helygen' means 'willow moor' in Welsh. To get to the 'front' door at the back of the house you walked around the side between the end wall and the bush. The first edition of *Rees Howells Intercessor* (1952) shows a cropped image from the same photo; however this one has been digitally enhanced as have all images within this book.

- 133 -

You need to learn this life of faith. You must live very near to God. He will tell you when you are to be delivered [when the prayer will be answered] and the amount to pray for.

You think you would like to learn a life of faith and you think you can work it at once. A thousand times, no! You have to start at the bottom. The moment you come and begin at the bottom, the sums may not be very great, but you know you are moving God.

The way to learn the life of faith is to be sure each time that you move God. How do you know you have moved God? By not being satisfied with anything, but what you need being supplied. If you need 15 shillings get 15 shillings not £1. [20 shillings = £1]. Anything more than you need is a gift and not your gained position of faith. [£1 in 1938 is worth £72 in 2022].

The Holy Spirit never gave me money to give while I was in the school of faith [often living hand-to-mouth daily]. I was delivered to the exact time and the exact amount, and what a blessed life it was! If I needed £5, He would not give me £10. If you need £10 and you have £2, you only need to ask the Lord for £8.

STATEMENT.

Manufacturer of the TEE DEE Neckwear.

9 St. Mary's Street, SWANSEA,

Jan. 1924.

Mrs. Rees Howells

Bible College Blackhill

DR. to

T. DRINKWATER

Manufacturer, Agent & Warehouseman

TERMS: 3¾% 7 days. 2¼% on 10th month following date of dispatch.

Dec.	To a/c rendered.	15	1	5
19	To Goods. Mrs. Thomas		7	6
	£	15	8	11

Goods Invoice, January 1924, ordered by Mrs Thomas. Her husband, John, was the first Principal of the Bible College of Wales. £15-8-11 (pounds, shilling and pence) is worth £995 in 2022.

It is not trying "stunts" (daring, hazards) that we shall get a life of faith, but only as we allow the Holy Spirit to do things through us. It will be by abiding, giving the Holy Spirit an opportunity through us. The money you are going to receive is an outcome of your walk. Expect the hundredfold. If you planted potatoes, you would not allow weeds to grow all over them because you did not expect the outcome.

There were two brothers. One studied many things and failed to apply any; the other learnt mining and did well at it. In the same way you may study many things in the Bible and yet be unable to live a life of faith. [This is probably from Rees Howells' own family experience or from his home village of Brynamman. Also, some students gave away their College fees as a "stunt" to test God's provision, only to learn, the money was God's provision!].

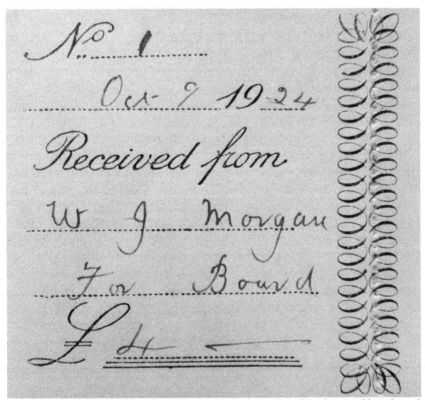

Cashbook 1, Receipts Board and Lodgings for Students. Number 1, October 9, 1924, £4 for Board (and Lodgings: accommodation and food) from W. J. Morgan. £4 in 1924 is worth £260 in 2022.

The Bible College of Wales (BCW) did not charge for education and subsidised everything by half. This made poor business sense because as the ministry grew, so did the liability. However, Rees Howells was acting under the guidance of the Holy Spirit to make training accessible to all. He was called to train men and women for the ministry at home and abroad who had a call on their life, but not necessarily the financial resources to get a university education. In the school of faith at BCW, they could learn the life of faith and equally apply it to wherever they served in the world.

In 1924, the fee was £40 (£2,600 in 2022) per annum (or £14 per term x3). £14 x3 = £42, therefore I conclude that by signing up for the year, or perhaps paying up front there was a discount. This used to be a common business practice, the same as when Rees Howells signed up for Livingstone College for his medical course in 1913. Pay up front and save money, which also helps with internal planning.

After the *cleavage of 1925, the Bible College of Wales' annual fee was reduced to £30 (£10 per term). In 1926, there was a General Strike which hit the mining communities of Wales hard, followed by the Great Depression. For a few years after the cleavage until 1929, women students paid a few pounds per term less than men.[3] In 1944, the cost per term was still only £10, unchanged for nineteen years and less than when BCW opened!

*The cleavage began in autumn 1925 and was a disagreement over the 'life of faith' which caused the Senior Lecturer to leave, alongside approximately 85% of the students. The Holy Spirit told Rees Howells that He was going to smash the College and rebuild it, as He was unhappy with certain things. Rees conveyed this in a letter to one of the trustees before the cleavage. For one year, the Bible College was shut in with a handful of students, but out of it God was able to rebuild a 'Gideon's Army,' as He had a core who believed in the fundamental truths and aims of the College in the walk and life of faith. This public death of the College, coupled with Rees' silence, who refused to comment or be drawn by journalists, and BCW's restructuring, resulted in an atmosphere where the Holy Spirit could move.

If you fail to move God for your personal needs you will never take a great part in this Vision. It is finance which is the Goliath of the day. Allow God to help you. It is only right that He should keep you, and He wants to do so, only you must have faith to take it.

Chapter 13

The Laws of Living By Faith

Jesus said, "Do not worry, saying, 'What shall we eat?' or 'What shall we drink?' or 'What shall we wear?' For after all these things the Gentiles seek. For your Heavenly Father knows that you need all these things. But seek first the Kingdom of God and His righteousness, and all these things shall be added to you" (Matthew 6:31-33).

Paul wrote: 'Indeed I have all and abound. I am full, having received from Epaphroditus the things sent from you, a sweet-smelling aroma, an acceptable sacrifice, well pleasing to God. And my God shall supply all your need...' (Philippians 4:18-19).

Rees Howells' laws in the life of faith were explained a few at a time, or mentioned singly in passing. The numbers (1-12) have been added to aid the reader.

There are laws in this life of faith that you must learn:
1. No needs are to be made known.
   I refused a deliverance when someone had come to know my needs, or if in some way I had made them known. God is watching you every second of the day to see if you break this.

2. Do not question a deliverance if you have not attempted to influence the donor and have not made the need known.
   'And my God shall supply all your need according to His riches in glory by Christ Jesus' (Philippians 4:19).

3. Natural deliverance before extraordinary deliverance.
   God covers me all the time with His hand and that quite naturally. 'Moses stretched out his hand over the sea and the Lord caused the sea to go back by a strong east wind all that night, and made the sea into dry land, and the waters were divided' (Exodus 14:21).

Do not be disappointed if a friend, church or family member gives you the money you have been praying for, assuming they do not know your need (no undue influence as above). However, if you receive an anonymous letter with money enclosed, or money posted through your letter/mail box, that is extraordinary.

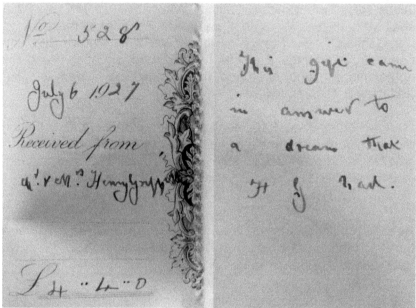

Receipt collage, 6 July 1927, #528 received from Henry Griffith, one of the first trustees of the Bible College of Wales. Written on the reverse in Rees Howells' hand: 'This gift came in answer to a dream H G had.' £4-4-0 (pounds & shillings) is worth £270 in 2022.

4. No debt.

You are not to take a single thing unless you can pay for it. 'Owe no one anything except to love one another, for he who loves another has fulfilled the law' (Romans 13:8).

Rees Howells used natural means to leverage the money he needed to purchase different estates. It is one thing to buy an estate to start (or expand the College), but money and manpower were also needed to make each property suitable or even habitable (Penllergaer). Rees took out private mortgages when led by the Holy Spirit to do so. He also declined private loans on occasions, as led by the Holy Spirit. He wisely used the standard fiscal provisions offered by businesses in the 1920s and 1930s of paying for items or good after, thirty days, sixty days, three months or six months. This helped balance the books whilst students were praying in their College fees for each term. Many businesses have cash-flow issues. The Lord often provided for the College on the day money was needed, sometimes down to the hour! Rees' warning of "No debt," is don't go into debt to fund your great ideas and expect God to bail you out. He pays *His invoices,* that which He has commissioned and sanctioned, which must be obeyed in His timing, which is equally important. The call is not always the command to commence. Rees was called to start a College, but after the visit to Moody Bible Institute in 1922, a year passed before the Lord spoke again about it! Rees received outstanding deliverances – answers to prayer – before taking on further responsibilities because he knew the leading of the Spirit. It was a miracle first, then deeper faith and risk.

When Rees Howells was involved in village ministry a strike was imminent, which could have lasted for months, the last had continued for eight months and the longest in Wales was nearly three years! The villagers were notorious, former drunkards who pre-conversion had barrels of beer in the street on the Sabbath where they openly drank and revelled! Rees Howells took responsibility for credit in two shops for up to £100 as the villagers were unable to run up a tab, to obtain credit. Rees told those in the village that not one person would be in need of bread and cheese, tea and sugar, therefore they need not fear. £100 in 1908 is worth £12,900 in 2022. In the end the strike was settled and Rees was not liable for the £100 credit for the villagers, but it sent a powerful message of Christianity in action, showing his faith by his works (James 2:14-26).[1]

5. First need, first claim.

In the life of faith you tend to keep for essentials instead of buying non-essentials, but it is not right to keep money (Matthew 6:25-34, do not be anxious about money, God will look after you).

Rees Howells taught that it is wrong to pray for money for someone in need when you have the means to provide already. Why pray for £100 to give when you already have £1,000 in the bank? You are the answer to your prayer.

Jesus said, "Do not lay up for yourselves treasures on earth, where moth and rust destroy and where thieves break in and steal; but lay up for yourselves treasures in Heaven, where neither moth nor rust destroys and where thieves do not break in and steal. For where your treasure is, there your heart will be also. The lamp of the body is the eye. If therefore your eye is good, your whole body will be full of light. But if your eye is bad, your whole body will be full of darkness. If therefore the light that is in you is darkness, how great is that darkness! No one can serve two masters; for either he will hate the one and love the other, or else he will be loyal to the one and despise the other. You cannot serve God and mammon" (Matthew 6:19-24).

The apostle James wrote: 'What does it profit, my brethren, if someone says he has faith but does not have works? Can faith save him? If a brother or sister is naked and destitute of daily food, and one of you says to them, "Depart in peace, be warmed and filled," but you do not give them the things which are needed for the body, what does it profit? Thus also faith by itself, if it does not have works, is dead. But someone will say, "You have faith, and I have works." Show me your faith without your works, and I will show you my faith by my works' (James 2:14-18).

6. When essentials and non-essentials come at the same time you must take for the essential *before* the non-essential.

During World War Two the Bible College of Wales and Bible Schools (later known as Emmanuel Preparatory School and Emmanuel Secondary/Grammar School) prepared nearly one thousand meals a day for pupils, students and staff. It was often deemed more essential to pay the food suppliers than the rates or other bills, as the rates could be deferred for a time, but food was needed daily. Visiting speakers were always sent away with financial gifts: 'Send them forward on their journey' (3 John 1:16), which was a greater priority than paying the water bill. Some visiting speakers had no money and lived by faith and to wish them "God speed" without money in their pocket was wrong.

An ounce of experience is worth a ton of theory. When I got married [December 1910], we lived on faith for two years from meal to meal. We were never able to compel the Holy Spirit to do what we liked, but He always delivered us. The things He did in healing were beyond the medical. When I went to Livingstone College [in 1913], there was an entrance fee of £75 [£9,250 in 2022] to pay down; else it would be £90 [£11,100, an additional expense of £1,850 in 2022]. I went there with only my single fare [money for train ticket]. The Lord told me, "You cannot afford to lose that £15, get through at once." When my wife came to

Livingstone College [to visit before her Maternity Course in City Road Hospital, London], I prayed for £26-10 [£26 and 10 shillings is worth £3,200 in 2022] and had it to the day.

Livingstone College Hospital, Leyton, East London, postcard, 1915. British soldiers playing croquet during World War One (1914-1918). From 1913, Rees Howells in preparation for the mission fields of Southern Africa spent nine months at Livingstone College learning elementary medicine, surgery and hygiene. The College was requisitioned in August 1915 and known as the Livingstone College Relief Hospital, a place for soldiers to convalesce. It closed at the end of 1918 and resumed its function for training missionaries until 1939, when the British Army resumed its use.

7. You cannot claim deliverance until you have gone to your extremity.

God will not send money when you are not in need. Any money that comes when you are not in need is money that would have come whether you prayed or not. I never prayed for anything that I was not in need of, or before the time that I was in need of it. I would not waste my time and before all I would not waste God's time to do that. Unless you are really in need and must be delivered, you will not pray through. God will never give to me unless I believe.

Rees Howells was often delivered on the day he needed the money, sometimes within an hour of paying the workmen or other bill. One supplier of construction material used to come to the College every Friday for some months during autumn and winter 1936 to collect payment, when the College Hospital extension was being built. Their business invoices were received at the Bible College on Thursday afternoon or Friday morning stating that Mr – would arrive on Friday afternoon to take payment.

INVOICE.

GEO. H. CANN

BUILDERS' AND PLUMBERS' MERCHANT,
HYDRAULIC PRESSED CONCRETE BLOCK MANUFACTURER,
SLATING & TILING CONTRACTOR,
SOUTH DOCK, SWANSEA.

M   The Bible College of Wales,

Derwen Fawr,   Swansea.

Month ending SEPTEMBER 193 6   No. 2

DATE	DLY TICKET NO.		RATE	DEBIT			CREDIT	TOTAL		
		Brought Forward.........						14	15	5
28th	6195M	48. B.G. 6" Pipes.	2/-	4	16	0				
		1. " 6" Slow Bend	3/-		3	0				
		40. " 4" Pipes.	1/4	2	13	4				
		6. " 4 Asstd. Sq. Bends	2/-		12	0				
		3. " 6x4 P. Gully & Gds	6/6		19	6				
		120. Blue 20x12 Slates	44/-	2	12	10				
		3. lbs Zinc Slate Nails	7d		1	9				
		1. Ton Cement	47/-	2	7	0				
		Dly Our Lorry. HM						14	5	5
29th	6213M	1. Load Ashes.			12	6				
		120. 20x12 Slates	44/-	2	12	10				
		3. lbs Slate Nails.	7d		1	9				
		276. ft 2x½ Battens.	2/8		7	5				
		Our Lorry. HM						3	14	6
								36	15	5

Builders' invoice, material for the Hospital extension, located at Derwen Fawr, September 1936. This is the second invoice for September from two deliveries on the same day. Items include: 240 slates (120 x 2), 6 lbs (3 lbs x 2) of slate nails, 276 ft of battens (wood), 1 ton of cement and more than 100 ft of various types of pipes. Prices in pounds, shilling and pence. £36-15-0 is worth £2,710 in 2022. This invoice with its slate tiles for the roof reveals that the exterior work was near completion. To use the Corporation's (Council's) water for construction you had to obtain permission and the water fee was set at a different rate.

8. Claim on your abiding.

You cannot live on gifts. [Money that you did not pray for, see point 7.]. There is a claim on a continual supply, it is on abiding. Jesus said, "If you abide in Me and My words abide in you, you shall ask what you will, and it shall be done for you" (John 15:7).

> The flesh can move people with emotion. Stories can be told of hardship, tests and can show images of devastation, destruction and emaciated children; people will give from an emotional response. Other people are moved to give because of their generous nature and abundance, like the woman who wanted to give Rees Howells £1,200 for the farm in Portuguese East Africa to start a mission base. Rees declined her generous offer.

9. Claim your wages from God.

Faith is better than a salary. Banks may fail, you may lose your job, but faith once gained can never be lost. If God is the Creator and could feed two million people in the desert, He can feed you (Exodus chapter 16, bread from Heaven in the wilderness). Believe what you have a claim on.

10. Whatever the Lord will order you to do, you can go back to Him and ask Him to pay for it.

You need to know where you have a claim. You cannot believe a 'plot' (a historical event in the Bible) unless you are in the same situation.

> Rees Howells was alive to Jesus Christ and obedient to the Holy Spirit. The Bible College of Wales (BCW) was God's College and He paid His own invoices. If Rees had stepped out on his own and bought the estates or erected buildings outside of the express will of God he would have failed in his own strength and enthusiasm. However, God kept the Bible College and the School for boarders, both of which were subsidised by Rees Howells and the staff who claimed their wages from God, and not from man or an institution. There was no solicitation for finances or goods, but trust in the living God to supply all of one's needs by prayer, faith and abiding, keeping the commandments of God.
>
> Spanning the mid-1930s into the late 1940s, staff and Bible College students numbered around 200-250 adults. It was a lot of mouths to feed, especially during the war (1939-1945), when many foods were rationed, including bacon, ham, preserves, butter, cheese, eggs, cooking fats, tea and sugar. Ration books

were issued for every registered citizen, which for BCW staff and students were surrendered to the Bible College. BCW registered each person who lived on site with the local authorities, and a designated butcher, grocer and other shops thus enabling each shop-keeper in theory, to be able to purchase enough stock for his or her batch of customers. Rationing was phased out in Britain from 1953-1954, eight years after the end of the war!

The Bible College of Wales

CASH STATEMENT
for the year ended 31st March 1939.

Dr.

Receipts.	Year to 31st March 1938 £	£ s d	Year to 31st March 1938 £
To Balance at Bank 1/4/38	—	2 3 4	
" Receipts from College, Day School, Boarding School, Missionary Home, Hospital & Conference Fees	5,435 435	5,327 17 9	7,849
" Capital receipts	600	—	3,831
" Gifts received	6,080	18,771 12 3	11,680
	£12,115	£24,101 13 4	£12,115

Cr.

Payments.	£ s d	Year to 31st March 1938 £
By Expenses in connection with the College, School, Missionary Home & Hospital, including Rates, Taxes, Fuel & Lighting, Repairs, Salaries & Wages, Provisions & Miscellaneous Expenses	12,270 13 0	
" Purchase of land, New buildings, Additions & Equipment of a Capital nature, & Bank Balances	10,804 10 4	£23,075 3 4
" Gifts to Missionaries & others	982 13 6	435
" Balance at Bank 31/3/39	43 16 6	—
	£24,101 13 4	£24,101 13 4

I certify the above CASH STATEMENT to be in accordance with the books and vouchers of the Bible College and Missionary School.

Derwen Fawr,
Swansea.
11th April 1939.

H. S. W. Seward,
Chartered Accountant.

Bible College of Wales Cash Statement ended 31 March 1939. Receipts £24,011-13-4 (£24,011 13 shillings and 4 pence in old English money) and Payments £24,011-13-4, of the exact amount! The 1937 Cash Statement was less, but also the exact amount.

11. You must have victory on a point in private before you are tested in the open (1 Kings chapters 17-18, Elijah predicts a drought and confronts King Ahab).

12. Do not run on the spoil.
You always get a chance and you do not know it is a chance. The old man will run on the spoil every time. When I joined the South Africa General Mission (SAGM), I did not know that I should receive a salary [money had no hold on Rees]. I also refused to use my salary to provide for my family in the future, for I trusted God for our daily bread. A retired bank manager, one of the Directors, quoted, "If a man neglect to provide for his own, he is worse than an infidel" (1 Timothy 5:8). I replied, "That means for the present, not for the future; I shall never make a penny out of the Mission." We decided on the spot to give back £10 a month and keep growing in the life of faith. [Many were preaching after you were tested on a life of faith it was fine to stop].

£10 in 1915 is worth £1,100 in 2022. At the SAGM Rees Howells was told that he would have to take out an insurance policy for his wife in case of his death on the mission field. He flatly refused, this not being faith and was duly rebuked by one of the staff members, probably the above Director. As Rees and Lizzie Howells gave half of their wage back to the Mission, it was later revealed that a sum of this had been set aside in case of Rees Howells' death. At home Rees had once paid in for an insurance policy, Rechabites Sick Benefit Club, to keep him out of the Workhouse. After more than sixteen years of payments the Lord told him not to keep up the policy but to trust in Him. However, Rees was called to pay the arrears on a Benefit Club for a man who had deserted his children! He was a convert of the Mission, but had sinned and left the area in shame. When he heard what Rees had done, it broke him and he came home a repentant man and lived at his dad's home for five months until his passing. His four children received a payment of £38 in 1908, which is worth approximately £4,900 in 2022.
In relation to the above incident Rees said, "We cannot say a thing is wrong for others just because we have been called to give it up; it depends on our position or grade in life."[2]

When I went to Africa, I walked to the queue [in Llanelli, Wales] without my train fare to London. In Africa I touched faith as I did at home. When I returned from Africa, I had only 2 shillings [20 shillings to £1], that God might have all the glory. The day we left, the Mission we had less than £1. [£1 in 1923 is approximately £65 in 2022]. We went up to the mountain [Black Mountains in Wales] and everything was very cold. The moment we [Rees and Lizzie Howells] went on our knees everything changed.

The Black Mountains, leaving the houses behind, through an iron gate onto the mountain. This photo was taken after a 15 minute walk from the Howells' family home at Brynamman, 2016.

'...Unto You I lift up my eyes, O You who dwell in the Heavens. Behold, as the eyes of servants look to the hand of their masters, as the eyes of a maid to the hand of her mistress, So our eyes look to the Lord our God...' (Psalm 123:1-2).

'Moreover it is required in stewards that one be found faithful' (1 Corinthians 4:2).

After a few days a cheque came from the Mission [SAGM]. I returned it. They sent it again, since it was for the previous month. But God told me, "Don't take it. Go back to your room. You have left the Mission and are responsible to nobody but, Myself." I spent every day on my knees from 6am to 5pm. I had only one meal a day at 5pm. The Lord sent an average of £38-10 a month. [£38 and 10 shillings from 1924 is worth £2,500 in 2022, this would have been towards Rees and Lizzie's upkeep and money towards the purchase of Glyn Derwen as it was then spelt].

The College also grew vegetables and salad in its fields and owned a tractor, plough and petrol rotavator. From the mid-1930s, BCW kept chickens for fresh eggs on the Derwen Fawr Estate, plus a goat, presumably to help keep the grass down. The runner beans were picked and moved in a wheelbarrow, such was the quantity and weight. One year, a ton of beans were picked! Staff (and students during practical workouts) used to prepare them for cooking or freezing. It was faith and works!

Tobias Bergin c.1970, preparing runner beans. "Toby" was a student in the 1930s and a faithful friend to Samuel R. Howells

Chapter 14

Trials and Tests of Faith

'My brethren, count it all joy when you fall into various trials, knowing that the testing of your faith produces patience. But let patience have its perfect work, that you may be perfect and complete, lacking nothing' (James 1:2-4).

The Lord said to Moses, "Behold, I will rain bread from Heaven for you. And the people shall go out and gather a certain quota every day, that I may test them, whether they will walk in My law or not. And it shall be on the sixth day that they shall prepare what they bring in, and it shall be twice as much as they gather daily" (Exodus 16:4-5).

The only point of trials and tests is to prove you. You must be tested on every point before you are proved. You are tested, not when there is a straight fight and you have to get through, but when there is a choice. After you have been delivered in a test, God gives you the opportunity to walk into the same kind of test by choice.

It is in the small tests that you make mistakes, for it is in them that you have confidence in yourself. ['Songs of Solomon 2:15 '…The little foxes that spoil the vines…']. When a thing is big, you know you must have God to help you; when it is small, you think you can do it yourself (Joshua chapters 6-8, the fall of Jericho and the defeat at Ai).

I never make mistakes when I am tested; I might step on a thing in the flesh if delivered. The greatest tests come through gifts of faith coming when the grace of faith is needed (Exodus 17:1-7, water from the rock. Numbers 20:1-13, the waters of Meribah and Moses strikes the rock when he should have spoken to it).[1]

Maintain faith in spite of appearances.

Suggestions are not doubting.

Temptation is not sin.

'No temptation has overtaken you except such as is common to man; but God is faithful, who will not allow you to be tempted beyond what you are able, but with the temptation will also make the way of escape, that you may be able to bear it' (1 Corinthians 10:13).

'Blessed is the man who endures temptation; for when he has been approved, he will receive the crown of life which the Lord has promised to those who love Him' (James 1:12).

A blind faith never questions God. It is blind to the test, to the accomplishment, blind to everything and never sees any difficulties because it is not faith. A living faith always questions. When God tells you a thing, you do not go under in a test.

'If you have run with the footmen and they have wearied you, then how can you contend with horses? And if in the land of peace, in which you trusted, they wearied you, then how will you do in the floodplain of the Jordan?' (Jeremiah 12:5).

'If thou faint in the day of adversity, thy strength is small' (Proverbs 24:10). It is the Lord who calls for this position. He would not be the Creator and create creatures to starve, would He? [God feeds the birds of the air and you are more value, Matthew 6:26]. I am going back, not on any feeling, but on what I told you, that I stepped out at His bidding and have been going on all these years. In every new position there is a higher test (Jeremiah 37:5-10, the Chaldeans besieging Jerusalem).

The Lord tests you to see whether you will take less than He originally promised you (Exodus 33:11-23, Moses desiring the Presence of God to go with the people of Israel from Sinai). In any trial now, don't give way. Go back to God. I am here to move God. I am not up when I am delivered and down when I am not. [Rees was even-tempered; he did not live by feelings, but on the promises of God]. It is when you are sane, quiet and in peace that you believe, not when you are in panic. You can never prove the deliverances of God until you face disaster.

You are not tested on a believing when it is far off. Only when you come to the final test do you know if you have believed (Genesis 22, Abraham called to sacrifice Isaac). It was in believing that these people were tested, before the actual point of entering in (Numbers chapters 13-14, twelve spies into Canaan, the people's rebellions, God's judgment on the nation and Israel defeated in battle). Any courage or bravery you have does not stand when the test is on believing (1 Samuel 7:3-12, Samuel judges Israel at Mizpeh for demanding a king to rule over them).

PENLLERGAER, GORSEINON

Penllergaer Mansion from a postcard, 1904. The property had been vacant from 1927 and in great need of repair when Rees Howells bought it in late 1938, early 1939. Often ownership of a property was not when an agreement had been made, contract signed or when a deposit had been handed over, even a significant sum, but when the Title Deeds were given to the new owner. Rees Howells spent around £6,000 getting the place habitable, including many miles of cables to electrify the house, and renovation of rooms and outbuildings. £6,000 from 1939 is worth approximately £440,000 in 2022. There had always been a grounds-man who looked after the 270 acres of land including two trout lakes, the Mansion and outbuildings to deter vandals and poachers. Rees continued this man's employment for some years. He may have also collected the rent from a number of habitual dwellings across the site, including a Farm House and Lodges. These were later sold.

God leads you into these tests to find your character. If you had gone there to fight the enemy and the Lord had not called you, you would have run away to a place, where the Philistines could not get you, not knowing that it was God who brought the Philistines. I could have said when I heard that the Roman Catholics were after Glyn Derwen [in late summer into autumn 1923], that they were the people to get it, since they had the money, but no, I said, "My God was the owner of the silver and the gold!"

The only thing you can do these days to keep yourself up in faith is to fill your mind with these 'plots' in the Bible. (Spoken during the Palestine test, 25 November 1947, when the nation of Israel would be 'born in a day' Isaiah 66:8).

> 'For whatever things were written before were written for our learning, that we through the patience and comfort of the Scriptures might have hope' (Romans 15:4).[2]

Never let the essentials go beyond the time. If you do go beyond the time, go back to God and see why you are not delivered. You must find out whether it is faith being tested, or whether it is unbelief. There is a burden in each case, but it is not the same burden. Say, "Make it known to me whether I am abiding, whether I am doing what You tell me and whether I have the faith which is necessary for this particular test."

You are in something for a week [a prayer or intercession], and you think that all is wrong. Measure yourself with Joseph [wrongly accused and thrown into prison]. This is the mistake you make all the time because God does not deliver you, you think He is not with you, but it is He who put you there and it is then that He is with you.

> God 'sent a man before them – Joseph – who was sold as a slave. They hurt his feet with fetters, he was laid in irons. Until the time that His word came to pass, the word of the Lord tested him. The king sent and released him, the ruler of the people let him go free. He made him lord of his house and ruler of all his possessions, to bind his princes at his pleasure, and teach his elders wisdom. Israel also came into Egypt and Jacob dwelt in the land of Ham' (Psalm 105:17-23).
>
> '...You meant evil...but God meant it for good' (Genesis 50:20).
> 'Surely the wrath of man shall praise You...' (Psalm 76:10).

Although the Lord is delaying my deliverances, I do not take that as due to unbelief. Oh no! I would not take it, for I am to be delivered! I do not go into unbelief because the answer to last night's prayers has not come today. No, it will probably come tomorrow. Do not come to the end and resort to physical effort and striving.

You say, "If only I had another day." But it is never too late for the Lord. Sometimes when you are in your darkest hour you are nearer the dawn (28 November 1947, United Nations voting on the partitioning of Palestine, the nation of Israel being born). Through the delay the Lord made display of the victory.[3]

> Queen Esther said, "If I have found favour in the sight of the king, and if it pleases the king to grant my petition and fulfil my request, then let the king and Haman come to the banquet which I will prepare for them, and tomorrow I will do as the king has said" (Esther 5:8).

The Holy Spirit told me, "If you look to agents [trusting in man and clever schemes] that will justify Me to let you down." There is a tendency when you are without something to cater to some source, but I never fell into that snare.

> Rees Howells could have sold the Half Way House (Pub) on the Glynderwen site with its alcohol license for a large sum of money, but knew it was wrong. During the Welsh Revival (1904-1905), many drunkards became sober and instead of getting inebriated nightly were able to feed and clothe their families. Lots of Public Houses lost trade, many went bankrupt and some were closed by converted landlords. When Rees was involved in his village ministry in Tir-gwaith nicknamed Hell-Fire Row, drunkards were converted and became sober for Christ. The apostle Paul wrote: 'Do not be drunk with wine, in which is dissipation; but be filled with the Spirit' (Ephesians 5:18). Rees Howells did not take the quick, easy option to sell the Half Way House with four acres of land. He closed it down, forfeiting the value of the alcohol license, worth more than £1,000 in 1923 (or £64,400 in 2022) and reimbursed the landlord for loss of livelihood![4]

The flesh is tempted to trust in man and his methods and any weakness I had, I had to walk back [to faith]. If God sees that you will take an easy way of deliverance. He [the old man of flesh] will make you take it every time. You have no excuse for not being delivered. If you do anything you go against the very confirmation that God wants to give you. If you do anything with the idea that God cannot do it for you, He will let you carry it. The moment God sees that you try to protect yourself or deliver yourself, He drives you to your extremity (1 Samuel chapters 27, 29 and 30, David flees to the Philistines and is later rejected by them. Ziglag is attacked and the wives, children and livestock are taken whilst his fighting men are considering stoning him to death).

A friend offered me £4,000, [£257,500 in 2022] repayable when convenient for taking over Glyn Derwen. During a two-hour train journey from a Conference at Birkenhead the Lord showed me from 2 Chronicles 25:5-9 that I was not to take the money.

'Amaziah gathered Judah together and set over them captains of thousands and captains of hundreds, according to their fathers' houses, throughout all Judah and Benjamin, and he numbered them from twenty years old and above, and found them to be three hundred thousand choice men, able to go to war, who could handle spear and shield. He also hired one hundred thousand mighty men of valour from Israel for one hundred talents of silver. But a man of God came to him, saying, "O king, do not let the army of Israel go with you, for the Lord is not with Israel – not with any of the children of Ephraim. But if you go, be gone! Be strong in battle! Even so, God shall make you fall before the enemy; for God has power to help and to overthrow." Then Amaziah said to the man of God, "But what shall we do about the hundred talents which I have given to the troops of Israel?" And the man of God answered, *"The Lord is able to give you much more than this"* ' (2 Chronicles 25:5-9).

Glynderwen Estate with four boarder children, c.1939. The photo shows the school field which was later cleared, levelled and fully grassed, and the tiers of land up to the "Millionaires' View" (rooms that overlooked Swansea Bay). The building on the back left is the edge of Glynderwen Mansion. The building on the right contained classrooms, behind that is El-Shaddai: classroom, library and laundry room on ground floor with accommodation on second floor and in the attic, including a play room for the male boarders.

It was exactly as though that 'plot' had been written for me. That is the Bible. I was always dead to money except as the Lord wanted me to use it. But the Lord gave me instead the promise: "The Lord shall open to thee His Treasury." No man is to take authority in the College. My friend said, "I will give you £200 instead." This I gave to the South Africa General Mission for the missionaries they were sending out in my stead.

Missionaries trekking with a wagon in Southern Africa, c.1918. Rees Howells is sitting with his pith helmet in hand and is wearing glasses. The lady missionaries are sat inside, Mrs Lizzie Howells is on the right. Depending on the weight of the wagon it would have been pulled by donkeys, oxen or bullocks. In the 1840s, some merchants and hunters would travel with 8000 lbs with 14 oxen across level ground, though 2000 lbs was common with inclines.[5]

Man's extremity is God's opportunity.[6] Allow God to deliver you when you are in your extremity. Although you go to your extremity, go back to God, and then you will not fail the second time.

What you think is your extremity is not what God thinks is your extremity of believing. When the time comes the Lord makes the need and the test comes on the same day and you cannot retreat. No excuse for failure. (1 Kings 12:25-33, after the Kingdom of Israel was divided; King Jeroboam *compromised* and made golden calves so that the people would not worship in Jerusalem). If God appoints a man to a position, that man must trust God to keep him in it and make him a success in it.

When God has a work that only He can do, He takes you to your extremity first (Exodus chapter 5 and 6:1, making bricks without straw and God's promise to deliver the Israelites from Egyptian bondage). When this work went beyond me [the founding and expansion of the College] it went into God's hands. [Some of the local newspapers referred to the work as "God's College"].

The College Vision.

GO YE INTO ALL THE WORLD

AND PREACH THE GOSPEL TO

Every Creature.

The Bible College of Wales' Vision/Motto, 1935. Paraphrased as "The Gospel to Every Creature" (Mark 16:15)

Chapter 15

The Sin of Unbelief

'Beware, brethren, lest there be in any of you an evil heart of unbelief in departing from the living God; but exhort one another daily, while it is called "Today," lest any of you be hardened through the deceitfulness of sin' (Hebrews 3:12-13).

'Do you have faith? Have it to yourself before God. Happy is he who does not condemn himself in what he approves. But he who doubts is condemned if he eats, because he does not eat from faith; for whatever is not from faith is sin' (Romans 14:22-23).

Once God has spoken I never doubt (Joshua chapter 1, God commissions Joshua and assumes command over the nation of Israel). I only needed to be shown the light once. Forgiveness I never doubted once. God needs to speak to me only once. But God speaks to you and you fall in the same place and you do not see it.

There is only one sin: rejecting the remedy for sin, for all the rest have been put away at Calvary. 'For He made Him who knew no sin to be sin for us, that we might become the righteousness of God in Him' (2 Corinthians 5:21). Unbelief is the greatest sin you can commit against God.

Jesus said, "For God so loved the world that He gave His only begotten Son, that whoever believes in Him should not perish but have everlasting life. For God did not send His Son into the world to condemn the world, but that the world through Him might be saved. He who believes in Him is not condemned; but he who does not believe is condemned already, because he has not believed in the name of the only begotten Son of God. And this is the condemnation, that the light has come into the world, and men loved darkness rather than light, because their deeds were evil" (John 3:16-19).

If you live in unbelief, you live in sin. The moment you fail to believe what God offers you to believe, you commit sin and live in sin. Until the old man is worked out of you, you will continue in unbelief which is sin. If you fail to do what God asks you to do, sin reigns in your mortal body (Romans chapter 6). It is not yourselves you are doubting, it is the Word of God. It is not you that promised, it is God (Exodus chapter 16, Israel in the wilderness complaining and God providing manna from Heaven).

These people began to murmur before God had time to show what He was going to do (Exodus 16:2-3). Do not rebel against anything that has been revealed to you. Do not fail God after you have seen all these things.

The twelve spies 'spoke to all the congregation of the children of Israel, saying, "The land we passed through to spy out is an exceedingly good land. If the Lord delights in us, then He will bring us into this land and give it to us, 'a land which flows with milk and honey.' Only do not rebel against the Lord, nor fear the people of the land, for they are our bread; their protection has departed from them and the Lord is with us. Do not fear them" ' (Numbers 14:7-9).

You may not think you are too serious about certain things you say, but everything is recorded up there (Matthew 12:35-36, for every idle word you will give an account). God took these people at their word. As soon as they disbelieved, God turned them down. If you disbelieve, I believe that as far as God is concerned, you die. No medical man can help you if you doubt. You are all tested like these.

'For as the body without the spirit is dead, so faith without works is dead also' (James 2:26).

'These things we also speak, not in words which man's wisdom teaches but which the Holy Spirit teaches, comparing spiritual things with spiritual' (1 Corinthians 2:13).

The strange part is that two believed. God knew who they were, Joshua and Caleb, and He knows who among you believe. Unless the Holy Spirit is in you, you are no different from these people who died in the wilderness. As long as you are doubting, you are down, you are miserable, you do not know what to do, you throw your doubts on others, you play with a few shillings or pounds. See what a report they made! Some people are so wise with worldly wisdom and all the time the Holy Spirit can see behind it that there is unbelief. They are after this, after that and the main thing is left out. [They know theology and argue against men of the Spirit, but don't know God. When they resisted Moses they resisted God for he was doing His will]. The moment you come to the place that you refuse to believe what God offers you, you go out of this. If you have really believed and have seen the value of a soul, surely you will do anything to get to your countries. There will be no time for trifling. Consider the apostle Paul and David Livingstone, who said, "I am not leaving till I have finished what God has given me to do."

EVANGELICAL UNION OF SOUTH AMERICA

The Bible College of Wales

A Missionary Conference

AT

THE BIBLE COLLEGE OF WALES

Derwen Fawr, Blackpyl, Swansea

June 24th to 28th, 1932

1932, Evangelical Union of South America (EUSA), Missionary Conference at the Bible College of Wales, *Blackpyl. *Welsh spelling of Blackpill, yet Derwen Fawr was located at Sketty, whilst Glynderwen was located at Blackpill. Rees Howells held a Summer School for Ministers at Derwen Fawr from 2nd-8th July 1932, a precursor to the Every Creature Conferences from 1936-1964.

When God says a thing, you are not to be anxious about it (Exodus 4:19-20, Moses was given powerful signs, but was not eloquent in speech). God all the time tries to drive you out of all this striving and struggling and bring you to be quiet. You always fail about an hour before you must be delivered. It is victory where God is. The moment you believe, your faith becomes substance (Hebrews 11:1), and nothing can stop you from continuing to believe, the moment you believe, it is yours. You will have from God only what you believe for.

'When Jesus departed from there, two blind men followed Him, crying out and saying, "Son of David, have mercy on us!" And when He had come into the house, the blind men came to Him. And Jesus said to them, "Do you believe that I am able to do this?" They said to Him, "Yes, Lord." Then He touched their eyes, saying, "According to your faith let it be to you." And their eyes were opened...' (Matthew 9:27-30).

But man tries to get evidence before his faith becomes substance. That is where all the striving comes in. If you believe, you do not doubt; if you doubt, you do not believe. Where faith begins, anxiety ends; where anxiety begins, faith ends. People are ill because they worry.[1] Ask yourself, "If I have given my body to the Holy Spirit, why do I not trust His guidance?"

Showing you are carrying a burden is your own burden [like the Pharisees who looked sad and disfigured their faces to appear as if they are fasting, Matthew 6:16-18]. You try this and that and you don't believe God. So you appear very serious and have no joy just because you do not believe. If you want the joy of God, it is the joy of believing. "Blessed are those who have not seen and yet, have believed" (John 20:29). Do you know that every time I believed God I am thrilled? I am swept off my feet for days. Come and trust God.

An old lady carrying a heavy basket was given a lift by a carter (one who worked on a cart, carrying loads). He noticed that while sitting in the cart she balanced the heavy basket on her lap which was a burden to her. He enquired why and said she could put it down, she replied, "I am sure you have enough to do to carry me without having the basket too." – It was an unnecessary burden.

It is only unbelief that can stop you from being delivered. God changed His mind in Kadesh Barnea (Numbers chapter 14, the people rebelled, God wanted to destroy the Israelites and to start a new nation through Moses, but he stood in the gap on behalf of the Israelites. Numbers 32:8-9, the spies are sent out of Kadesh Barnea to see the land of Canaan). He is a Sovereign God (Numbers chapter 12, Miriam and Aaron oppose Moses. Numbers chapter 14, the Israelites rebel and God's promise of judgment, not entering into the Promised Land).

God will not deliver you in your doubts. The Holy Spirit will not live with doubt. If you find yourself doubting He is not dwelling in you. God does not run ahead to help you not to doubt, but every time there is real believing He delivers.

"And Elijah said to Ahab, get thee up, eat and drink; for there is a sound of abundance of rain" (1 Kings 18:41). If God told Elijah that the rain was going to stop, the same Person was able to tell him when it would come back. What you say is, "If I go to Ahab, the rain may not come." The moment you say it, the rain will not come. It is just this shade of doubt that stops you from being delivered. 'For the thing which I greatly feared is come upon me, and that which I was afraid of is come unto me' (Job 3:25).

Moses said, "The people whom I am among are six hundred thousand men on foot; yet You have said, 'I will give them meat, that they may eat for a whole month.' Shall flocks and herds be slaughtered for them, to provide enough for them? Or shall all the fish of the sea be gathered together for them, to provide enough for them?" And the Lord said to Moses, "Has the Lord's arm been shortened? Now you shall see whether what I say will happen to you or not" (Numbers 11:21-23).

Unbelief is the Root of all Failure

The Lord said, "Whatever your need, all I ask is that you prove your faith to Me. The only thing that can make you fail is that you are not up in faith."

The root of all failure is unbelief.

The only reason for failure is unbelief.

By being a failure, I mean that you gave it up [a prayer] & left it.

If you are a failure, you are the only cause of it.

If you fail in money, you will fail in all the signs [e.g. healing].

Jesus said to the woman with the issue of blood, "Daughter, be of good cheer; your faith has made you well. Go in peace." While He was still speaking, someone came from the ruler of the synagogue's house, saying to him, "Your daughter is dead. Do not trouble the Teacher." But when Jesus heard it, He answered him, saying, "Do not be afraid; only believe and she will be made well" (Luke 8:48-50).

Ask yourself, "Why is it that God has not delivered me regularly?" I never expected failure. If you have the faith of God it never fails. If you can believe, He can move these donors for you. You need to be alone. 'I am your portion' (Numbers 18:29, R.V.).

I shall be sorry if you continue to live like paupers and put it down to humility – the humility of the old man! You let me fail once. I am sure to recover and go on from there.

At the first test, when responsibility was put on Aaron, he failed (Exodus chapter 32, the golden calf, the people were unrestrained when Moses was on the mountain with God and Aaron was left in charge). When Moses was there he could not fail, because Moses shielded him. The Bible is silent in regard to fasting up to that time, so when Moses failed to return, the people thought that something had happened to him. You may say that Aaron lost his head. So would you, if you were asked to do something beyond man.

You cannot lose what you have gained. Men who have gained positions, if they fail on a high point, do not lose what they have gained, but one who has never gained anything cannot afford to fail (Numbers 20:7-13, Moses failed at the waters of Meribath as he hit the rock instead of commanding the water to come out. Numbers 27:12-14, this disobedience cost him entry into the Promised Land). Do not take criticism from a person who has not done a greater thing than you have done yourself.

Monday, 2 June 1941 was the 17th anniversary of the Bible College of Wales. The following day, an article in the *Evening Post*, a local newspaper, was printed. The journalist recounted much of what Rees Howells had said and achieved over many years and concluded with: 'Impossibilities have happened in the College, and it would not fail. Unless his [Rees Howells'] critics were men of faith, they are not qualified to criticise him.'

"Therefore said I, the Philistines will come down now upon me to Gigal and I have not made supplication unto the Lord; I forced myself therefore, and offered a burnt offering" (1 Samuel 13:12). Do not pray prayers of unbelief, like King Saul did. This was putting prayer instead of believing and that is what you are doing all the time. You weary God with your words. Saul did not trust

God. A man would be a lunatic to preach this man's failures when in failures himself. Saul's own son Jonathan condemned him throughout countless ages (1 Samuel 18:1-4, Jonathan and David made a covenant. 1 Samuel 19:1-7, Jonathan defends David before his dad, King Saul).

The stories of the prophets have the same effect on you as do the histories of great men like Napoleon [Bonaparte of France] and General Gordon [of England who died in Khartoum, Sudan. He refused to leave when he had the opportunity to escape, but stayed to defend the indigenous people from being enslaved and died a martyr]. They stir up the old flesh to do something – and you cannot touch it.

You are a failure in the life of faith without the Holy Spirit. Although you have been failures in the past, do not believe that you must be so now. There is power in the blood to cleanse away all your unbelief. When you have only God to look to, there is no failure there (Joshua chapter 1, God commissions Joshua and assumes command of Israel). There is no failure where God is.

Satan will take no notice of our own efforts, prayers and gossip, but directly when God begins to do anything he is up in arms at once. Whatever God will say to you, will be the centre of Satan's attacks. The Devil attacks every advance (Daniel 10:12-13, the Prince of Persia withstood an angel for twenty-one days who had the understanding for Daniel. Michael the Archangel had to come to the aid of the angel).

The Devil attacks only those whom he sees will be used to attack his kingdom. The Devil can sway millions, but he has no power over a man of God.

Elijah repaired the altar of the Lord that was broken down and took twelve stones, according to the number of the tribes of the sons of Jacob, to whom the word of the Lord had come, saying, "Israel shall be your name."

'And it came to pass, at the time of the offering of the evening sacrifice, that Elijah the prophet came near and said, "Lord God of Abraham, Isaac, and Israel, let it be known this day that You are God in Israel and I am Your servant, and that I have done all these things at Your word. Hear me, O Lord, hear me, that this people may know that You are the Lord God, and that You have turned their hearts back to You again." Then the fire of the Lord fell and consumed the burnt sacrifice, and the wood and the stones and the dust, and it licked up the water that was in the trench. Now when all the people saw it, they fell on their faces;

and they said, "The Lord, He is God! The Lord, He is God!" ' (1 Kings 18:30-31, 36-39).

Rev. Archibald. E. Glover and his wife were missionaries in Shansi Province in northern China. During the Boxer Revolution of 1900, they endured sixty-seven days of captivity as they were driven one thousand miles under the sentence of death, amidst, threats, violence and much physical and mental deprivation. They were also robbed and stripped of their clothing. Many of their co-workers were severely injured or martyred and the strain on his wife led to her eventual death and the loss of their ten-day old baby. Rev. Glover was a lecturer at the Bible College of Wales from October 1927 and financially supported the College.

Rev. Archibald. E. Glover wrote: 'That our God was behind the persecution and would make the wrath of man to praise Him, was a fact in which we found true rest and comfort. Through all the evil, He was working out His own good and glorifying His own name. Had He not a gracious purpose in view? For –

1. Was He not granting us the high privilege of knowing in measure the fellowship of the suffering of His own beloved Son?

2. Was not the persecution His call to the pastors and teachers, native and foreign, to fulfil their ministry in filling up that which is behind of the afflictions of Christ for His body's sake?

3. Did He not design by the persecution the purification of His Church in China?

4. Was it not the only way known to His wisdom in which the answer could be given to our constant prayers for the opening of 'a great door and effectual' to the Word of His grace?

5. Was it not His opportunity in us for proving to the native converts the power of the truths we had so often preached, namely, that we should 'take pleasure in necessities, in persecution, in distress, for Christ's sake,' and 'rejoice that we are counted worthy to suffer shame for His name'?

6. Was it not meant to be, to ourselves individually, an evident token of salvation, and that of God, a seal of our sonship and a means by which we might become 'partakers of His holiness'?

7. And was it not, after, all, only what He told us to expect as the appointed portion of all who will live godly in Christ Jesus and enter the Kingdom of God?

Yes, there was a needs-be for our sufferings. The silver lining to the cloud out of the sea, was 'the eternal purposes of Him who worketh all things after the counsel of His own will,' the cause behind the causes. And in Him we had peace.'[2]

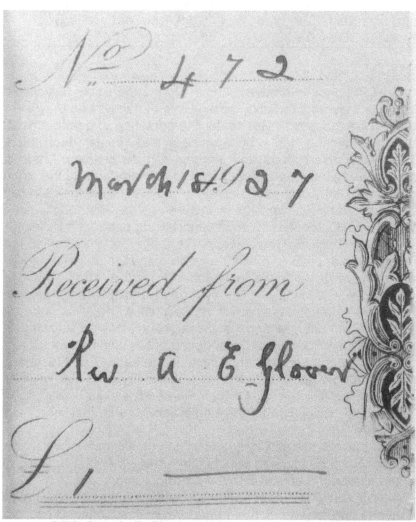

#472, Rev. A. E. Glover's gift receipt, 18 March 1927
£1 in 1927 is worth approximately £67 in 2022

When the Holy Spirit is fighting, the Devil always tries to draw attention to something which is of no importance. The glory in this life, is that the very thing that the Devil brings against you helps you to go through.

'Now it happened when Sanballat, Tobiah, Geshem the Arab, and the rest of our enemies heard that I had rebuilt the wall, and that there were no breaks left in it (though at that time I had not hung the doors in the gates), that Sanballat and Geshem sent to me, saying, "Come, let us meet together among the villages in the plain of Ono." But they thought to do me harm. So I sent messengers to them, saying, "I am doing a great work, so that I cannot come down. Why should the work cease while I leave it and go down to you?" But they sent me this message four times and I answered them in the same manner' (Nehemiah 6:1-4).

What God has said will be the very thing that troubles the enemy and the very thing he will attack you on, and say, "Has God said it?" (Genesis 3:1, the serpent speaking to Eve in the Garden of Eden. Genesis 37:8-28, Joseph and the telling of his dreams antagonised his brothers who sold him as a slave).

The enemy comes to you so subtly, getting at your intelligence: "Use your commonsense." It is as though a man living in the country sold a £100 note for £5 to a person knowing the value of it. [£100 notes/bills were issued by the Bank of England from 1775 to 1943 and ceased to be legal tender on 16 April 1945. £100 in 1943 is worth £4,900 in 2022, and £5 is worth £245]. The Devil makes you willing to take less than your due because you do not believe. Satan wants you to do things he knows you will fail on.

The Devil will help you to do things if he sees that by so doing, he can put a rope round your neck to hang you. You do not realise that it is the old Devil pushing you to do it badly, because he is a liar from the beginning (father of lies, John 8:44). So you just turn it round the other way. The Devil said, "What about that donor you were going to move first." I never allowed the Devil to give me a suggestion of failure. God allows the Devil to have every chance and then He steps in (Job's tests, Job 1:9-22, Job 2:3-10). You say the Devil is strong. He is. You say it because you are on this side, but the Holy Spirit and the new man are living on the other side (He who is in you is greater, 1 John 4:4). If the Devil takes power without authority, you have the right to cast him out. Do not look at the enemy, look at God.

Jesus said, "All authority has been given to Me in Heaven and on earth" (Matthew 28:18).

Jesus said, "Go into all the world and preach the Gospel to Every Creature. He who believes and is baptised will be saved; but he who does not believe will be condemned. And these signs will follow those who believe: In My name they will cast out demons; they will speak with new tongues; they will take up serpents; and if they drink anything deadly, it will by no means hurt them; they will lay hands on the sick, and they will recover" (Mark 16:15-18).

Jesus said, "Now is the judgment of this world; now the ruler of this world will be cast out" (John 12:31).

Jesus said, "Of judgment, because the ruler of this world is judged" (John 16:11).

Paul wrote: 'Having disarmed principalities and powers, He made a public spectacle of them, triumphing over them in it' (Colossians 2:15).

Opening of Twelfth Session, September 1935. Estates: The Bible College, Derwen Fawr. The Missionary Home of Rest, Glynderwen. The Missionary School, Sketty, before its extension.

Chapter 16

Believe – Trust and Obey

'Trust in the Lord with all your heart and lean not on your own understanding; in all your ways acknowledge Him and He shall direct your paths' (Proverbs 3:5-6).

A boy had an unclean spirit which tried to kill him, and the father pleaded for Jesus' help. He replied, "If you can believe, all things are possible to him who believes" (Mark 9:23).

It all depends on your believing. You all the time want to put something beside the believing. You know you must not do that for salvation, but you do it for other things. No, it depends just on believing. "Now the Lord said unto Abram, get thee out of thy country and from thy kindred, and from thy fathers house, unto the land that I will show thee and I will make of thee a great nation and I will bless thee, and make thy name great; and be thou a blessing, and I will bless them that bless thee and him that curseth thee will I curse, and in thee shall all the families of the earth be blessed" (Genesis 12:1-3, R.V.). God said this before Abram did anything.

It is God who is to lead in this battle. When you are fighting against principalities and powers (Colossians 2:15), you have to come out of fighting against the flesh (1 Corinthians 15:50).

'...Be strong in the Lord and in the power of His might. Put on the whole armour of God that you may be able to stand against the wiles of the Devil. For we do not wrestle against flesh and blood, but against principalities, against powers, against the rulers of the darkness of this age, against spiritual hosts of wickedness in the heavenly places' (Ephesians 6:10-12).

It is God planning, God speaking, God showing. He said to Joshua, "I have given Jericho into thine hands" (Joshua 6:2). It was not the marching and shouting that brought the walls of Jericho down, but the Unseen Captain. All Joshua and the people did was to believe. It is only believing (Joshua 5:13-6:27, the Commander of the Lord's Army and the fall of Jericho). The trouble is that we are not simple enough to believe God. The blessing makes us like a child, so that we can believe.

Jesus said, "Let the little children come to Me and do not forbid them; for of such is the Kingdom of God. Assuredly, I say to you, whoever does not receive the Kingdom of God as a little child will by no means enter it" (Luke 18:16-17).

To a man, real faith and mental assent seem very much alike. Faith untested is ninety percent imagination. God will never uphold anything but real faith. He may deliver in a test, but will bring another test later to show that the believing was not real (Exodus 17:1-7, water came from the rock at Horeb. Numbers 20:1-21, the water from the rock at Meribah which Moses *should* have spoken to, and the Edomites refused the Israelites passage through their country).

If you say you are believing something at a distance, as a rule, He will test you on something visible and never at hand. You think you can believe by simply going on your knees, but you have to spend time until every difficulty is removed. With the Holy Spirit's believing there is an accomplishment. You have to discern between real faith and presumption.

Mrs P. Syres was a missionary who was trained under Rees Howells at the Bible College of Wales. She spoke at the College in October 1961, relating to an experience from her student days in the early days of the College, late 1920s or early 1930s.

One evening, the Director Rees Howells and the men students were out at a meeting and the women students were having a prayer meeting by themselves. The burden at the time was for a large sum of money and during the meeting they 'came through' to a great believing. The next morning she went to dust the furniture in the Director's room. Students always did practical duties which helped keep the fees as low as possible and were half actual cost, subsidised to help train more people. The Director greeted her with a curt, "Good morning," and his eyes were like fire. "I hear," he said, "that you believed last night!" "Yes," she replied, "we had a wonderful believing." "All right then," he said, "would you like to sign this paper?" (A contract). As she stood there her faith fled from her. That morning when the students went into the meeting the men had their heads up, but the women's heads were drooping. The Director stood up and spoke to them on the difference between faith and presumption.

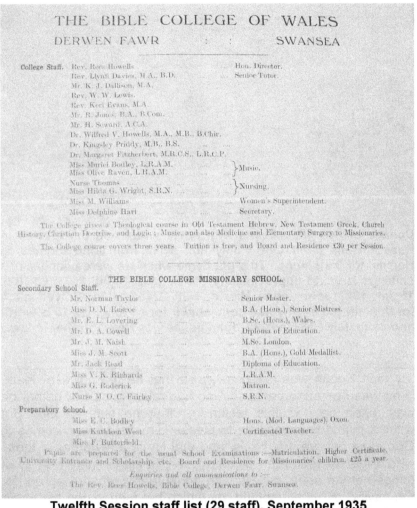

Twelfth Session staff list (29 staff), September 1935

Rees Howells spoke to a preacher friend in Carmarthen:
"Why don't you trust the Lord? You can't trust Him to supply your needs, if you don't trust Him to forgive your sins. If you ask God to forgive your sins, why don't you take forgiveness and never ask again? 'He carried our sins in His own body on the tree' (1 Peter 2:24). It's in the Bible. Do you believe the Bible?"
The preacher friend responded, "Yes."
Rees Howells asked, "Do you believe this then?"[1]

Faith is believing what God tells you. Abraham believed God and did not mix himself with the plan. You are not going to do much unless you believe. Begin to trust God.

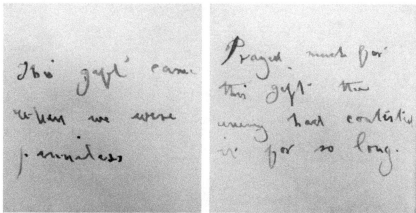

Collage of two gift receipts with notes written on the reverse in Rees Howells' hand. Left: 9 July 1927, #530, from John Thomas, St. Helens, for 3 shillings. 'This gift came when we were penniless.' 3 shillings is worth approximately £10 in 2022. Right: #531, £2-10-0, 16 July 1927, John Jones, Mission Hall, Brynamman. 'Prayed much for this gift the enemy had contested it for so long.' £2-10 is worth approximately £168 in 2022. John Jones was Rees' brother-in-law.

'By faith Enoch was taken away so that he did not see death, "And was not found because God had taken him." For before he was taken he had this testimony, that he pleased God. But without faith it is impossible to please Him, for he who comes to God must believe that He is, and that He is a rewarder of those who diligently seek Him. By faith Noah, being Divinely warned of things not yet seen, moved with godly fear, prepared an ark for the saving of his household, by which he condemned the world and became heir of the righteousness which is according to faith' (Hebrews 11:5-7).

'And he believed in the Lord and He accounted it to him for righteousness' (Genesis 15:6). 'For what does the Scripture say? "Abraham Believed God and it was accounted to him for righteousness" ' (Romans 4:3).

Be dead to anything the world or the Devil may say to you. In that way you will prove to the Lord that you believe what He has said (Romans 8:1-5, no condemnation in Christ, walking in the Spirit, not according to the Law or in the flesh). Do not listen to people; believe God and not the thing, which is in the impossible (Genesis 16:1-4, Sarai, Abram's wife, asked her husband to have sexual relations with her Egyptian maidservant so they could have a child). Live in the love of God and believe that He wants to deliver you. When God finds that you are believing, He will come down to deliver.

Do not limit God. 'Yes, again and again they tempted God and limited the Holy One of Israel. They did not remember His power: The day when He redeemed them from the enemy' (Psalm 78:41-42). A man cannot take in the greatness of God. His mortal, limited mind cannot contain Him. Some men of the old dispensation came up to believe Him, but generally He spoke to them in the form of an angel like a man. If faith can quench fire, it can quench anything (Moses and Daniel).

God does not need to repeat Himself. He is an Almighty Person. All He needs is to find faith (Exodus 12:29-52, the tenth plague, death of the firstborn, plundering the Egyptians and the Exodus. Daniel 9, Daniel's prayer for his people, the Angel Gabriel's sent from God with a message and wisdom for Daniel to understand. Ezra 1:1-3, King Cyrus of Persia was called to build the House of the Lord in Jerusalem, fulfilling the word of the Lord through Jeremiah – the Jews were told to go and build.

Isaiah was strong in challenging because he saw God (Isaiah chapter 6, his vision of the Lord. Isaiah chapter 7, sent to King Ahaz and the sign of Immanuel. Isaiah chapter 9, for to us a Child is born, and judgment on arrogance and oppression. Isaiah chapter 37, King Hezekiah seeks Isaiah's help and Sennacherib's Fall. Isaiah chapter 38, Hezekiah's sickness and recovery).

Faith is the greatest weapon (Hebrews 11, by faith…). The faith of God can move mountains. People have not moved mountains in this generation because they have their own faith and not the faith of God. You do not believe more than you believe God can do through you.

Norman Brend was a BCW student from 1935 whilst Nollie (later Mrs Brend) joined BCW in 1937. During the war, Norman was one of the lumberjacks at Penllergaer for a few years before he left the area. Nollie was conscripted into war work as a nurse in a T.B. sanatorium alongside a handful of other BCW women. Nollie left the area later than Norman, but they corresponded and married in August 1947. On 10 October 1957, the anniversary of Rees Howells' birthday, they became staff members at Emmanuel School and with their children lived on campus. The following was told to me by "Mr Brend" as he was known.

At one prayer meeting, staff and students at the Bible College of Wales were praying for some missionaries (probably one was a former student) in the Far East. The problem was in relation to the isolation of the community and the difficulty in reaching them. As the College body prayed audibly for God to make a way, Norman Brend prayed, "For the mountain to be cast into the sea." Afterwards, a senior staff member, Dr. Kingsley Priddy politely rebuked Mr Brend for his prayer. Weeks passed and then news reached Swansea from the isolated community. In a dramatic moment, the earth moved and part of the mountain collapsed allowing easier access into the remote community! Norman Brend received an apology from the humbled staff member. I can still see Mr Brend outside Glynderwen Mansion as he told me this story with a smile on his face and a glint in his eyes. For the author, it was a lesson of faith, to trust God even when things appear impossible.

Jesus said to his disciples, "If you have faith as a mustard seed, you will say to this mountain, 'Move from here to there,' and it will move; and nothing will be impossible for you" (Matthew 17:20).

Norman Brend was promoted to glory on 10 October 2012, age 98, 55 years to day of his arrival as staff and 133 years to the day of Rees Howells' birth. He was the last of the "120" students and staff who surrendered all in March 1936, in the cause of the Great Commission, to intercede and to help train up others to go. Mrs Brend was promoted to glory on 15 August 2015, age 100, she was the last of the pre-war students.

It is God doing it and you are believing that He is doing it. And that is the chance that God is giving you, to believe Him. But flesh and blood cannot believe. God has to work you out of yourself, put you back, disappoint the flesh until you know that you can do nothing. It is not any activity, not anything that you can do only what God does. It was revealed to Rebekah that the elder son should serve the younger (Genesis 25:20-34). Joseph believed the promise and made mention of the carrying up of his bones out of Egypt (Genesis 50:25-26, Hebrews 11:22).

An Ethiopian Proverb quoted by the Emperor of Ethiopia to Rees Howells and often quoted by Rees Howells, "The man who has only God to look to, can do all things and never fail."

There is nothing that pleases God more than you take Him at His word. When did I believe for the College? – The moment He told me. When I believed for Glyn Derwen, the Lord asked me, when I was on the tennis court, "Do you believe for it?" I said, "I do believe." "Then it is yours." And I praised Him for it then and there.

One with God is in the majority.

One with God will do more than millions without Him.

I never believed He could fail.

Glynderwen Estate showing the tennis court area c.1947 with four students and a large tree stump. The tennis ground was marked with chalk when in season and was later enclosed with a high wire fence for Emmanuel School. To the right, just beyond the conifer trees was an unnamed stream.

Chapter 17

Faith, Not Feelings

Jesus said, "...I say to you that even Solomon in all his glory was not arrayed like one of these. Now if God so clothes the grass of the field, which today is and tomorrow is thrown into the oven, will He not much more clothe you, O you of little faith? Therefore do not worry, saying, 'What shall we eat?' or 'What shall we drink?' or 'What shall we wear?' " (Matthew 6:29-31).

Jesus went to the region of Tyre and Sidon and a woman of Canaan came from that region and cried out to Him, saying, "Have mercy on me, O Lord, Son of David! My daughter is severely demon-possessed." But He answered her not a word. And His disciples came and urged Him, saying, "Send her away, for she cries out after us." But He answered and said, "I was not sent except to the lost sheep of the house of Israel." Then she came and worshipped Him, saying, "Lord, help me!" But He answered and said, "It is not good to take the children's bread and throw it to the little dogs." And she said, "Yes, Lord, yet even the little dogs eat the crumbs which fall from their masters' table." Then Jesus answered and said to her, "O woman, great is your faith! Let it be to you as you desire." And her daughter was healed from that very hour (Matthew 15:21-28).

It is all believing. Once you believe, no delay can put a doubt in your mind. Once the Holy Spirit believes through you, He believes forever. Faith does not change; it is feelings that change. Feelings have nothing to do with believing and if you believe you have no need of feelings. You might have thought I ought not to have closed the meeting last night when I was on the point of going through [in prayer – victory]. No, if I could have gone through last night, I can go through tonight. We start from where we left off. Once faith, faith forever!

Only that which is faith endures. God kept no record of what happened in Egypt from the time of Joseph to the time of Moses [the Word of God is mostly silent on those years].

> 'For who has despised the day of small things? For these seven rejoice to see the plumb line in the hand of Zerubbabel. They are the eyes of the Lord, which scan to and fro throughout the whole earth' (Zechariah 4:10).

If one has not faith for a small thing, one cannot pray for a large thing. If one has attained a high degree of faith, one can carry burdens easily when they are of lower degree. When one makes a venture, one must be sure of one's ground, and have a series of answers to prayer leading up to that point. But after a great deliverance one must not despise smaller things and imagine they are to be obtained without real guidance, faith and prayer. Faith for personal needs must be kept effectual by constant exercise when intercession has risen to higher grades.

Never go beyond your faith.

Believe the essential.

You must have complete victory in one position before proceeding to the next.

> Jesus said, "He who is faithful in what is least is faithful also in much; and he who is unjust in what is least is unjust also in much. Therefore if you have not been faithful in the unrighteous mammon, who will commit to your trust the true riches? And if you have not been faithful in what is another man's, who will give you what is your own? No servant can serve two masters; for either he will hate the one and love the other, or else he will be loyal to the one and despise the other. You cannot serve God and mammon" (Luke 16:10-13).

Learn faith in one thing at a time, cover the ground and apply it only from gained positions. You are not going to win these positions lightly. Unless you become men of faith for money, do not try Divine healing, for you cannot do it, especially in a test case. You cannot rise in faith in an emergency.

With Divine healing you cannot expect another to believe for you unless you believe for yourself.

With financial needs, if you allow your needs to pile up and continually add to the sum you are praying for, you may go beyond the limit of your faith. I must never go beyond the grade of my faith. I must certainly walk up to a new position, but when I have gained it, I must keep within it.

The Lord said, "In building the College like the Second Temple (Haggai chapter 1 and Haggai 2:1-9). I can go on with it at once.

As Owner, I give you permission to come back every time you are in need, whether it is £100, £200 or £500. All I expect is for you to have the faith for it. Do not tempt Me to break a law. 'According to your faith be it unto you' " (Matthew 9:29).

LIST OF CHARGES FOR CALLS

FROM .... SKETTY .... EXCHANGE TO THE
UNDERMENTIONED EXCHANGES AND RURAL CALL OFFICES.

TIME	UP TO 5 MILES	5 TO 7½ MILES	7½ TO 10 MILES	10 TO 12½ MILES	12½ TO 15 MILES
7 a.m. to 2 p.m.	1¼d.	2½d.	4d.	5d.	6d.
2 p.m. to 7 p.m.	1¼d.	2½d.	3d.	4d.	4d.
7 p.m. to 7 a.m.	1¼d.	2½d.	3d.	3d.	3d.

Bishopston	Clydach	Pontardawe	Porteynon	Rhossilly
Pentrefach	Penclawdd	Reynoldston	Aberdulais	Cymmer
Gorseinon	Penmaen	Cwmavon	Ammanford	Resolven
Gowerton	Pontardulais	Neath	Burry Port	Garnant
Llansamlet	Skewen	Port Talbot	Llangennith	Glanamman
Morriston	Briton FerryLlanelly		Bryn	Gwaun-cae-
Mumbles	Llangennech	Llwynhendy	Llannon	Gurwen
Swansea		Pemberton		Llandebie
Three		Gorwich		Up.Cwmtwrch
Crosses				Ystalyfera
Treboeth				Ystradgyh-
Bonymaen				lais
Pentrechwyth				Crynant
Skewen				Cross Hands
				Pontyberem
				Pontyates
				Tumble
				Up.Brynamman
				Caerau
				Kenfig Hill.
				Maesteg
				Trimsaran

List of Charges for Telephone Calls c.1929, for Sketty, where the Derwen Fawr Estate was based, known locally as Lower Sketty. Notice the three designated time charges 7am-2pm, 2-7pm and 7pm-7am. And the cost by distance, up to 5 miles (8.04 km), then in 2½ mile increments (4.02 km), up to 15 miles (24.14 km). The typed towns and villages reveal how far they are located from Sketty, Swansea. Rees Howells' home village of Upper Brynamman was in the furthest charge zone, to distinguish it from Lower Brynamman. Rees believed God for his daily bread and for payment for essential phone calls. The College had its first phone in the late 1920s, the internet in 1999 (dial-up) and in 2001 a private landline was first installed for a student.

I knew the moment I had faith for £20, then for £50. Now when you have faith, you have the evidence of it, not before. When I had to get through for £300 [from 1923, this is worth £19,400 in 2022] I knew I had prayed through [got the assurance] the night before. Oh the joy! I knew the next day I came through for the £500 [from 1924, this is worth £32,400 in 2022]. No need to regain it.[1]

The next place I had to get was £1,000 [from 1929, this is worth £67,700]. The £1,000 was most wonderful, when I turned the workmen back and stopped the lectures; we devoted every hour to waiting upon God. In three days, on the Friday, the £1,000 came. Afterwards, £1,000 did not test me.[2]

Then came the second, third, fourth, fifth, sixth, seventh and eighth gifts of £1,000. Then the Lord stopped me and said, "I am not going to give you any more at £1,000. Pray for £2,000." To gain it, I had first to give away £2,000; I did it in two sums: £1,200 and £800. The next step was £10,000.[3]

The £10,000 arrived in July 1938 and in 2022 is worth approximately £717,000, however, if it was invested into an estate at a conservative estimate the value would be five or six times as great.

As soon as I sent out the first pamphlet concerning the Vision three years ago [in 1935, thus speaking in 1938], I wrote: "The first gift to the Vision is £10,000." The Lord told me: "I will open unto you My Treasury." I wondered all the time how I should prove to the Lord that I had faith for £10,000. I would give £10,000 on the property. The Lord told me, "You have got £10,000. If you like you can take the money from the College and give it to the Vision." I acted on it at once.

Nobody except my family knew that I had an income on a capital that had been given to the College. [This was an investment, possibly shares where dividends or interest was paid to Rees Howells, which he put into the College funds. Rees and Lizzie Howells did not take a wage from the College and to use his own words, "Did not run on the spoil" (take advantage).

The question now is to change the income for capital. The position is gained whether He will sell it or not, but He will watch me to see if I do all I can to sell it. Why did the Holy Spirit do it? You cannot get people to give £10,000. The Holy Spirit must get people to use their capital. That is why He used capital belonging to the College.

WESTMINSTER BANK LIMITED

Date 22 FEB 1937

Credit ... Howells ...

THE BIBLE COLLEGE OF WALES.

Gold				
Notes £1				
1 Notes 10/-		10		—
Silver				
Copper				
£		10		—
Bank Notes £5 and over				
Scotch or Irish Notes @ £5		5	—	—
Cheques, Postal Orders, etc.				
Annuity.		16	18	4
Paid in by £		22	8	4

Westminster Bankbook statement 22 February 1937, £16-18-4 annuity (a fixed sum paid each year), worth approximately £1,235 in 2022. Some staff paid regular sums to the College from legacies, whilst many paired up and prayed in money for the College.

I used to wonder how the Vision could ever become so dear to me as the College. Now that I have gained the intercession over

£10,000, I can never come up to it again. It is wonderful to think that the Treasury has been opened for £10,000. All I have to do is to remain quiet and allow it to come over me. If the Bible is true, the hundredfold on £10,000 is £1,000,000.[4]

No person is greater in this College than what he is able to move God for. It is only as much of the positions as you have believed for in this life that you will have credit for in eternity.

I do not wish to hear confessions [of sin or lack of faith etc.]. If there is anything I need to know, the Holy Spirit will tell me of it.

Will you put such a glory in this life of faith that people like Tommy [Howells from Brynamman, not a relative, but Rees Howells' prayer partner from 1921] will step out and follow in it? The value I put on Tommy is that I would rather have half of you go than for him to go, because I am always able to trust him. In a test he has never crossed me once. It is not what you do, but the fellowship you have. Many and many a time he had £50. Once I was praying for £100 and Tommy for £20 without our telling each other, and we were both delivered on the same day and from different sources. [Rees and Tommy met in the evenings to pray together for the founding of the College. £100 in 1923 is worth £6,500 in 2022].

You ought to pray for people in your homes to follow you [to take an interest in your ministry]. If people have followed you and believe in your calling, when they are tested you can never have the same feeling towards them as you have towards other people.

The majority of students that arrived in 1936 and 1937 on a three or four year course of studies stayed through the war years (1939-1945). Those conscripted to government duties were only released by the government in 1946 or 1947 depending on their duties. During the 1930s and into the 1940s, there were at least twenty-three sets of relatives (more than sixty people) living at the Bible College of Wales (BCW) and the Bible School, later known as Emmanuel School. It was a large community of 'one in Christ Jesus' (Galatians 3:8), where students and staff tried to 'esteem others better than oneself,' and to 'look out not only for his own interests, but also for the interests of others' (Philippians 2:3-4). As in the Gospels, relatives often served together, think of the Twelve Apostles: Simon Peter & Andrew and James & John.
 These family relations in Swansea included:
A dad and four children (mother and baby later joined them).
A mother and three daughters.
Mum, dad and two daughters.

Mum, dad, son and daughter.
A mother and two daughters.
Uncle, nephew and niece.
Father, mother and son.
Mother and daughter.
Husband and wife.
Brother and sister.
Aunt and niece.
Two brothers.
Two sisters.

When my faith becomes equal to the substance of the thing prayed for, I have the evidence (Hebrews 11:1). You try to get the evidence without the substance and you forget it, unless it be by chance. Striving in prayer comes because you use effort to obtain evidence when you have not believed. You want evidence, but God wants faith, not praising when you have not believed. Do not get into bondage by trying to obtain the evidence before faith has become substance. Your deliverance will always be found on the Mount (Genesis chapter 22, Abraham and Isaac on Mount Moriah). Think about believing for your salvation. It was fear that you had, although the deliverance [atonement] was there. The moment you believed you had the joy of revelation [Christ died for my sins]. The moment you believe, you have forgiveness of sins. You might think that then it was given; no, it was given at Calvary. ['...He has appeared to put away sin by the sacrifice of Himself' (Hebrews 9:26), Cf. Ephesians 1:4].

Praise flows naturally from believing. When God speaks and you believe, you praise before the victory (2 Chronicles 20, people of Moab, Ammon, Ammonites and others came to battle against King Jehoshaphat). The cloud of witnesses are always watching; they see if you praise more after the deliverance than before. [Rees often mentioned the 'cloud of witnesses' during his preaching and teaching at the College meetings].

'The Spirit of the Lord came upon Jahaziel the son of Zechariah...in the midst of the assembly. And he said, "Listen, all you of Judah and you inhabitants of Jerusalem, and you, King Jehoshaphat! Thus says the Lord to you, 'Do not be afraid nor dismayed because of this great multitude, for the battle is not yours, but God's. ...You will not need to fight in this battle. Position yourselves, stand still and see the salvation of the Lord, who is with you, O Judah and Jerusalem!' Do not fear or be dismayed; tomorrow go out against them, for the Lord is with you."

'And Jehoshaphat bowed his head with his face to the ground, and all Judah and the inhabitants of Jerusalem bowed before the Lord, worshipping the Lord. Then the Levites of the children of the Kohathites and of the children of the Korahites stood up to praise the Lord God of Israel with voices loud and high. So they rose early in the morning and went out into the Wilderness of Tekoa; and as they went out, Jehoshaphat stood and said, "Hear me, O Judah and you inhabitants of Jerusalem: believe in the Lord your God and you shall be established; believe His prophets, and you shall prosper." And when he had consulted with the people, he appointed those who should sing to the Lord, and who should praise the beauty of holiness, as they went out before the army and were saying, "Praise the Lord, for His mercy endures forever." Now when they began to sing and to praise, the Lord set ambushes against the people of Ammon, Moab, and Mount Seir, who had come against Judah; and they were defeated' (2 Chronicles 20:14-15, 17-22).

'Therefore we also, since we are surrounded by so great a cloud of witnesses, let us lay aside every weight, and the sin which so easily ensnares us, and let us run with endurance the race that is set before us' (Hebrews 12:1).

Unless you come to the place to act on your believing, you cannot go very far. Never let your action betray your believing. Believing means trusting and applying. All I believed I had to put through. Whatever I believe I make known. When the influenza came in Africa [1918 onwards, after World War One, and is referenced in the *SAGM Pioneer Magazine* from 1919], I believed that no one would die and made it known.[5]

The moment I believed the College I acted on it. I believe it is almost unknown for a man to buy a property when he had only two shillings, but when I bought Derwen Fawr I acted in the open. [People were notified that he was going to buy the property and 4,000 booklets were sent out. His believing was not private; he staked his reputation on it]. In believing you must step out on something. I remember walking round this great property and the Spirit saying, "You are going to buy this." So I began to shut the gates at night. It became mine the moment I believed it."

Lady Ruthen gave the first refusal on Derwen Fawr to Rees Howells in the presence of her daughter and son-in-law, but had not told her agent or solicitor. Rees went to the solicitor's office on Saturday, 21 December 1929, to make payment and sign papers for the property, but was told to return on Monday. Rees knew that he was being fobbed off and asked his cousin, Dr. John Howells, a medical doctor to accompany him on Monday. The solicitor was unwell at home and had instructed the clerk in the office to tell Rees that Derwen Fawr was sold! Dr. Howells was none too pleased and said things that Rees would not have said. Outside, Rees was given strength by God and declared to his cousin, "Derwen Fawr is not sold!" Dr. Howells disagreed, believing the word of the clerk over Rees' word from the Lord months before. Rees had already put into print that the Bible College *would* buy Derwen Fawr.

Rees Howells and Dr. John Howells went to see the solicitor at his home, who was an old patient of Dr. Howells. The daughter opened the door and refused entry because her father was too unwell. Dr. Howells said, "It's the first time I ever heard that a patient was too ill to see a doctor" and walked inside! It transpired that a Syndicate had sent a cheque to the solicitor's office. If he had been at the office that day he would have cashed it and Derwen Fawr would have been sold! He then agreed to turn down the Syndicate who had plans to build a housing estate.

The following day, Tuesday, 24 December, the Lord said to Rees Howells, "You must buy Derwen Fawr tonight or never." That night, on Christmas Eve, Rees and Lizzie Howells visited Lady Ruthen just as the lights were being put out. The door was unlocked and they were invited in. She was seriously considering keeping the house, but Rees reminded her of her promise of 'first refusal' which her son-in-law confirmed. Rees then offered £500 more than the Syndicate, which in 2022 is worth £33,900. A deposit of £25 (£1,700 in 2022) was handed over, all the money that Rees possessed, which had come from two gifts that day.[6]

If you cannot believe the impossible in secret, how will you believe it in the open? If you believe this Vision [the Gospel to Every Creature] God will use you every day to bring about its fulfilment. When you believe the Vision you have no time for anything else. Oh, the joy of believing! It is not through doing. Doing is alright, but doing is an outcome of believing.

In this life numbers are not to count. If one believes it is enough (Judges chapters 6 and 7, Mideon oppresses Israel and Gideon is called to defeat them). When God speaks to a man, it is that one that does the believing; others merely believe it from him.

Did Isaac need the same faith as Abraham? No, Abraham believed the Covenant as did his seed after him [Isaac and Jacob etc.]. When Abraham was on the Mount, the Lord confirmed the Covenant without a single condition to Isaac (Genesis 17:9-14, 19 and Genesis 22:16-18).

'But without faith it is impossible to please Him: for he that cometh to God must believe that He is and that He is a rewarder of them that diligently seek Him' (Hebrews 11:6).

The Holy Spirit dealt with me first, not with the donor. Whatever objections the donor [the person who will give to Rees Howells or BCW, as directed by God's command] may have towards this College, the Lord can do away with them all. I do not try to move the donor. If I did, I should have to move every other donor and have to do everything all over again. No, I try to move God and again a proof that I can do so. [Rees did not try to influence the giver by solicitation or emotional appeals etc. but trusted God to move them to give].

The Lord told me once to move a certain donor for £1,000. [From 1929, £1,000 is worth £67,700 in 2022]. At first, £200 came from that donor, then £1,000 from another donor. I could have taken it as the answer, but the Lord told me to pray that the first donor would complete the amount and soon afterwards I had £800 from that donor.

Rees Howells prayed that the Holy Spirit would speak to the donors to give, whether by name, e.g. Joe Bloggs or John Smith, or that God would speak to a person or to give x amount. There were many incidents where parcels of money or envelopes had been left at the front door at one of the estates. Rees Howells would often meet the postman in the morning. Back then, the postal service made multiple deliveries a day across Britain. Mrs Howells, money in hand, would walk into Sketty to buy essential provisions. At other times, banks abroad e.g. New York or Chicago, America, were instructed to send Rees Howells or the College money, from anonymous donors. Foreign cheques were also received. There are thousands of gift receipts which I have seen, ranging from the widow's mite to wealthy individuals. Some merely state 'anonymous' and the amount received. Others give the name of the donor, mission hall, ministry, chapel or just the area it was received from. Some people asked for an acknowledgement of the gift or a receipt by post.

Glynderwen Mansion obtained its first letterbox in 2002, with a wire box attached to collect the mail, seventy-nine years after it was bought by Rees Howells in 1923. The residents now in their 70s and 80s no longer had to bend down and pick up the envelopes from the porch floor outside.

What God is doing is not man's doing. An advance in faith is ordered and given by God. It is from a position of poverty that an advance in faith has to be made otherwise it would not be God who ordered it. If God wants you to do anything, surely He will go to all lengths to help you. God always works in the impossible (Isaiah 43:1-2, the protection of Jacob/Israel who has been redeemed. Daniel chapter 3, the Jews refused to bow down before Nebuchadnezzar's golden image. Shadrach, Meshach, and Abednego were thrown into the fiery furnace as an example but were protected by God). God shows you that you can do nothing; then He works. God is working and He is telling you what He is doing.

It is not what you try to do; it is God working and you believing. 'Let us labour therefore to enter into that rest' (Hebrews 4:11). This is the rest where God is working and you are trusting. This is what you have not seen, it is not you, but God behind you and in you, and He told you not to premeditate (Luke 12:29-30). The world is to be evangelised; I do not know the way God will do it, but He will do it* (September, 1937).

*This was decades before TV satellites, the internet, video-conferencing, social media and smartphone Apps. In 2000, a former BCW student, Rheinard Bonnke, founder of CFaN, led the largest evangelistic meetings in history, where on one night, one million people made a profession of faith and more than 1.6 million attended. From 1967 until his promotion to glory in 2019, he saw 79 million professions of faith!

Jesus said, "Do not seek what you should eat or what you should drink, nor have an anxious mind. For all these things the nations of the world seek after, and your Father knows that you need these things. But seek the Kingdom of God and all these things shall be added to you. Do not fear, little flock, for it is your Father's good pleasure to give you the Kingdom. Sell what you have and give alms; provide yourselves money bags which do not grow old, a treasure in the Heavens that does not fail, where no thief approaches nor moth destroys. For where your treasure is, there your heart will be also" (Luke 12:29-34).

Chapter 18

Guidance

'For the eyes of the Lord run to and fro throughout the whole earth, to show Himself strong on behalf of those whose heart is loyal to Him...' (2 Chronicles 16:9).

'Trust in the Lord with all your heart and lean not on your own understanding. In all your ways acknowledge Him and He shall direct your paths' (Proverbs 3:5-6).

When I was in a railway compartment on the way to a conference at Llandrindod [during the summer holiday week of 1906] with about eleven people from the village ministry, I heard God speak to me, although the others did not hear. He said and I remember the words He said, "When you will be coming back this way, you will be a new man." I protested, "But I am a new man." No, it was to be something far more real than that!

Do you know that God has been speaking to me from that day to this? Does God speak to you? Does He tell you what to do? Or is everything you do guesswork? He spoke to me (on the Friday of the Conference) on the way to a district Workers' Meeting. His voice was as loud as any other. He said, "I will give you till six o'clock to make your decision. It is your last chance. For two years you have told people that you want the best. I showed you the best last Sunday. At six o'clock you will either accept Me or reject Me. Your no or your yes."[1]

The voice of the Holy Spirit is unmistakable.

To hear God speaking is a delicate thing.

Ninety-nine percent of people let things crowd over them and lose it. [You must renounce and put away *all* that hinders you from hearing the Spirit's voice clearly].

If you have made the same surrender as Abraham, why do you not expect God to speak to you? (Genesis 12:1-3, the call of Abraham and the promise of blessing). A man called, chosen and anointed has a claim on God for daily guidance (1 Samuel 23:1-14, David saves the city of Keilah from the attacking Philistines after asking God. 1 Samuel 30:1-8, David's wives are captured as Ziglag is plundered and he seeks God's guidance whether to pursue the enemy or not). Come and get God to speak to you. What you try to do is to pray. No, no! Wait upon God. [Being still before God, listening, not petitioning].

You do not need to be before the Holy Spirit five minutes before He will tell you what to do, if you are still. And He will not speak to you again until you have obeyed Him on that point. [Cf. Acts 5:32, '...The Holy Spirit whom God has given to those who obey Him'].

The guidance of the Holy Spirit stops the moment there is sin in a company or an individual (Joshua chapter 7, Israel defeated at Ai due to the sin of Achan, coveting illicit goods). It is not your striving; it is knowing God's will; it is knowing God's voice. Leave off your effort. Stand before God and know His voice. It is not your intelligence. It is not any attainment. It is knowing God's voice and it will take you years to learn this. When you fall, you ought to learn from it (1 Kings 16:13, the sins of Baasha and the sins of Elah his son, with their idols encouraged Israel to sin, provoking God to anger).

'Love suffers long and is kind; love does not envy; love does not parade itself, is not puffed up; does not behave rudely, does not seek its own, is not provoked, thinks no evil; does not rejoice in iniquity, but rejoices in the truth; bears all things, believes all things, hopes all things, endures all things' (1 Corinthians 13:4-7).

'Let all that you do be done with love' (1 Corinthians 16:14).

'Let nothing be done through selfish ambition or conceit, but in lowliness of mind let each esteem others better than himself. Let each of you look out not only for his own interests, but also for the interests of others. Let this mind be in you which was also in Christ Jesus, who, being in the form of God, did not consider it robbery to be equal with God, but made Himself of no reputation, taking the form of a bondservant, and coming in the likeness of men' (Philippians 2:3-7).

'Let your speech always be with grace, seasoned with salt, that you may know how you ought to answer each one. ...Therefore, as the elect of God, holy and beloved, put on tender mercies, kindness, humility, meekness, longsuffering; bearing with one another, and forgiving one another, if anyone has a complaint against another; even as Christ forgave you, so you also must do. But above all these things put on love, which is the bond of perfection' (Colossians 4:6, 12-17).

Peter asked Jesus, "Lord, how often shall my brother sin against me and I forgive him? Up to seven times?" Jesus said to him, "I do not say to you, up to seven times, but up to seventy times seven" (Matthew 18:21-22).

'He who covers a transgression seeks love, but he who repeats a matter separates friends' (Proverbs 17:9).

'The discretion of a man makes him slow to anger and his glory is to overlook a transgression' (Proverbs 19:11).

Before going out to the mission field you need to learn not to take a single step unless God speaks to you. This life becomes as natural as the other. He does not speak unless you believe. Drop the excuse, "If God speaks to me, I will do this," believe the other. God will never speak to you unless He sees that you have faith. First you learn faith, come up in believing and learn to know God's voice. God will never speak to you on a higher grade than your gained position has given you (Genesis chapter 22, Abraham offering up of Isaac).

Unless you have completely gone out of yourself, you will never be tested like this. Ninety-nine people out of a hundred hide under the cloak of saying, "I don't know whether it is God speaking to me."

If the Holy Spirit has come into your body, it is only right that He should speak to you and speak to you every day. Something outside of you, a voice, not your own thoughts. Live a natural life until God tells you to do something, keep the morning watch [your quiet time with God before the day's work, duties and distractions overtake you].

'Commit your works to the Lord and your thoughts will be established' (Proverbs 16:3).

Never try to do anything, but know God's voice. One thing I want to bring before you and that is that you need to know God's voice. [Learn the difference between the voice of the Spirit, the world, the flesh and wishful thinking/good ideas]. It will be years and years before you do anything important. You will not do big things for twenty years. [The students were age eighteen plus, and the majority were in their early twenties].

Rees Howells then told the story of how enroute to the village (in 1907 or 1908) he was instructed by the Holy Spirit, "Go to that house and knock at the door." This was a house in Llandeillo

Road, Brynamman, the same street that Rees Howells lived in and was about a five minute walk from the family home. For Rees it seemed too strange because he did not know who lived in the row of houses. He ignored the word and carried on towards the village before being told *not* to go to the meeting unless he went to the house first. One of his friends returned to the house with him, they knocked the door and were invited in by a young girl. Her mother was in the last stages of consumption (T. B.). She had been praying for Rees to come and God had answered her prayers! Rees led her to the cross of Jesus Christ where she passed from death to life, the New Birth, being born again. Every Thursday evening a meeting was held in her home until her mortal body passed from life to death.[2]

This was perfect guidance. You will have to be at this every second of the day. You have a long way to go. You must begin like babes. Test it in your own case, not in mine. Do not think that God must speak to this man or that woman. If you become like a little child and spend much time with Him, He will speak to you. There is no need to shut yourself up in your room.

I did most of my praying while walking. As soon as I left people I entered into His Presence again. I want you to still these thousand voices speaking in you. You will have to begin this now, else you will be the same in ten years time. Let God appear to you and speak to you. Let Him tell you what He is going to do through you (Exodus chapter 3, Moses and the burning bush, God was going to deliver the people of Israel from the Egyptians).

Jesus said, "My sheep hear My voice and I know them and they follow Me" (John 10:27).

Jesus said, "However, when He, the Spirit of truth, has come, He will guide you into all truth; for He shall not speak on His own authority but whatever He hears He will speak; and He will tell you things to come. He will glorify Me, for He will take of what is Mine and declare it to you. All things that the Father has are Mine. Therefore I said that He will take of Mine and declare it to you" (John 16:13-15).

You ought to be ashamed if God does not speak to you. [Rees Howells was told to "build a College" but one year passed before he was told where to build, in Swansea; there are times of silence]. When God speaks, He speaks like God. When a man speaks, he speaks like a man. Sometimes I hear voices, but I can pick out the voice of God at once. You must come to the place to know the difference between the voice of God and all other voices. You must get clear of all other voices and know the voice of God, that He may instruct you. Only one mistake I need to make in this, only a thought, and an acting on it, that is all I need to do to fail, and you can never retrace your steps. [Moses was commanded to *speak* to the rock to bring forth water at Meribah, but struck it as commanded on a previous occasion; this was a mistake and a failure on his part, Numbers 20:7-13]. If you make one mistake, you are open to make another. But I have never found the Holy Spirit making one mistake.

Imagine you are in the countryside. Nature is speaking, but other sounds are drowning it out. You're chatting with a friend, listening to music, scrolling through your phone or your phone is pinging with notifications. You can't hear the birds singing, the sway of the trees, leaves rustling, a rabbit running for cover under a bush or amongst long grass. The other sounds, those of the world are drowning out nature's orchestra. It is the same with God's Spirit. What opinions, sounds and distractions are filling your mind so that you cannot hear from God? Shut the noise out and be still before the Holy Spirit. A young Samuel said, "Speak Lord, for Your servant listens" (1 Samuel 3:7-10).

Do not take guidance unless it is clear. If it is uncertain ask the Lord to make it clear [Gideon needed certainty and reassurance before victory over the Midianites, Judges 6:36-40 and Judges 7:9-15]. In cases of uncertainty give God the benefit of the doubt. Where there is a doubt as to whether He tells you to do a thing, test the motive: "Is it to exalt my Master and to extend His Kingdom?"

Wait before God otherwise you will fail before you begin. Leave all self-confidence. If a thing is not clear, do not let the Throne go until it is clear. The thing He tells you is what He expects you to believe and that only.

Rees Howells told the story how in August 1912 his wife Lizzie was gravely ill after giving birth to their only child, Samuel. God said that she was not to take medicine. Yet at least three members of Rees' relatives were medical doctors! This was a real test of obedience and faith. He said to his wife of just two and a half years, "You are not to take medicine and you are not to die." The phrase 'Have Faith in God' (Mark 11:22), stood out in golden letters.[3] In the 1930s, the phrase was made in concrete, using individual bold protruding letters (approximately 7 inch/18cm high) on the outside of Derwen Fawr wall. It was probably painted in gold as the phrase "Ebenezer" on the exact reverse of the wall was originally covered in gold paint.

"Ebenezer" (stone of help/Hitherto hath the Lord helped us), photo taken in the 1960s on the Derwen Fawr Estate. 'Samuel took a stone, and set it between Mizpeh and Shen, and called the name of it Ebenezer, saying, Hitherto hath the Lord helped us' (1 Samuel 7:12, A.V.). The section of the wall in the quadrangle was opposite the Bake House. The wall is about 15ft tall with one door onto Derwen Fawr Road and the Sketty Estate opposite.

He whispered to me in a way I could have said was not clear, but I trusted Him. What God tells me comes only as a word or an impression and then it comes to be a fact.

Come and understand God's will, come and know His voice so that you may trust Him. If you find a thing does not come to pass, you must admit that you do not know His voice. You do not struggle by hearing a voice. You can pick one voice out of a thousand, so you can pick out God's voice. You have been doing [things yourself] and not God. When God acts, He acts like God. In this life you must not expect to do things in the same way as you did on a previous occasion (2 Samuel 5:17-25, King David defeats the Philistines on two occasions, seeking guidance on whether to fight and battle tactics). I have never acted on promptings from this self. Through living with God you come to know His voice. Once God has spoken, you know His voice again.

Do not ask God to speak to you but to wait, otherwise you may hear other voices. Do expect Him to speak to you. If He does not speak, enjoy fellowship with Him. When He first speaks it is generally in a whisper and it is very easy to quench or grieve Him. You should first spend plenty of time with Him.

When God speaks to you, He uses very plain words and you need no one to interpret them for you. When God speaks to you, you not only hear it but see it. [Rees Howells could visualise a College and the new buildings etc.].

A man wants God to act and before He has time to act, the man has done everything himself, and done it all wrong. You try to work. Where there is a need you jump into it whether God wants you in it or not. Your 'strength is to sit still' (Cf. 2 Chronicles 20:17, '...stand still and see the salvation of the Lord...'). If you make your little plans and go before Him, He soon catches you. Hands off until you know God's voice. You cannot do things unless God gives them to you. Never try to open a door that God has shut. If a door is open, push, but never pull strings.

The apostle Paul wrote: 'For this reason I also have been much hindered from coming to you' (Romans 15:22).

The apostle Paul wrote: 'Furthermore, when I came to Troas to preach Christ's Gospel, and a door was opened to me by the Lord' (2 Corinthians 2:12).

The apostle Paul wrote: 'Continue earnestly in prayer, being vigilant in it with thanksgiving; meanwhile praying also for us, that God would open to us a door for the word, to speak the mystery of Christ, for which I am also in chains, that I may make it manifest, as I ought to speak' (Colossians 4:2-4).

Jesus said to the Church at Philadelphia, "I know your works. See, I have set before you an open door, and no one can shut it; for you have a little strength, have kept My word, and have not denied My name" (Revelation 3:8).

Bible College Future

One or two other aspects of the lengthy "account of the work" of the Bible College at Blackpill prepared for the anniversary services may well be of sufficient general interest mentioned here in addition to the extracts that have already appeared in "Leader" news columns.

The number of students in the college is now given as thirty, and the directors says "we are impressed that the Lord will give us faith to take on another large property, so as to have separate places for the men and the women, and also to be near enough to share in the same lectures."

"The college, like any other public institution," it is commented elsewhere, "is open to public criticism; but where that criticism has been adverse the Lord has never allowed us to make a defence because we have felt that it has largely come from men who have not been able to trust the Word of God for daily needs as He has called us to do."

Newspaper article clipping from a religious paper, c.1928/9, found inside Lizzie Hannah Howells' Schofield Reference Bible. The Bible was given to her by Rees Howells, on her thirty-seventh birthday, 2 August 1921, when they were at Llandrindod Wells. The article speaks of buying a property (Derwen Fawr) and public criticism.

If I do a thing myself I pay the price for it, but if He did it, I cast my care upon Him (1 Peter 5:7). The man of faith is not to do anything unless God tells him that He can do it through him. The man of God waits till He knows God's will (Joshua chapter 1, God commissions and commands Joshua. Joshua chapter 3, Israel cross the Jordan River into the Promised Land). One hundred percent in the hands of God, one hundred percent guidance.

I am always very careful with essentials, careful about God's will. I know beforehand what I am going to do. I never do anything at random. Get your plan from God. He gives me something to do every day and afterwards I have something to show for it.

God can speak through a dream but be discerning. There is often nothing in a dream, but, this one was different. 'Now Joseph had a dream, and he told it to his brothers, and they hated him even more' (Genesis 37:5). How real were Joseph's dreams to him? Were they more real than circumstances? When God speaks it is more real than circumstances. The life with the Holy Spirit is one of perfect guidance. Don't trust every dream. King Solomon said, "For a dream cometh through the multitude of business [much activity]..." (Ecclesiastes 5:3).

Very often God will speak to you through the Word [Scriptures from the Bible]. I have always been a man of one Book. [Rees is referring to test cases and how to pray, guided by 'plots' in the Bible. Rees was well-read and on occasions in College meetings he would make reference to what he was reading or had read].

For help, guidance and advice I use the Bible. These people who wrote the Gospels never tried to make a show, never brought in their own opinions, but facts only. Other books die out – not this! This Person is so steady, so great, that everything He tells you to do prospers. But how are you to know the difference between these voices? You may say, "It is in the Word." But you are not able to use the Word. The only test is that you fail to believe where you are (Exodus chapter 3, Moses at the burning bush).

As a rule, God speaks to you through men who have done a thing similar to what God is calling you to do. You ought to read the lives of these men. [You may quote The Bible in your believing, but do you have God's power and will behind it?].

The College library in Rees Howells' day (and later Samuel Rees Howells) was well stocked with Victorian era mission biographies and many inspirational Christian paperbacks from the 1930s. It was customary for visiting speakers who had a book published to donate a copy to the College, as did many past students and staff. Some staff members specifically prayed in money so that they could purchase Christian publications on a variety of genres. Cases of books were also left in people's wills for the College, whilst some retiring pastors thinned down their own collections and BCW was the recipient of their generosity.

Say to yourself, "God spoke to Moses. Does He speak to me?" I was always quick at taking things from God. I have never got into bondage by speculating on the Word of God or going beyond what the Holy Spirit has told me. There is no need for Him to speak to you in a case where He has already spoken from His Word. [Obey God's revealed will in the Bible]. Seek confirmation of verbal messages from the written Word.

Discerning the voice of God comes through experience, but even mature Christians make mistakes and on occasions get things wrong. God will never tell you to do anything that contradicts His Word, as revealed in the Holy Bible. Any so-called 'word' can be from God, the Devil, a demon or from one's own imagination, wishful thinking (Jeremiah 14:14 and Jeremiah 23:25-36). Some people speak with two spirits; the Holy Spirit, but are also influenced by another spirit (Job 26:4), an evil spirit, this is often because their lives are polluted and they have compromised in an area.
The Holy Spirit speaks lovingly, reassuringly, encouragingly and will guide you into all truth and inform you of things to come (John 14:26 and John 16:13). God's Word will bring peace into your life, even if it is a rebuke (Colossians 3:15). Whereas the Devil accuses, nags, and speaks in a mocking manner; he will try to confuse you with regards to God's will by sowing doubt, fear and discouragement into your mind, "Did God really say?" (Genesis 3:1-7).[4]

God told Joshua, "Be strong and of good courage. Meditate on My law to do according to all that is written therein" (Joshua 1:6, 8, one of Rees Howells' compounded Scriptures where extracts of two verses are placed together). The man to whom God is not speaking is always seeing difficulties, seeing things like mountains, he is always under. The man to whom God speaks is never under defeat. I can go back and say, "You told me." So I can expect Him to do it. Does God tell you things and you believe Him, and that's done? (2 Kings 2:19-22, Elisha by throwing salt

- 194 -

into the spring that has caused death and barrenness, declaring the Word of God, the water was healed and became safe).

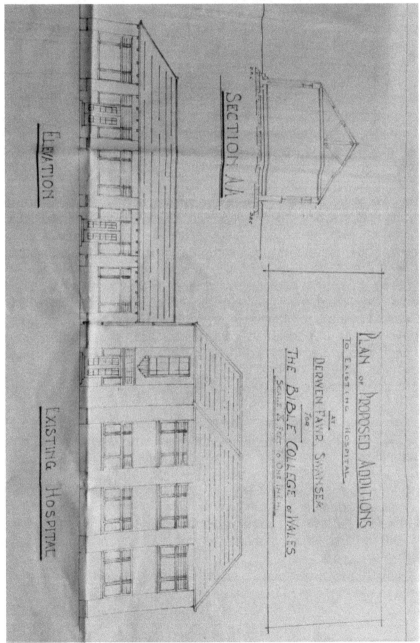

Architect's drawing for proposed Hospital extension, 1936. Borough Engineers, date stamp 24 August 1936 (not in photo). The extension (left) was actually two-storeys, see photo in chapter 11.

God's plan: All He tries to do is to train a man so that He can speak to him and reveal it to him. This is the only place where you are a child, where you do as you are told. Have you seen this wonderful plan, or are you after some position you have not got? What kills many Christians is that they have an ambition to do something that God has not given them.*

*It is outside of their calling, e.g. the evangelist decides to become a pastor. The missionary decides to leave their mission organisation or their field of labour without knowing the will of the Lord. The pastor leaves his flock to take up a new pastorate with better wages and benefits. A Christian leaves their employment for another without God's express approval. A promotion is accepted without seeking God on the matter; it may be better pay, but extra hours and more stress. Someone decides to marry without God's permission, or worse, marry when God has said, "Do not marry this person." You decide to move to a new area to rent or buy a larger property without God's direction. Who is Lord of your life? Whose will are you following?

Jesus said, "Not everyone who says to Me, 'Lord, Lord,' shall enter the Kingdom of Heaven, but he who does the will of My Father in Heaven. Many will say to Me in that day, 'Lord, Lord, have we not prophesied in Your name, cast out demons in Your name, and done many wonders in Your name?' And then I will declare to them, 'I never knew you; depart from Me, you who practice lawlessness!' " (Matthew 7:21-23).

God has a plan and He does not want you to do anything else, or to act before the time. That is where darkness and breakdowns come in. When God has spoken, to you, He does not go on repeating the same thing. Once you believe it, there is no need to repeat it (Genesis 25:22-34, Rebekah's children struggled together in her womb and she asked God why. Genesis 27:27-46, Jacob receives a blessing from his dad, Isaac, who was blind, which was reserved for the firstborn son).

Chapter 19

Being Guided by God

'...We also, since the day we heard it, do not cease to pray for you, and to ask that you may be filled with the knowledge of His will in all wisdom and spiritual understanding, that you may have a walk worthy of the Lord, fully pleasing Him, being fruitful in every good work and increasing in the knowledge of God' (Colossians 1:9-10).

'I beseech you therefore, brethren, by the mercies of God, that you present your bodies a living sacrifice, holy, acceptable to God, which is your reasonable service. And do not be conformed to this world, but be transformed by the renewing of your mind, that you may prove what is that good and acceptable and perfect will of God' (Romans 12:1-2).

If you tell people a thing [e.g. a vision from God, or what He has said to you and you relay it], you are responsible for the consequences. Whatever you say in the name of God you must stand to it. If God has told you, you can make a stand; if He has not, you cannot. To do these things a man must know the voice of God (1 Kings chapter 17, Elijah prophesies a drought, oil and flour not running out and raises a boy from the dead. 1 Kings chapter 18, Elijah confronts Ahab and the prophets of Baal are defeated). If you act only as God tells you, you do not shake (1 Samuel 9:7, 15-16, Saul and his servant looking for direction from the man of God at Zuph. 1 Samuel 13:8-14, the prophet Samuel rebuked King Saul for his unlawful sacrifice, thus forfeiting his kingship).

The Holy Spirit uses men who have made a stand for God (Daniel chapters 1-2, Daniel's faithfulness in Babylon and interpreting Nebuchadnezzar's dream which leads to promotion).

The man of God from Judah and the old prophet of Bethel from 1 Kings chapter 13. In a straight fight with the Devil you come through, [but doubters and deceivers are the deeper tests]. It is these people who come round you that deceive you like the old prophet at Bethel. If his guidance was right, why did God send a man from Judah to deliver the message? You must find where you are mistaken. When God speaks to you, not even an angel can shake you. But this was a lie of the Devil. I want you to be alone with God. You want plenty of time to fight with this old self of yours. He is your worst enemy. Don't listen to people when they tell you something contrary to what God has said. God uses you and yet they want you to do what they think! [Rees is speaking from personal experience].

Do not copy. Do not think that God will deliver you in the same way as He did another person, look at the difference of ministry between the prophets Isaiah and Jeremiah. Do not think that you will prevail upon God to do a thing which is not His will. You say, "Come, and pray this and that." And when the prayer is not answered you are not touched. You do not know that you are dragging the name of Jehovah in the dust. God told Israel (Jacob, cf. Isaiah 41:8) to do what He had forbidden Isaac.

The Lord God to Isaac, "Do not go down to Egypt; live in the land of which I shall tell you" (Genesis 26:2).

God spoke to Israel in the visions of the night, "Jacob, Jacob!...I am God, the God of your father; do not fear to go down to Egypt, for I will make of you a great nation there. I will go down with you to Egypt, and I will also surely bring you up again, and Joseph will put his hand on your eyes" (Genesis 46:2-4).

When God speaks to a man, He speaks through that man when he speaks to others (Genesis 37:5-9, Joseph's dreams. Genesis 41:25-41, Joseph interprets Pharaoh's dreams and his rise to power). You will never lead a person with a bigger blessing than yourself.

The life of faith is one of perfect guidance. The whole secret of the life of faith is knowing God's voice. If you can consult Him and obtain answers, Satan is unable to touch you all day (1 Samuel 23:1-12, David saves the City of Keilah from the Philistines but the people of Keilah were prepared to hand David over to King Saul! 1 Samuel 30:1-19, David's wives are captured and the inhabitants of Ziklag are taken captive by the Amalekites. David inquired of the Lord whether to go after the enemy and recover his people and their livestock). Take God's way of victory in a test not your own. When one follows God, one always falls into testings, but He always, delivers (Exodus 14, crossing the Red Sea. Exodus 15:1-21, the Song of Moses, praising God for the defeat of the Egyptians at the Red Sea).

The Holy Spirit knows where the battle is: 'Then the King of Israel went out and attacked the horses and chariots, and killed the Syrians with a great slaughter. And the prophet came to the King of Israel and said to him, "Go, strengthen yourself; take note, and see what you should do, for in the spring of the year the King of Syria will come up against you" ' (1 Kings 20:21-22).

> The Lord condemned King Ahab who was in the vineyard of Naboth, for taking illegal possession of land and property belonging to another family (1 Kings 21:17-24). Ahab said to Elijah, "Have you found me, O my enemy?" And he answered, "I have found you, because you have sold yourself to do evil in the sight of the Lord: 'Behold, I will bring calamity on you. I will take away your posterity, and will cut off from Ahab every male in Israel, both bond and free' " (1 Kings 21:20-21).

Some people are always fighting when there is no battle and when there is a battle they are not there! 'The children of Ephraim, being armed and carrying bows, turned back in the day of battle' (Psalm 78:9), Cf. Judges 5:15-17, 23. Why not ask God the way He is going to deliver you? Something outside you, instead of your thoughts going like a machine all day. Once you know it is God then you can be happy.

> Under the South Africa General Mission (SAGM), Rees and Lizzie Howells hoped to start a new Mission Station in Portuguese East Africa (PEA), present day Mozambique. PEA was under Roman Catholic influence who did not want Protestant missionaries in their country. Some of the converts from Rusitu, men full of the Holy Spirit converted in the Rusitu Revival (1915-1917), used to trek into PEA, as did SAGM missionaries annually. However thirty-two Christians, local converts including women and children and some of Rees Howells' indigenous fellow labourers were imprisoned for their faith. They were arrested in their place of worship by PEA soldiers. After four months, the women and children were released, but the men were kept in prison for two years because they refused to promise that they would not preach! Their leader, *Mathew caught smallpox and died in prison. (*Original documents spell his name 'Mathew' with one 't' the same spelling format from the Gospel of Mathew from the first six English translations of the Bible, beginning with William Tyndale's 1526 New Testament).
>
> Rees Howells told the above story whilst on furlough at a convention in 1921 and explained that to gain a permanent footing in PEA you had to own land. A Frenchman had already

offered them a farm for £1,200. From 1920, this would be worth £56,100 in 2022, though the value of the land would be far greater. The farm was situated between Rusitu in Gazaland, present day Zimbabwe, and the Port of Beira, in present day Mozambique. People from Rusitu had already promised sums of money, as had Rees and Lizzie Howells. At the convention, Rees did not mention money, when a woman stood up and said that she would pay for the farm in full! The Lord told Rees not to accept it as she was influenced by the meeting. After the meeting he told her, "I don't expect you to give more than I give – £100 (worth £5,220 in 2022). Three other people said they would give gifts of £100 each and a gift of £100 each was received in Birmingham, England, and in Dundee and in Glasgow, both in Scotland. Eleven gifts of £100 in total! The farm was never purchased, but the territory was opened via several centres.[1]

Rees Howells once received a gift for the College from a Christian minister. The Lord told him not to accept it. He took it back to the minister and said, "I do not know why it is; but the Lord will not allow me to accept your gift. Is it because you are in debt?" He replied, "Yes, I am."

During the cleavage of autumn and early winter 1925, which led the College to close for one year, Rees Howells wiped out many of the students' debts, simply because they left and were not going to pay. By erasing the debt and thus offering forgiveness, the students' fiscal sins could not be held against them as their debts had been erased.

You have to be quiet in your spirit to take revelation. As a rule, your reason and intelligence are against taking a revelation. I have never argued a revelation with anyone. If you enter into the realm of argument, you are only in the realm of intelligence and reason. I have always refused that a man should touch any revelation I received with his reason and intelligence, because I have these two myself. No one could have known the Son of God unless it was revealed to him, and it was revealed to Peter by the Father (Matthew 16:13-20, that He was the Christ). The Saviour called Himself the "Son of Man" (Cf. Daniel 7:13 and Matthew 8:20), not, the "Son of God" (Cf. John 10:36), and that in itself would put people off. Every time you are "put off," your reason and intelligence are put aside until God reveals a thing to you, and the moment you see it, your reason and intelligence wonder why you did not see it before. If God wants to do a thing, He will reveal it to you. If you believe what God tells you He will always give a proof, but it may not come for many years (Genesis 25:23-34, Rebekah's twins, the older would serve the younger. Esau despised his birthright and sold it to Jacob for a meal).

'So Gideon said to God, "If You will save Israel by my hand as You have said – look, I shall put a fleece of wool on the threshing floor; if there is dew on the fleece only, and it is dry on all the ground, then I shall know that You will save Israel by my hand, as You have said." And it was so. When he rose early the next morning and squeezed the fleece together, he wrung the dew out of the fleece, a bowlful of water. Then Gideon said to God, "Do not be angry with me, but let me speak just once more. Let me test, I pray, just once more with the fleece; let it now be dry only on the fleece, but on all the ground let there be dew." And God did so that night. It was dry on the fleece only, but there was dew on all the ground' (Judges 6:36-40).

God will never reveal His will to you on a higher grade than your gained position of faith. When God gives a revelation, some, like Mary and Elizabeth, believe it and live in the joy of it, others, like Zacharias, disbelieve and are dumb (Luke 1:5-15).

There is difficulty in believing when there is no revelation. The New Birth is a revelation (John 3:3-7), not a teaching. Do not make the Vision [Every Creature Vision] a teaching, it is a revelation and cannot be received through commonsense. A proof given only after there has been a revelation (Genesis 32:2, Jacob said, "This is God's camp" calling it Mahanaim. Genesis 32:24-32, Jacob wrestled with God and prevailed, calling it Peniel. 2 Kings 6:8-17, the city of Dothan was surrounded by the enemy and the eyes of Elisha's servant were opened. He saw the mountain full of horses and chariots of fire to protect them).

Only those in whom self has been completely dealt with can see the Heavenly Host. Only those who can take revelation can be greatly used. One who has received a revelation can never be shaken (Numbers 16, Korah's rebellion against Moses and Aaron).

When I was on furlough from Africa God spoke to me about the College (1922). It only came about in a very off-hand I way. A minister [R. B. Jones] asked me to come and pray with a few others about training the young people who had received the call in my meetings [Rees and Lizzie were on deputation work, on furlough from the mission field]. While we prayed God spoke to me and said, "I want to build a College in Wales through you, so take care what you pray." I had no idea God was going to speak to me like this. I went home and told my wife what God told me. I asked Him to confirm it through the Word and He did so. He gave me three promises:

1. "Be strong and of good courage, and do it...for the Lord God...will be with thee; He will not fail thee, nor forsake thee, until thou hast finished all the work for the service of the house of the Lord" (1 Chronicles 28:20).

2. "There shall be with thee for all manner of workmanship every willing, skilful man, for any manner of service (1 Chronicles 28:21).

3. "I will give you a *talent of gold*." [£6,150 according to the margin note of the *Schofield Bible*, 1909, 1917, referring to 1 Chronicles 29:4 and 2 Chronicles 8:18].

Then the Holy Spirit told me to ask for one more confirmation. I was going to America [on a private visit in three days time] and He told me to ask for my passage money. So I prayed, "Deliver me of the money for two passages to America tomorrow." The following day I had £50 [worth £3,050 in 2022] from a man who told the Lord that if he ever met me again he would give me £50. That's God! The money my wife and I both had that day, was, £138 [worth £8,400 in 2022]. As a thanksgiving we gave £100 away.[2]

When God spoke to me in the Moody Bible College Institute, I was on the platform in front of nine hundred young people and they were singing a hymn. They were standing up and I was sitting down before I spoke. The noise they were making was not sufficient to prevent God from speaking to me.

I prayed, "O Lord, if ever You have used me, use me to bless these young people." Then He spoke to me in a low voice, quietly, "Do you believe that I can build a College like this in Wales?" I said, "Yes You can, You are God." He said, "If you say I can, can I ask you another thing, can I do it through you? You are going to tell these young people that I came to dwell in you. Before you speak, answer Me. Do you believe that I can build a College through you, without money, without a Council and without an appeal to man?" I said, "Yes, You can do it through me." He continued, "Have I failed you in the past? Can I fail you in the future?" I answered, "No, You are God." Then He said, "Go back, do this for Me and do not consult man." The moment I gave my word to Him I had faith for the College and no Devil nor man could stop it from being built. It was that moment my faith became substance for the College and I had the evidence of it. It was there the College was built.

**Moody Bible Institute Auditorium, from a postcard c.1920
Rees Howells spoke at the Institute in spring 1922**

Nearly twelve months after He told me to build the College, He had not made a single move. He gave a few confirmations in the August [1922] and He did not make a move till the following July

[1923]. How can you go on unless He continues to speak to you? After God has spoken, He gives you every chance to doubt His word. I asked Him when He was going to make a move and it seemed He did not hear me. It was God testing one as to whether He had spoken or not. I did not even know the town where He wanted to have the College. It was in July [1923], before I went to Keswick, that I said, "Don't You think You ought to speak now and show me where the College is to be?" and He said, "Yes, I will show you tomorrow." The next day while we were walking along Mumbles Road, I saw a house without any curtains in the windows, so we went up to look at it. When I stood in front of Glyn Derwen God said, "This is the College."

The Lord told me not to buy freehold even if it was nine hundred and ninety-nine years! I did not put these buildings up because of any impression I had, but because He told me.

It was important that as the College belonged to God the land also belonged to Him as well. With ownership of the land Rees Howells could build subject to local planning rules and acceptance, and sell plots of land when surplus to requirement. Rees said that he "never bought land to speculate," to make a future profit, but much agricultural land was later sold with planning permission for entire estates. The cost per acre of building land was considerably more valuable than farm land for animals to graze.

The Swansea Corporation (local Council) made compulsory purchases of land on at least two occasions: to widen Derwen Fawr Road, formerly a lane in the westward direction and nearly 6 acres for a Park Scheme, which became playing fields off Ashleigh Road and Mumbles Road. This also caused the loss of Derwen Fawr Lodge, a small cottage near the bottom of the Derwen Fawr Estate with an entrance on Ashleigh Road. The Corporation undervalued this property and Rees wrote letters to state the cost to build a new lodge and asked for more money to compensate for the financial loss. On the Sketty Isaf Estate, small sections of woodland on the northern edge were swapped with the Corporation's woodland to square up boundaries.

Rees Howells led the College in prayer for China on many occasions and in 1936, he sold land for £900, worth around £70,000 in 2022, and gave it to evangelise one thousand villages in China! This was faith in action towards the Every Creature Vision.

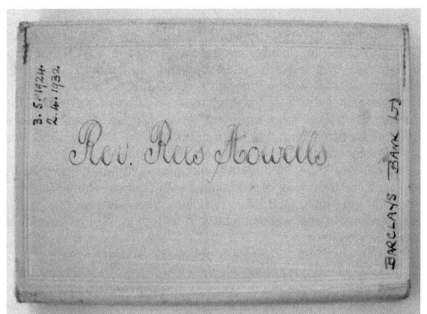

Rees Howells' Barclays Bankbook 3 May 1924 to 2 April 1932

This section of page is from Barclays Bank Ltd, Swansea, from February 1931. The dates are on the left (2-14 February) and the amount on the right is in pounds (£) and shillings. £5 to China Mission February 1931, worth £365 in 2022. The first name is: Gregor, Thanett, self (Rees Howells), China Mission, Hughes and self. Rees Howells was praying in money, the fees of one term £10, as he identified with the students who were praying in their fees.

The College meeting notes for 29 January 1948, regarding China: 'Prayer for missionaries and Christians who are being persecuted by the Reds' (Communists). Ten months later the concern needed to be engaged at a deeper level as Rees Howells called them to 'the beginning of prayer for China.' The burden continued for years and when Samuel Rees Howells became Director upon the death of his dad in February 1950, the intercession proceeded to a further untapped level.

10 February 1955. "We were thinking of Abraham pleading with the Lord for the cities of the plain," said Samuel Rees Howells. "Concerning Isaac, God said, 'Is anything too hard for the Lord?' We believe He spoke those words to us too. In the Far East...we are believing for revival."

11 February 1955. "There are countless millions outside of the fold," prayed Samuel Rees Howells, "we ask Thee to lay their burden upon us. We thank Thee for the prayer Thou hast given us this week for the millions in the Far East. We thank Thee for the many parts Thou hast already visited with revival and Thou wilt (will) visit these places again!"

Paul Backholer in Richard Maton's book *Samuel Rees Howells: A Life of Intercession* wrote: 'After a month of prayer, [March 1955] Samuel Rees Howells challenged the College to prepare for the battle ahead. "Paul stood out for the Gentiles. Christianity was dependent on the revelation of this man. They were coming out of heathenism. He had seen the atonement and he knew there was enough power to keep these converts without any outward restraints." Just as Paul had stood for the Gentiles, the College had to stand for China. "Special meetings are starting tomorrow for prayer," said Samuel. "As we pray these things we want Him to inspire those servants of His who are praying for revival in China. If there is a release of the Spirit in one place, He can be released in other places." Samuel was speaking of the principle of a gained intercession. Once a position of intercession has been gained, the Lord can apply it again for any other situation that He chooses.'[3]

Were the prayers and intercessions of Rees Howells, Lizzie, Samuel and other members of the Bible College of Wales answered? Emphatically yes! *The China Chronicles* series by Paul Hattaway reveals province by province 'how the Living God brought about the largest revival in the history of Christianity.' Many other books also document revivals in China.

OUTLINE PROGRAMME

FRIDAY, June 24th, at 6.30 p.m.

WELCOME MEETING.

Chairman : **Dr. COCHRANE.**

SATURDAY.

8 a.m., Prayers.	10—11, Bible Reading.	11.30—12.30, Missionary Session.	Afternoon, Free.

7—9 p.m. **GREAT MISSIONARY MEETING.** (Open to the Public.)

SUNDAY.

8 a.m. Prayers.	10 to 10.45, Missionary Session.	11.0, Service.	3 p.m. YOUNG PEOPLE'S RALLY.

6.30 p.m. **SERVICE** followed by Praise and Thanksgiving Meeting.

MONDAY.

Arrangements for Monday will be announced at the Conference.

MEALS.

Breakfast, 8.30. Dinner 1 p.m. Tea 5 p.m. Supper 9 p.m.

TERMS: Friday to Tuesday, **25/-** ; Friday to Monday, **21/-**.
Saturday to Tuesday, **21/-** ; Saturday to Monday, **18/-**.
(With 2/6 registration fee in addition.)
(Friends desiring to remain for a longer period may do so at the rate of **7/-** per day by arrangement with Mrs. Howells.)
Also any attending for the day and desiring meals at the College must advise Mrs. Howells *beforehand.*

1932, Evangelical Union of South America (EUSA), Missionary Conference at the Bible College of Wales, from Friday 24 June until Tuesday 28 June. This invitation notes the Chapel and Conference Hall. The College Chapel could seat two hundred and was opened in January 1931, whilst the Conference Hall was completed in April 1931 and could accommodate five hundred. These two projects were built simultaneously. The four-page invitation (A4 card folded in half) notes that the EUSA has 80 missionaries at work in South America, each country is now open and 'the society is calling forth 50 new missionaries – men of God – to respond to the clamant [urgently demand] call of South America.' One of Rees Howells' objectives was to be in contact with leaders of mission organisations, to help fulfil their need for trained men and women of faith (BCW graduates) and to bring the claims of world missions to believers. The first conference at BCW was in the summer of 1925 and a missionary weekend in 1931.

Chapter 20

The Call and Plan of God

'I thank my God, making mention of you always in my prayers, hearing of your love and faith which you have towards the Lord Jesus and towards all the saints. That the sharing of your faith may become effective by the acknowledgement of every good thing which is in you in Christ Jesus' (Philemon 4-6).

'Take heed to the ministry which you have received in the Lord, that you may fulfil it' (Colossians 4:17).

Spend time in the Presence of God. Let Him appear to you and call you (Genesis 28:10-15, Jacob's dream of the angels ascending and descending the ladder, and the promise of his descendants and the land). Do not think of what you have done. Have you made the surrender? It may be that one who thinks himself very insignificant [like Gideon or David] is the one whom God will choose. But what you think is your cleverness is the very thing that will hinder God from using you.

It is not because of what you have done that the Lord has called you, but for what He is going to do through you. You are like an instrument, a dead thing in the Master's hand. It is not a man giving a call to himself or seeing a need somewhere. You must come to know God's voice. It is strange that in the case of men whom God chose, there was something in their lives that could have made them doubt they had been called. Moses was a murderer, and Jacob a deceiver in the eyes of the world. When Jacob went to Laban, he might have thought he was out of the will of God, since Laban deceived him, and God did not deal with him for many years. God can clear away every objection to your being used (Exodus chapters 3 and 4, the burning bush, the call of Moses and the powerful signs).

God has called all Christians to a specific work for Him, but the call to service is the summons of God to your spirit, for special service. It is not for you to commence this special work until He tells you. The call of God is not the command to commence. God told Rees Howells he was to build a College, but Rees did not know where it would be located until a year had passed. This service for God may be in your normal day job (secular) or it may be a specific call (sacred) to the ministry. The terminology of 'secular and sacred' is not disparaging to one or used to uplift the other, as we are all called to 'do all for the glory of God' (1 Corinthians 10:31). If all Christians left their secular jobs to go into Christian ministry, where would the evangelical witness be to the vast majority of the population? The mechanic must be a good witness in his or her job (and to one's neighbours) as the teacher, checkout assistant, minister, influencer or the financial advisor. As a Christian, you should try to meet the spiritual needs of your colleagues. You are the light at work and should be the evangelist/missionary to them. Show forth the love of Christ and use wisdom and discernment when sharing the Good News. Some believers are called into full-time Christian ministry, more are part-time whilst the majority have normal day jobs and support the others in prayer, finances and encouragement.

The revivalist Duncan Campbell of The Faith Mission, Scotland, had been used in the Hebridean Revival (1949-1952) and was promoted to glory in 1972. He was a near-annual speaker at the Bible College for around fifteen years. He spoke of a farmer, "God in dungarees!" This man exuded the Presence of God because the Spirit possessed him and shone through him! He was a working-class man who toiled outside, but was intimate with God.

At one College meeting in 1955 under Samuel Rees Howells, as Duncan Campbell preached, the Conference Hall began to tremble as God's Spirit moved! Those present were in awe of a man who was in touch with God, others were frightened, as when Mount Sinai shook in the days of Moses.[1]

The call of God is an 'upward calling' (Philippians 3:14), and is on another level from all other interests and claims of life. The higher calling to fully obey God must mean more to you than anything else (see Luke 14:25-35).

The call of God is a 'holy calling' (2 Timothy 1:9), something that is sacred and needs to be protected from compromise or defilement.

The call of God is a 'Heavenly calling' (Hebrews 3:1), a voice from Heaven which calls you to Christian service, whether it comes as 'a still small voice' (as in Elijah sheltering in the rock, 1 Kings 19:9-12), or as 'the sound of many waters' (Revelation 1:15), it is the voice and calling of Almighty God.[2]

When God calls a man, He speaks to him and gives him promises (Genesis 12:1-3, the call of Abram to a new land and blessing). The moment you have the call, the Holy Spirit will guide you, but you will not get guidance before then. I allowed God not only to break me down but to build me up before I went out. I had no space behind me to fall back into. I did not intend to be a missionary; Mr James Middlemiss [Superintendent of SAGM in Durban], was baffled that I should go [leave the SAGM]. But all I knew was that God called me. When God called me to build the College, the only things I was afraid of were:
1. Was there anything of my own thoughts in it?
2. Was it the need that prompted me?
Thank God I found nothing of these! But you are living in suggestions and feelings. [Because self-interest still rules you].

The Seal on Your Call
If God calls you to work, He will confirm it in every shape and form. Study the call of the prophets. Forget all pride now and what you are going to do. Why don't you ask the Lord to sanction your call by £100? [£100 in 1936 would be worth £7,625 in 2022].

FOR THE MISSION FIELD

A missionary conference will be held at the Bible College of Wales, Derwen Fawr, Swansea, from July 11 to July 16. There will be delegates from India, Peru, Colombia, the heart of Africa, West Africa, and the frontier of Nepal.

Students of the college going as missionaries to Colombia, India, the Ivory and Gold Coasts, the Congo, Arabia, and Spain will be given a farewell.

1936 newspaper clipping, Missionary Conference (Every Creature Conference) held at the Bible College of Wales, from 11-16 July, *Western Mail* (3 June 1936). 'Students of the College going as missionaries to Columbia, India, the Ivory and Gold Coasts (West Africa), Congo, Arabia and Spain will be given a farewell.'

The altar must be as real in your life as that of Isaac. If you are on the altar you can claim your £100 seal on your call. Spend all your time with God. Do not let the Throne go until you have that £100 seal on your call.

When God calls a man, be quiet that He may give him a plan, it will not be written down here in the Bible. It will be something new. In the case of Elijah not a single person could have guessed what God was going to do (1 Kings 17, Elijah prophesies a drought, the jar of oil did not run dry and a boy is raised from the dead!). There is nothing outside of God's reach if He will find His man, such as founding this ministry. To the man whom God has anointed there comes a chance which only he can take (1 Samuel chapters 16 and 17, David the shepherd, Samuel anointed the future king and David's battle with Goliath a giant).

Be up to the first plan: "This is the Father's will...that of all He hath given Me I should lose nothing" (John 6:39). A man whom God has called endures all things and never rests until his goal is achieved.

Never give up what the Spirit has given to you, but first test the spirits to know if it is He who speaks and not a deceiving spirit or a word from a false prophet or false teacher.

You'll never take a better thing to the mission field than a knowledge of the Scriptures in the light of the Holy Spirit. I used to live in Romans, Corinthians and Ephesians.

'All Scripture is given by inspiration of God and is profitable for doctrine, for reproof, for correction, for instruction in righteousness, that the man of God may be complete, thoroughly equipped for every good work' (2 Timothy 3:16-17).

'Now all these things happened to them as examples and they were written for our admonition, upon whom the ends of the ages have come' (1 Corinthians 10:11).

You must read the Bible to apply it (James 1:22-25), God may lead you down strange paths, think of Moses and the rod (Exodus 4:1-4, his staff became a snake). These Scriptures appeal when you are called to do a similar thing. God will use the words that He used to another man, whom He asked to do a certain thing, only when He has asked you to do a similar thing.

Some of the staff members of the Bible College of Wales and Emmanuel Schools in 1950. Most taught at the Bible College and/or at Emmanuel Preparatory or Emmanuel Grammar School. All these men and women lived on the College Estates (Glynderwen, Sketty or Derwen Fawr), except Rev. Ieuan Jones, an early 1920s BCW student and then missionary to China, before the Reds (Communists) took over. (Names over the page).

From photo, left to right, front row: Eva Stuart (Samuel Rees Howells' personal secretary), Mary Henderson (Rees Howells' personal secretary), Mrs Winifred Jones, Doris M. Ruscoe (first Headmistress of the School), Matron Roderick (medical, in charge of Hospital), Mrs Lizzie Howells (mother of the College), Margaret "Aunty Peg" Williams (an early 1920s BCW student), Miss Scott "Scottie," Gwladys Thomas and Dr. Joan Davies (medical).

Centre row: Judy Jenkins, Jessie Harris, Judith FitzHerbert, Olwen Evans, Tommy Howells (known as "Uncle Tommy" to school students and no relation to Rees Howells), Samuel Rees Howells (Honorary Director), Dr. Kingsley "Doc" Priddy (medical, then Headmaster), Valerie Sherwood (teacher, then Headmistress), Audrey Potter, Olive Raven, Ceturah 'Kitty' Morgan and Hanns Gross.

Back row: Archie Jones, John Rocha, Tobias 'Toby' Bergin (mechanic and handyman), Charles Ridgers, David Rees (gardener), Leslie Lee, Geoffrey Crane (first compiler of this manuscript and able printer), Dr. Kenneth "Symbo" Symonds (medical), Rev. Ieuan Jones (local minister) and Norman Madoc.

Most of the above staff members served in Swansea to help train others for Christian work or were teachers in the Schools. From the 1950s until the late 1970s, some of the above workers left or retired from BCW/Emmanuel to serve in various mission fields including Vietnam, Ramallah, north of Jerusalem (a BCW adopted work, under Jordan's jurisdiction), Greece and Israel. H. Gross went to America and became a Professor of History.

It is not you reading history, but coming up to the prophets and knowing that you are the channel in God's hands, for Him to do exactly the same through you.

You are responsible for your call (Acts chapter 26, Paul's defense before Agrippa, Ephesians chapter 3, the mystery of the Gospel revealed and prayer for spiritual strength). You who are called are responsible to be on the mission field (Matthew 19:16-30, the rich young ruler, and the hundredfold for forsaking all for the Kingdom of God).

Jesus said, "Peace to you! As the Father has sent Me, I also send you." And when He had said this, He breathed on them, and said to them, "Receive the Holy Spirit. If you forgive the sins of any, they are forgiven them; if you retain the sins of any, they are retained" (John 20:21-23).

Do not trample on your call (1 Samuel chapter 16, David anointed as king and in King Saul's service. Isaiah chapter 6, Isaiah's vision of the Lord and call to serve Him. Jeremiah chapter 1, the call of Jeremiah in his youth). [The Holy Spirit does not send doubt to you, that is the work of the enemy, do not listen to the enemy of souls]. Is it within the veil you are living? – Not that you can push yourself there – Are you longing to get out to the mission fields and take your part? Or do little things call your attention? (Numbers chapters 13 and 14, the twelve spies went into Canaan and the people rebelled after hearing a bad report from ten of the spies).

BIBLE COLLEGE MISSIONS

Mrs. Rees Howells, wife of the Rev. Rees Howells, hon. director of the Bible College of Wales, Swansea, and Mrs. Cowman, author of " Streams in the Desert," have left for Egypt and Palestine. They hope to visit many mission stations, and expect to be away for two months. There are four students of the Bible College doing mission work in Palestine and Arabia.

1937 Newspaper clipping, Mrs Lizzie Howells and Mrs Lettie Cowman left Wales on a mission trip visiting Egypt and Palestine (Holy Land/Israel), though they visited many other countries (7 April 1937). 'There are four students of the Bible College doing mission work in Palestine and Arabia.'

Do you live entirely for these countries? Are you as though you are the only man in the world who is responsible for them? Have you seen yourselves in these countries? Do you have victory every day? What kind of lives will you live if you are really in it? Can you say at the end of each day that you have brought this Every Creature Vision nearer to its fulfilment by believing? What we say is that God will do it for us. But here (Joshua chapter 1) we have God telling a man to be strong. We cannot say we have no part in it, for this man had a big part in it, equal to God's part, for it was through him that God did it. You do not obtain a good report unless you fulfil what God has given you (Hebrews 11:2).

'Jesus said to them, "Go into all the world and preach the Gospel to Every Creature. He who believes and is baptised will be saved; but he who does not believe will be condemned. And these signs will follow those who believe: In My name they will cast out demons; they will speak with new tongues; they will take up serpents; and if they drink anything deadly, it will by no means hurt them; they will lay hands on the sick, and they will recover." So then, after the Lord had spoken to them, He was received up into Heaven and sat down at the right hand of God. And they went out and preached everywhere, the Lord working with them and confirming the word through the accompanying signs. Amen' (Mark 16:15-20).

When you preach, the nations know nothing of what you mean. You are preaching another world, which they do not know. It only becomes real to them in the measure to which you can demonstrate it. They ask you: "Does God do such things today?" Then you feel very simple. Get people to watch you, and preach nothing you cannot prove.

In Madeira, the Holy Spirit proved He was stronger than Consumption (T.B.) and Joe Evans was healed on a specific day as foretold by Rees Howells. In Rusitu, Gazaland, the Holy Spirit proved to the natives in Africa, that the true God was stronger than death (influenza/Spanish flu). The witchdoctors failed and some died, but God showed His protection on the Mission Station, no-one died as Rees Howells had proclaimed and the natives sought refuge at Rusitu. The estates that Rees Howells bought by faith in Swansea were testaments and evidence of believing faith, because faith is substance.
The apostle Paul wrote: 'For the Kingdom of God is not in word but in power' (1 Corinthians 4:20).
'Truly the signs of an apostle were accomplished among you with all perseverance, in signs and wonders and mighty deeds' (2 Corinthians 12:12).

Without being called and commissioned, without God revealing Himself, it is only the work of a man you can do. [Theology and education can't save you, only believing faith can]. God will always use the man who has tried to do the thing at his own expense. When the Apostles were commissioned (after the Resurrection) they must have felt their failure very much. But can you find a weakness in Peter after Pentecost? The man whom God has commissioned has authority (1 Kings chapter 18, Elijah confronts King Ahab and the prophets of Baal are defeated. 2 Kings chapter 1, Elijah denounces King Ahaziah for sending messengers to inquire of Baal-Zebub, the god of Ekron as to whether he would recover from his injuries).

Rees Howells often spoke about Moses and Dr. Barnardo, both men he greatly respected and often cited their works, alongside: J. Hudson Taylor, China Inland Mission, General William Booth, Salvation Army, George Müeller, Bristol orphanages, and William Quarrier, Orphan Homes of Scotland, near Bridge of Weir and Sanatorium.

If you have gone to the altar and are commissioned in the Vision, you have authority (Exodus chapters 33 and 34, the command to leave Mount Sinai, Moses making new tablets and the Covenant renewed). You can only believe God according to the commission He has given (Numbers 16:1-33, Moses and Aaron stood firm in their leadership against the son of Korah's rebellion). God will never give you power further than He has commissioned you. Any one who has obeyed this call is greater than the greatest who has disobeyed it (Mark 16:15-16, go into all the world and preach the Good News).

Jesus said, "And I will give you the keys of the Kingdom of Heaven, and whatever you bind on earth will be bound in Heaven, and whatever you loose on earth will be loosed in Heaven" (Matthew 16:19).

Epilogue

Jesus said, "Go into all the world and preach the Gospel to Every Creature" (Mark 16:15).

Jesus said, "You shall receive power when the Holy Spirit has come upon you; and you shall be witnesses to Me in Jerusalem, and in all Judea and Samaria, and to the end of the earth" (Acts 1:8).

Rees Howells lived a life of faith, but came from humble beginnings. As a child, he had a short window of education before starting work in a Tin Mill aged twelve in late 1891, though he attended evening classes when he was older. After ten years he took a ship to America, to work in the mines, where the pay was superior. It was in America that he met the Saviour and returned to Wales during the Welsh Revival (1904-1905). Rees began evangelising and fully gave of himself to the Holy Spirit to glorify Jesus Christ and to extend the Kingdom of God. He was led into a number of intercessions and began a local Mission, where fellow like-minded labourers joined him in the evenings to witness and hold open-air meetings in different villages in and around Brynamman. Some evenings they met in a believer's home (a cottage meeting as it was then known), at other times they rented a hall until they had their own basic Mission Hall.

Rees Howells was led to lay the Mission down, to hand it over to his future brother-in-law, and was set apart to God in the hidden life. In December 1910, Rees married Lizzie Hannah Jones and in August 1912, a son was born, Samuel, their only child. Rees was already in training to be a Congregational minister which was in preparation for a call to Southern Africa. Samuel was handed over to Moses and Elizabeth Rees, relatives of Rees, and further training began until Rees and Lizzie sailed for Cape Town, arriving in late August 1915.

Rees and Lizzie Howells began work at a Mission Station in Rusitu, Gazaland, where they saw revival within six weeks of arrival! They annually trekked into Portuguese East Africa with local Christians to share the Good News and to strengthen fellow believers. They also saw revival in other places as they travelled across Southern Africa for two years under the auspices of the South African General Mission (SAGM) and ten thousand souls were won to the Lord, whilst many were filled with the Spirit. They covered more than 11,000 miles in total, by train, car, on horseback, on foot, and with wagons pulled by oxen or donkeys. They ministered in five countries: Swaziland, Pondoland, Bomvanaland, Tembuland and Zululand.

The Howells served nearly a decade with the SAGM, including training before their arrival, and deputation work from 1921, before resigning in June 1923 to be obedient to their future call of God. Now, they were going to do something new, as led by the Spirit in acts of faith, to start a Bible College in Wales where men and women could train for Christian work, for service at home or abroad, regardless of their previous education or lack of finances.

The Bible College of Wales was inaugurated in June 1924 and from 1927 went from strength to strength, growing in student numbers and staff. The College was born without a committee or a denomination, but trusted in the living God who said He would 'provide for all your need according to His riches in glory' (Philippians 4:19). The mid-1930s were years of highlight for the College, spiritually and numerically with times of revival, alongside intense spiritual battles.

Rees Howells lived a life of faith because he had faith in the finished work of Jesus Christ at Calvary. Rees was a surrendered vessel, fit for the Master's use because he was full of the Spirit of God and obedient to Him. Rees trusted explicitly in God for his daily bread, and the meals of the students and staff, for many days this 'daily bread' was literally when the College had no money until the next post was delivered, an anonymous gift was left on the doorstep, or someone brought money and knocked the front door of one of the estates.

Rees Howells was not perfect, he had idiosyncrasies, and at times spoke what appeared to be sharp, like many of the Biblical prophets of old, but he walked in the Spirit and sought fellowship with all who loved the Saviour. Especially those who were faithful to the Every Creature commission with their prayerful concern for the Kingdom of God. On a few occasions, Jesus Himself appeared sharp in His words and actions, yet He was sinless and without reproach. Many of the Biblical prophets also had strong words. In the late 1930s, Rees had spoken sternly to a student inside Derwen Fawr Mansion and reduced her to tears. "Mair," said Mrs Howells, the mother of the College, "you know that he loves you." With moist eyes, Mair acknowledge this truth and went on to serve forty-two years in France at Rees Howells' Paris mission base. She also lived a life of faith and then returned to BCW for nearly two decades of service, where Mair (Mary) Davies told me the story, sixty years after the actual event.

Jesus' works testified of who He was and what He stood for, similarly so with Rees Howells. The College estates and student graduates were testimonies of faith. Faith in the living God, the Creator, the God of Truth (Isaiah 65:16), whose Son is the Way the Truth and the Life (John 14:6). They went forth to many countries of the world and a number were pioneers in their field of labour or work of service, some of whom kept in contact with the College for thirty, forty or sixty years after graduation! This is a testimony in itself.

Rees Howells was kind and compassionate, but running a College, Schools, Hospital, Home of Rest for Missionaries, multiple estates and their liabilities, conferences and supporting past students and other missionaries whilst training men and women for the mission field all takes its toll. Rees knew the consequences of failure, past and present, especially during the battles of intercession leading up to and into World War Two (1939-1945), with the rise of the Nazis, and then the nation of Israel being born in a day to fulfil biblical prophecy. Like Elijah, he was 'a man with a nature like ours' (James 5:17), and had great faith that could change world events, not because he was somebody great or special, but because he had given all of himself to the Master's service and had a team of faithful workers unto God who had done likewise. They all depended upon God and trusted Him implicitly. It was not Rees Howells who lived, but Christ in him (Galatians 2:20) through the power of the Holy Spirit (Matthew 3:11). His life was sown in weakness and raised in power (1 Corinthians 15:43), as he battled principalities and powers in the heavenly places during times of intense intercession and spiritual warfare (Ephesians 3:10 and Ephesians 6:12). The College body joining in, as a powerhouse of prayer, faith and intercession.

Rees Howells lived a life of faith, 'taking nothing from the Gentiles' (3 John 1:7), but trusted in God and His unchanging faithfulness. Rees imparted his life to those at the College in Swansea, to help advance the Kingdom of God, by prayers, finances and trained Christian workers who could trust God to provide for their needs. He lived what he preached and preached what he lived. Thankfully, these Christian principles, addresses, teaching and testimonies from an intercessor and missionary have been passed down to us, for such a time as this.

I never personally knew Rees Howells, he was promoted to glory some decades before I was born, but we have been introduced to his authentic voice in this book, so that we too can live a life of faith, walking in the Spirit, being faithful to our Heavenly calling, exalting Jesus Christ and advancing the Kingdom of God.

'...To ask that you may be filled with the knowledge of His will in all wisdom and spiritual understanding; that you may walk worthy of the Lord, fully pleasing Him, being fruitful in every good work and increasing in the knowledge of God; strengthened with all might, according to His glorious power, for all patience and longsuffering with joy; giving thanks to the Father who has qualified us to be partakers of the inheritance of the saints in the light. He has delivered us from the power of darkness and conveyed us into the Kingdom of the Son of His love, in whom we have redemption through His blood, the forgiveness of sins. He is the image of the invisible God, the firstborn over all creation. For by Him all things were created that are in Heaven and that are on earth, visible and invisible, whether thrones or dominions or principalities or powers. All things were created through Him and for Him. And He is before all things and in Him all things consist' (Colossians 1:9-16).

Thank you for taking the time to read this book. Could you be so kind to write a review on your favourite review site, and give a shout out on social media? Thank you.

Social Media
Instagram, Twitter and TikTok: @ByFaithMedia
Facebook, YouTube and Pinterest: /ByFaithMedia

Rees Howells and Samuel Rees Howells Related Books
Directors of the Bible College of Wales
(Hardbacks and paperbacks)

Samuel Rees Howells A Life of Intercession: The Legacy of Prayer and Spiritual Warfare of an Intercessor by Richard Maton, Paul Backholer and Mathew Backholer. An in-depth look at the intercessions of Samuel Rees Howells alongside the faith principles that he learnt from his father, Rees Howells, and under the leading and guidance of the Holy Spirit. With 39 digitally enhanced photos and images.

Samuel, Son and Successor of Rees Howells: Director of the Bible College of Wales – A Biography by Richard Maton edited by Mathew Backholer. The life of Samuel and his ministry at the College and the support he received from numerous staff and students as the history of the Bible College of Wales unfolds. With more than 110 digitally enhanced photos and images.

God Challenges the Dictators, Doom of the Nazis Predicted: The Destruction of the Third Reich Foretold by the Director of Swansea Bible College, An Intercessor from Wales by Rees Howells and Mathew Backholer. Available for the first time in 80 years – fully annotated. Discover how Rees Howells built a large ministry by faith in times of economic chaos and learn from the predictions he made during times of national crisis.

Rees Howells' God Challenges the Dictators, Doom of Axis Powers Predicted: Victory for Christian England and Release of Europe Through Intercession and Spiritual Warfare, Bible College of Wales by Mathew Backholer. This is the story behind the story of *God Challenges the Dictators* (GCD), Rees Howells' only published book during his lifetime, before, during and after publication which is centred around World War Two. Read how extracts of GCD were aired over occupied parts of Europe, and how Hitler and leading Nazi officials were sent copies in 1940! With 24 digitally enhanced photos and images.

Continued over the page

Rees Howells, Vision Hymns of Spiritual Warfare, Intercessory Declarations: World War II Songs of Victory, Intercession, Praise and Worship, Israel and the Every Creature Commission by Mathew Backholer. A rare insight into the prophetic declarations, hymns and choruses used in spiritual warfare by Rees Howells and his team of intercessors at the Bible College of Wales. Spanning the pivotal years of 1936-1948 and brought to life for the first time in more than seventy years. Many of the songs of worship reveal the theology, spiritual battles, and history during the dark days of World War II and the years surrounding it. With more than 30 digitally enhanced photos and images.

The Holy Spirit in a Man: Spiritual Warfare, Intercession, Faith, Healings and Miracles by R. B. Watchman edited by Paul Backholer and Mathew Backholer. One man's compelling journey of faith and intercession, a remarkable modern day story of miracles and faith to inspire and encourage. (One chapter relates to the Bible College of Wales and Watchman's visit).

Holy Spirit Power: Knowing the Voice, Guidance and Person of the Holy Spirit: Inspiration from Rees Howells, Evan Roberts, D. L. Moody, Duncan Campbell and Other Channels of God's Divine Fire by Paul Backholer. Jesus walked in the power of the Holy Spirit and declared His disciples would do even greater works. Today, God's power can still be released in and through Christians who will meet the Holy Spirit on His terms.

Rees Howells, Life of Faith, Intercession, Spiritual Warfare and Walking in the Spirit: Christian Principles, Addresses, Teaching, & Testimonies from an Intercessor & Missionary by Mathew Backholer and Rees Howells. The famed intercessor and missionary, Rees Howells, preached thousands of times, but until now his authentic voice has not been heard. This book was commissioned by Samuel Rees Howells in the 1960s as the sequel to his dad's biography but was lost in development until now. Discover the wonder as you listen to Rees Howells teach on the ministry of the Holy Spirit and learn how you can open yourselves to Him to become His channel for blessing, faith and intercession. Including anecdotes and contemporary quotes from men and women of God, friends of Rees and Lizzie Howells. With more than 70 digitally enhanced photos and images.

Books by Mathew Backholer

The majority of the following books are available as paperbacks and eBooks on a number of different platforms worldwide. Some are also available as hardbacks.

Historical
- God Challenges the Dictators, Doom of the Nazis Predicted: The Destruction of the Third Reich Foretold by the Director of Swansea Bible College an Intercessor from Wales (Rees Howells and Mathew Backholer).
- Rees Howells' God Challenges the Dictators, Doom of Axis Powers Predicted: Victory for Christian England and Release of Europe Through Intercession. (This is the story behind the story of *God Challenges the Dictators,* before, during and after publication which is centred around World War II. The book includes letters to Prime Minister Winston Churchill, Press Releases from Rees Howells, plus newspaper articles and adverts, and what Rees Howells said and wrote about his only published work within his lifetime, with Mathew Backholer).
- Rees Howells, Vision Hymns of Spiritual Warfare Intercessory Declarations: World War II Songs of Victory, Intercession, Praise and Worship, Israel and the Every Creature Commission.
- Rees Howells, Life of Faith, Intercession, Spiritual Warfare and Walking in the Spirit: Christian Principles, Addresses, Teaching & Testimonies from an Intercessor & Missionary. (Rees Howells and Mathew Backholer).

Christian Revivals and Awakenings
- Revival Fires and Awakenings, Thirty-Six Visitations of the Holy Spirit.
- Understanding Revival and Addressing the Issues it Provokes.
- Global Revival, Worldwide Outpourings, Forty-Three Visitations of the Holy Spirit.
- Revival Answers, True and False Revivals.
- Revival Fire, 150 Years of Revivals.
- Reformation to Revival, 500 Years of God's Glory.

Books by Mathew Backholer (Continued)

Christian Discipleship and Spiritual Growth
- Christianity Rediscovered, In Pursuit of God and the Path to Eternal Life. Book 1.
- Christianity Explored. Book 2.
- Extreme Faith, On Fire Christianity.
- Discipleship For Everyday Living, Christian Growth.

Christian Missions (Travel with a Purpose)
- Short-Term Missions, A Christian Guide to STMs.
- How to Plan, Prepare and Successfully Complete Your Short-Term Mission.

World Travel
- Budget Travel, A Guide to Travelling on a Shoestring, Explore the World.
- Travel the World and Explore for Less than $50 a Day, the Essential Guide.

Appendix A

Rees Howells and the Welsh Revival (1904-1905)

The meetings were often swayed by strong currents of emotionalism
and excitement . but beneath it all was the deep steady onflow of the
RIVER OF LIFE. When someone complained of the noise in the prayer meetings,
an old Minister answered, that "he prefered the noise of the city, to the
silence of the cemetry". During the next two years the Welsh people were
carried by a flood-tide of Pentecostal Blessing, and were literally, like the
beliggers of apostolic days , "found daily in the Temple Praising and Blessing n
God". I had the privilege of attending two meetings addressed by "The Revivalist himself(Mr Evan Roberts)"; on both occasions the Spirit of God was
upon him, so "clothing him" indeed, that , like Moses "though he wist it not
the skin of his face shone". No one who had been brought into contact with
him during that period , could ever question that he was the instrument by of
God's own choice for bringing in the great WELSH REVIVAL. He was the outstanding figure, his personality eclipsed all, the multitude went after him,
and his name probably will be the only one that will go down to history in
connection with the Welsh Revival of 1904. During the latter part of
the Revival , the remark was often heard, that"the children born into the
Kingdom of God during that time outnumbered the nurses (Spiritual)? It was
only too true ; the sad fact remains that, with but few exceptions , the
Ministry was incapable of feeding the new born babes with the sincere milK of
the WORD that they might grow thereby.

An unpublished account of Rees Howells talking about the Welsh Revival (1904-1905) and Evan Roberts, c.1936 (text below)

The meetings were often swayed by strong currents of emotionalism and excitement, but beneath it all was the deep steady onflow [sic] of the River of Life. When someone complained of the noise in the prayer meetings, an old minister answered that "he preferred the noise of the city, to the silence of the cemetery." During the next two years, the Welsh people were carried by a flood-tide of Pentecostal blessing and were literally, like believers of apostolic days, "found daily in the Temple praising and blessing God" [Luke 24:53]. I had the privilege of attending two meetings addressed by "the Revivalist" himself (Mr

Evan Roberts). On both occasions the Spirit of God was upon him, so "clothing him" [clothed with power from on high, Luke 24:49, A.S.V.], indeed, that, like Moses "though he wist it not the skin of his face shone" [Exodus 34:29, A.V.]. No one who had been brought into contact with him during that period could ever question that he was the instrument of God's own choice for bringing in the great WELSH REVIVAL. He was the outstanding figure, his personality eclipsed all, the multitudes went after him, and his name probably will be the only one that will go down to [sic] history in connection with the Welsh Revival of 1904.

During the latter part of the Revival, the remark was often heard, that, "the children born into the Kingdom of God during that time outnumbered the nurses" (spiritual). It was only too true; the sad fact remains that, with few exceptions, the ministry was incapable of feeding the 'new born babes with the sincere milk of the Word that they might grow thereby' [1 Peter 2:2].[1]

Appendix B

Articles by Rees Howells 1916 & 1919 on the Mission Field

Rees Howells' First Missionary Article 1916
Great Expectations
Rusitu, Gazaland. Rees Howells

In 1916, Rees Howells wrote his first article for the South African General Mission (SAGM). This is the first time it has been in print in more than a century:

We arrived in August 1915, and soon found out that the climate, environment, or natives were not the same as in England; on the other hand, we soon discovered that God, His Son Jesus, and the Holy Spirit were the same; and because they never change we could count on the same result in dark Africa as we witnessed in Wales. We went through the Welsh Revival and witnessed remarkable "demonstrations of the Spirit." We told the people about revival (language was no hindrance as we have many interpreters), and we, the missionaries, agreed as to the conditions of revival, and were willing to comply with them:

On the people's side the conditions were:

1. Confession of all known sin.
2. Full surrender to the will of God.

Thursday evening we (missionaries) not only prayed definitely for a revival but had the assurance that the prayer was answered. Sunday evening, October 10th [Rees Howells' 36th birthday], the Heavens opened. The Holy Spirit descended, and there was no room for the blessing. We witnessed the same result as in Wales. Rusitu was a transformed church; many young men had entered the "School of Faith."

An Evangelist Class of about fifteen was started, and our boarding school was more than doubled. So we proved, whatever the environment may be on the mission-field, our part is to look to God. The environment cannot change God, but God can change the environment.

Now I want to tell you of a trip to Portuguese East Africa. There is not a single missionary (except on the coast) in all this vast country. It is the stronghold of Satan, and this was another great challenge when we planned to go in there. On the first day of June, thirty-one of us started out on this evangelistic trip, the party made up of twenty-three boys, four girls, and four missionaries. We started out with great expectations, as men going to war, and the "Cross of Jesus" going on before. Our plan was to go along the bank of the Rusitu and preach at all the kraals [village of huts], but in the afternoon we were led to change this, and as the Holy Spirit was the guide we obeyed, and went in through the country. After we walked two miles we came to kraals and gathered the people for service. While the preaching was on they were spellbound under the convicting power of the Holy Spirit, and before the preaching was over some of them signified that they wanted to leave Satan and worship the living God. They all stood up and said they wanted God to be their Father, and to give them eternal life. We were all taken by surprise, and, like D. L. Moody, thought the people had not understood the invitation, but, after all, it was "the breaker had come up before" (Micah 2:13). From there we were led on to another group of kraals and had a service in the evening. Many gathered, and the preaching had the same effect as in the afternoon; all the people stood up and confessed their sin of "worshipping spirits," etc., signifying that they now wanted to serve the living God. We had quite a revival meeting at that place, many testimonies and much praying, until late in the night the boys made the forest ring with songs of Zion. Instead of giving an account of how we travelled daily, we give an account of what was accomplished spiritually, as we want the intercessors to follow in prayer the results of the preaching.

We visited the kraals of thirteen chiefs, four of whom were absent, but we preached to their people; the other nine gathered their people for services.

Most of the heathen worship ancestral spirits, etc., and are greatly in bondage because of the "fear of death" [Hebrews 2:15]. Through these weaknesses the Holy Spirit appealed to them, and revealed to them that fear was the effect of sin, and that the love of God in their hearts would cast out fear. When the preaching was going on we could see by their faces that the Holy Spirit was convicting them. In groups they would stand up and confess that Satan had deceived them, and that they were living in great bondage because of the fear of death. We walked for twenty-four days, preaching in every kraal and group of kraals and went from one chief to the other.

Apart from faith it will be impossible for all one to believe the results, but the reader has to bear in mind that the twenty-seven carriers were preachers, and most of them Spirit-filled Christians; the Bible says: "One man of you shall chase a thousand, for the Lord fighteth for you" [Joshua 23:10]. Getting the Lord to fight makes all the difference in the result. Nine chiefs and Over twelve hundred people stood up and confessed how Satan had deceived them and made them to spend their time in worshipping spirits, etc., keeping them in bondage; now they wanted to accept God as Father; the Lord Jesus as Saviour; the Holy Spirit as Comforter (Helper) and eternal life as a gift.

The question is: Does Jesus care that these people are without a teacher? Yes, "He cares." [1 Peter 5:7 with John 4:35]. Thousands of people are perishing; because it is not possible to get land to build missions or schools, and native evangelists are not free to witness and work for Christ.

May this closed door hinder the "Lord's Coming"? [2 Peter 3:12], Shall the intercessor force it open? We are co-workers with the Lord, and it only needs faith to get the Lord to open it, [James] Gilmour [1843-1891, of Mongolia] said, "The God of Elijah only waits for Elijah to call on Him."[1]

Rees Howells' Second Missionary Article 1919

In 1919, Rees Howells wrote his second article for the South African General Mission (SAGM). The front of the magazine notes it as a 'Special Article: God Versus Ancestral Spirits.' This is the first time it has been in print in more than a century:

God Versus Ancestral Spirits
Rusitu, Gazaland. Rees Howells

This is my first letter for over two years, and one reason for that is that we were away for over seventeen months. We visited all our Mission Stations in the movement of the Spirit in many places. We also saw a great movement in the compounds in Johannesburg, where we conducted a united mission for three weeks; we preached to thousands of natives, and hundreds were touched by the Holy Spirit.

In travelling over the country and conducting missions, we had varied experiences and gained more faith, knowing that what we had seen the Lord doing in other places, He could do to these Gospel hardened people in our own district. About four years ago we had a revival in this district; it was mostly among the Christians, and the heathen from a distance received blessing through it, while the heathen men and women of this district kept away, and have done so ever since.

The enemy often brought the thought to our minds that these people were too hard to be convicted of sin, but in Swaziland we used to sing,

> "There is nothing too hard for Thee, dear Lord,
> There is *no-one* too hard for Thee."

To-day it is a living fact in this district that there is "no-one" too hard for the Lord because some of the hardest cases have come through. A couple of months ago we began to prepare to build our house (which was given by Mr Alfred Head), and had six heathen from the district working for us. We made it plain if they were to work on the house they were not only to attend prayers every morning, but the Sunday services, and to the latter there was little objection. We gained our object in getting them to the services, and we prayed that the Holy Spirit would convict them of sin. After a few weeks the hardest case, as we thought, came to blessing, standing up and confessing Christ. An indescribable scene followed; it seemed that the Heavens had opened, and that the angels had come down to join in the triumphant song.

In another week the second confessed Christ and the third, fourth and fifth (five out of six). After these men yielded themselves to the Lord there was great power in the meetings, and we planned for an aggressive fight against the enemy, realising that the Holy Spirit was pulling down his strongholds because there was a movement among the dry bones. When we were ready for the fight we heard that the influenza was in the Mission next to us (Mount Silinda); we knew if it should come to this district the meetings and everything would be stopped, and it would give great advantage to the enemy. We took all precautions and prayed to the Lord to stop it, unless allowing it would bring more glory to Him. That week the magistrate ordered all schools and churches to be closed; it seemed that the Devil laughed at us: we lost sight of the fact that our extremity was God's opportunity.

The influenza came and in less than a week we had forty cases on the [Mission] Station. We turned the Church and the Girl's Boarding House into hospitals, and they came one after the other saying we must go to the Church (hospital). At first the sickness was only among the Christians, and the heathen would not come near the Station; they said this sickness was for the Christians and not for them. At the time we could not understand God's purpose in allowing all this; we were very much like the Psalmist: "Our steps had well nigh slipped; until we went into the Sanctuary of God, then understood we in the end" [Psalm 73:2,17].

In a week the Christians commenced to get well, and the heathen had the sickness in the kraals; in less than a week they had fifteen deaths and not a single death on the Mission Station. The talk changed, the heathen said that this was such a bad sickness that only the God of the Christians could deliver in it. The ancestral spirits were like the magicians in Egypt, they had failed with this new sickness, and the people had to admit it.

At this time the doctor was sent out by the magistrate. He asked if I would undertake the medical work in this district, attending the sick and inoculating, the medicines to be supplied by the Government. They sent to call all the people and over 600 came to be inoculated. It was a glorious opportunity, the talk was, "Why was it the Christians were not dying?" Over 50 cases had been nursed on the Station and not single death, while great numbers were dying in the kraals.

We told all the people that we had prepared plenty of room, and were willing to nurse them all on the Station. In coming they had to admit that the spirits had failed, and that God alone was able to deliver. The Christians could say: "Our God whom we serve is able to deliver us from this sickness." [Daniel 3:17 with Isaiah 38:9]. It was like the challenge on Mount Carmel: "God versus ancestral spirits" [1 Kings 18:20-40]. The test was who would be the first heathen to cross the line. In a day or two we saw a man coming in his blanket, and the wife carrying his mat. He said, "I am coming to the Church, Umfundisi" [Meaning: Pastor / teacher / missionary, among speakers of Xhosa and Zulu in South Africa]. We asked him if the spirits had failed, because they could not be worshipped in the house of God (Church), the answer was "Yes." I went into the house and thanked God *for the influenza.* In less than half-an-hour another man came in his blanket (walking slowly with a temperature of 104 degrees) [Fahrenheit or 40 degrees Celsius]. He asked, "May I go to the Church, Umfundisi?" and before this one had gone another one came; we had to laugh, and thanked God again for the influenza, because it had made things a reality to these people. Many others have come and are coming daily, but I want to give a little account of the first three men.

They were brought up in this district, and two of them had heard the Gospel through the first missionaries that came to Rusitu, but had hardened their hearts. In giving medicine, we pointed out that it was not the medicine in itself but God that would heal. They wanted both (medicine and God) and on the third day the three repented and received the "Gift of Eternal Life" [Romans 6:23].

These were great men among the heathen in our district. Space will not permit us to write much more, but we have had about twenty picked men and women out of this district turning to God. Knowing them, a person feels that one is worth a thousand. For twenty years they have hardened their hearts against the Gospel, and nearly all have been prayed for by the Christians.

We have cause to thank God for the influenza; more work has been done in a month than would have been accomplished otherwise in a couple of years.

In future, we shall aim at having a hospital on the Mission Station, knowing the confidence the people have in us, and the way the Lord has used it. We are beginning to prove that it matters not how hard the people are, nor how long they have rejected the Gospel; the Holy Spirit can convict, and make eternity a reality to them, and we only need to find that way out. Pray for these new converts.[2]

Sources and Notes

Within the Sources and Notes I frequently link to *Rees Howells Intercessor* by Norman Grubb, Lutterworth Press, 1952, so that the reader, if he or she desires can understand the context or the incident in greater detail of what Rees Howells is talking about. For staff and students at the Bible College of Wales, these stories, quotes and incidents in the life of faith were common and frequently shared from the pulpit and occasionally in the classroom. The context of Rees Howells' words was a discussion between Samuel Rees Howells and Norman Grubb as revealed from their letters of the 1960s (cited earlier on in this book) regarding the original manuscript *Go Through the Gates* from which this work is based. Some of the sentences without the additional information or footnotes could leave the reader with more questions than answers. I have used a 1952 first edition, but with some later editions, especially paperbacks the page numbers do not always align. With one 2015 edition the Postscript has been omitted and a Chapter 38 added. With this in mind, I have included the chapter number (or chapters, e.g. Rees Howells' village ministry) to help the reader, as well as the page number(s) when necessary.

The intended title of the book about Rees Howells was originally typed as *God's Dealing With the Bible College of Wales*, but was changed to *Rees Howells Intercessor* (1952), a more fitting title as a biography, rather than an institution. This book was first discussed in 1936 by Norman Grubb and Rees Howells, and commissioned in 1950 by Samuel Rees Howells. He assigned a handful of BCW staff members to collate and type a manuscript which Norman Grubb worked from and added to, especially the teaching on intercession.

Introduction

1. See *Samuel Rees Howells A Life of Intercession: The Legacy of Prayer and Spiritual Warfare of an Intercessor* by Richard Maton, Paul Backholer and Mathew Backholer, ByFaith Media, 2012, 2018, pages 141-142.

2. Geoffrey Crane was in charge of Missionary Press, later known as Emmanuel Press, for some in-house BCW publications. They also printed foreign language tracts, Scripture cards and envelopes for the mission fields, especially in various African and Indian languages, alongside Arabic, Hebrew, French, Spanish and Portuguese. Some pupils of Emmanuel Grammar School also assisted in this vital work and outreach from the 1950s for at least two decades. At least one former student who had served on the mission field and returned to the Swansea area, also assisted in the work for a time.

In 1982, the *Emmanuel Magazine* states that Geoffrey Crane is in Israel studying and working. In 1983, Crane and John Rocha (a former boarder at Emmanuel from 1940 and student-teacher from 1948) are noted as being in Cyprus (travelling together) and then return to Israel. In 1948, Crane visits the Bible College and the following year is in Greece. In July 1986, he visits the College again and returns to Greece. By 1990, in his 80s he retires in Athens, Greece, whilst John Rocha becomes an official Israeli citizen. In 1991, Geoffrey Crane, age 85 is in a retirement home and presumably is promoted to glory within a few years.

In the Vision
1. *Henan: Inside the Greatest Christian Revival in History* by Paul Hattaway, Piquant Editions, 2021, pages 23-24.
2. *America and World Evangelization* by Jacob Christoph Kunzmann, The United Lutheran Publication House, 1920, pages v-vi.
3. *Rees Howells, Vision Hymns of Spiritual Warfare, Intercessory Declarations: World War II Songs of Victory, Intercession, Praise and Worship, Israel and the Every Creature Commission* by Mathew Backholer, ByFaith Media, 2021, pages 120-121.

Chapter 1
1. *Rent Heavens, the Revival of 1904: Some of its Hidden Springs and Prominent Results* by R. B. Jones, The Bookroom, Bible Institute, 1931, pages 71-72.

Chapter 2
1. For more about the Holy Spirit see: *Holy Spirit Power: Knowing the Voice, Guidance and Person of the Holy Spirit* by Paul Backholer, ByFaith Media, 2013, 2017. Drawing from the powerful influences of many Christian leaders, including: Rees Howells, Evan Roberts, D. L. Moody, Duncan Campbell and others.
2. For the Divine-human partnership see: *Global Revival, Worldwide Outpourings, Forty-Three Visitations of the Holy Spirit: The Great Commission* by Mathew Backholer, ByFaith Media, 2010, 2017, chapter 5. Also: '...he has worked with God this day' (1 Samuel 14:45). '...Babylon was a golden cup in the Lord's hand...' (Jeremiah 51:7). Jesus said, "Go into all the world and preach the Gospel to Every Creature...and these signs will follow those who believe..." (Mark 16:15, 17).
3. David Wilkerson once held a crusade with Kathryn Kuhlman. He asked her how she maintained her vigour. She replied, "It's the Spirit. There's your answer. He is the Quickener, the Enlivener. When you work under the anointing, you work under power and life." From *Beyond The Cross and the Switchblade* by David Wilkerson, 1975, 1986, page 113
4. The Every Creature Commission/Vision: See *Rees Howells Intercessor* by Norman Grubb, Lutterworth Press, 1952, chapter 30, page 212.
5. See *Rees Howells, Vision Hymns of Spiritual Warfare, Intercessory Declarations: World War II Songs of Victory, Intercession, Praise and Worship* by Mathew Backholer, ByFaith Media, 2021.
6. *Understanding Revival and Addressing the Issues it Provokes* by Mathew Backholer, ByFaith Media, 2009, 2017, page 148.

Chapter 3
1. Baby Samuel Howells who was kept by God. He was given into the care of Moses and Elizabeth Rees, before Rees and Lizzie Howells began their preparation for the mission field of Southern Africa: See *Rees Howells Intercessor* by Norman Grubb, Lutterworth Press, 1952, chapter 22, pages 148-151.
2. For binding the strong man in relation to a person see *Rees Howells Intercessor* by Norman Grubb, Lutterworth Press, 1952, chapter 9. See also *Extreme Faith, On Fire Christianity: Hearing from God and Moving in His Grace, Strength and Power* by Mathew Backholer, ByFaith Media, 2013, 2017, chapters 49 and 50 (Deliverance, the Casting out of Demons and Demonised Places / Territorial Spirits).

3. See *Rees Howells Intercessor* by Norman Grubb, Lutterworth Press, 1952, chapters 6-11 (Loving an Outcast to The Consumptive Woman).

4. The pictures of BCW graduates are believed to have come from a WEC magazine, pasted into a small diary-sized book by Samuel Howells, with annotations.

Chapter 4

1. To pray the prayer that the Holy Spirit gave him: See *Rees Howells Intercessor* by Norman Grubb, Lutterworth Press, 1952, chapter 6, page 43.

2. Praying in the evenings, not going to the Mission and handing it over to his friend, his future brother-in-law: See *Rees Howells Intercessor* by Norman Grubb, Lutterworth Press, 1952, chapter 16, pages 106-107.

3. Not being distracted when walking the two-miles to the Mission, but praying and walking: See *Rees Howells Intercessor* by Norman Grubb, Lutterworth Press, 1952, chapter 16, page 103.

4. Not thinking bad thoughts about others, especially jealously: See *Rees Howells Intercessor* by Norman Grubb, Lutterworth Press, 1952, chapters 5 and 14, pages 39 and 98.

Chapter 5

1. *Hudson Taylor in Early Years – The Growth of a Soul* by Dr. and Mrs Howard Taylor, China Inland Mission, 1911, 1940, pages 372-373.

2. Rees Howells spent twenty-three months alone with the Bible was after he handed over the mission to his friend, his future brother-in-law (John Jones, also known as Johnny Jones), and also stopped attending chapel. He was shut in with God, being led of the Spirit.

3. *The Vision Lives – A Profile of Mrs Charles E. Cowman* by B. H. Pearson, Oliphants Ltd, 1960, 1964, page 49.

4. A handful of Rees Howells' relatives were medical doctors and this reference to cancer being healed may be the family cure of 'half starvation' and 'twelve months in bed,' plus any medicine which is not mentioned. In an unpublished manuscript of *Rees Howells Intercessor,* a section from chapter 1, states: 'On his father's side, his grandparents were very interested in medicine. His grandfather had discovered a cure for external cancer, and was known to cure scores of cases. The secret of this cure has been passed down in the family, three or four of whom are practicing in the medical profession today.' (1952).

Chapter 6

1. Jim Stakes (James Thomas) of whom the common saying was attached: "What Jim Stakes would not do, the Devil himself could not do!" See *Rees Howells Intercessor* by Norman Grubb, Lutterworth Press, 1952, chapter 6, pages 46-48.

2. See *Rees Howells Intercessor* by Norman Grubb, Lutterworth Press, 1952, chapter 23, pages 154-155.

3. See *Rees Howells Intercessor* by Norman Grubb, Lutterworth Press, 1952, chapter 5, page 39, chapter 14, page 98 and chapter 16, pages 106-107.

4. *This Is The Victory – 10,000 Miles of Miracle in America* by J. Edwin Orr, Marshall, Morgan & Scott, LTD, 1936.

Chapter 7

1. "Do not preach on being dead to the world until you have victory over it!" See *Rees Howells Intercessor* by Norman Grubb, Lutterworth Press, 1952, chapter 16, page 104.

2. See *Rees Howells Intercessor* by Norman Grubb, Lutterworth Press, 1952, chapter 30, pages 212-218.

3. See *Understanding Revival and Addressing the Issues it Provokes* by Mathew Backholer, ByFaith Media, 2009, 2017, chapters 15 and 23.

4. *For Sinners Only* by A. J. Russell, Hodder and Stoughton, 1932, 1940, page 163.

5. See *Rees Howells Intercessor* by Norman Grubb, Lutterworth Press, 1952, chapters 8 and 16-20.

Chapter 8

1. See *Rees Howells Intercessor* by Norman Grubb, Lutterworth Press, 1952, chapter 6, page 45 and chapter 8, pages 57-61.

2. See *Rees Howells Intercessor* by Norman Grubb, Lutterworth Press, 1952, chapter 20, page 131.

3. Based on work from: *Christianity Rediscovered, in Pursuit of God and the Path to Eternal Life: What you Need to Know to Grow, Living the Christian Life with Jesus Christ, Book 1* by Mathew Backholer, ByFaith Media, 2018, pages 118 and 120.

4. See *Reformation to Revival, 500 Years of God's Glory: Sixty Revivals, Awakenings and Heaven-Sent visitations of the Holy Spirit* by Mathew Backholer, ByFaith Media, 2017, pages 151-152.

5. See *Revival Fires and Awakenings, Thirty-Six Visitations of the Holy Spirit: A Call to Holiness, Prayer and Intercession for the Nations* by Mathew Backholer, ByFaith Media, 2009, 2017, pages 213-214.

6. For more about deliverance/exorcism see *Extreme Faith, On Fire Christianity: Hearing from God and Moving in His Grace, Strength and Power – Living in Victory* by Mathew Backholer, ByFaith Media, 2013, 2017, chapters 49 and 50.

Chapter 9

1. See *Rees Howells Intercessor* by Norman Grubb, Lutterworth Press, 1952, chapter 6, page 43 and chapter 15, page 99.

2. See Introduction in *God Challenges the Dictators, Doom of the Nazis Predicted: The Destruction of the Third Reich Foretold by the Director of Swansea Bible College, An Intercessor from Wales* by Rees Howells and Mathew Backholer, ByFaith Media, 2020, pages 18-22, but especially page 19.

3. For Rees and Lizzie Howells ministry in Africa see Appendix B and *Rees Howells Intercessor* by Norman Grubb, Lutterworth Press, 1952, chapter 24.

4. *America and World Evangelization* by Jacob Christoph Kunzmann, The United Lutheran Publication House, 1920, pages 23-24.

Chapter 10

1. See *Rees Howells Intercessor* by Norman Grubb, Lutterworth Press, 1952, chapter 8, pages 56-57.

2. The example of Rees Howells at Livingstone College praying with another student: See *Rees Howells Intercessor* by Norman Grubb, Lutterworth Press, 1952, chapter 23, pages 153-154.

3. Praying through the Bible: See *Rees Howells Intercessor* by Norman Grubb, Lutterworth Press, 1952, chapter 18, pages 113-115.

4. Rees and the Sermon on the Mount: See *Rees Howells Intercessor* by Norman Grubb, Lutterworth Press, 1952, chapter 7, pages 51. Praying through the Word: See *Rees Howells Intercessor,* chapter 18, pages 113-116.

5. The village untouched by the Welsh Revival (1904-1905). See *Rees Howells Intercessor* by Norman Grubb, Lutterworth Press, 1952, chapter 7, pages 53-55.

6. See *Rees Howells Intercessor* by Norman Grubb, Lutterworth Press, 1952, chapter 7, pages 53-55.

7. See *Rees Howells Intercessor* by Norman Grubb, Lutterworth Press, 1952, chapter 7, especially page 53 (giving up the last £1), and chapter 33, page 234, (the test of the £100,000 gift for the Jews, the value of three estates).

8. *Extreme Faith, On Fire Christianity: Hearing from God and Moving in His Grace, Strength & Power, Living in Victory* by Mathew Backholer, ByFaith Media, 2012, 2017, pages 61-62.

Chapter 11

1. Living off God's resources in the work of village ministry: See *Rees Howells Intercessor* by Norman Grubb, Lutterworth Press, 1952, chapters 7 and 8.

2. This was at Rusitu, Gazaland: See *Rees Howells Intercessor* by Norman Grubb, Lutterworth Press, 1952, chapter 24, pages 171-175.

3. Correspondence with Daniel 'Dan' Bavington (brother of Ruth Bavington), a boarder at the Bible School (later Emmanuel Grammar School) under Rees Howells then Samuel Howells. Thank you Dan for your time, May 2022.

4. For examples of Rees Howells during times of intercession, giving of himself for the Holy Spirit to work through so that lives can be touched: See the chapters concerning: For an outcast, tramps, consumptive woman and Joe Evans, the consumptive healed in Madeira: See *Rees Howells Intercessor* by Norman Grubb, Lutterworth Press, 1952, chapters 6, 8, 11 and 21.

5. *When God Came Down an account of the North Uist Revival 1957-58* edited by John Ferguson, 2000, Lewis Recordings, page 10.

6. For first-fruits: See *Rees Howells Intercessor* by Norman Grubb, Lutterworth Press, 1952, chapters 11 and 15.

Chapter 12

1. "The promises became equal to money in the bank," a claim on God's resources to do His work: See *Rees Howells Intercessor* by Norman Grubb, Lutterworth Press, 1952, chapter 7, pages 53-54.

2. Payments to Mrs Howells, Rees' mother, when he was called out from wage-earning: See *Rees Howells Intercessor* by Norman Grubb, Lutterworth Press, 1952, chapter 20.

3. The "cleavage" as it was known at the College in September/October 1925 was over a major difference of how it was run, a life of faith or not, with many other underlying issues, especially regarding holiness, living the Christian life and paying for board and lodgings (tuition was free). Many students were not paying their way, nor living the life of faith, which increased the financial burden on Rees Howells. This split the College, students and staff were divided over loyalties, whilst senior staff resigned. This led to its closure for one year, though just over a handful of students remained with Mr and Mrs Howells and were shut in with God for a year before the College reopened in 1926. From its opening in 1924 until 1929, women students at the Bible College of Wales paid a few pounds per term less than men. This was probably because many unmarried women living at home (i.e. not in service) did not have paid jobs, they helped out with family duties, though many did men's work during World War One (1914-1918), but when the soldiers returned, they wanted their jobs back. Many businesses in an effort to help returning veterans released their female staff force (who were also paid less than men) and hired those who had been conscripted for service. Chapels across Wales were generally open to female speakers during the Welsh Revival (1904-1905). Evan Roberts had a number of female singers and evangelists who travelled in teams across Wales, alongside

some men. However, after the revival, many pulpits and doors were closed to female ministry, regardless of their anointing and call on their life. In the time of Rees Howells (and later his son, Samuel), many chapel pulpits were still closed to female students to preach or teach, though they could give testimony, sing and speak to the children at Sunday School or give a children's story before the sermon when there was no Sunday School. (Please note that some chapels in Wales have Sunday Schools for adults). This is another reason why female BCW student fees were less than the men for a few years, as they were less likely to speak at a chapel, church or mission hall and therefore would not receive a financial gift as a labourer is worthy of his or her hire. Ironically, many chapel secretaries were women, but they were only permitted to book male preachers by the male elders. BCW policy was: after traveling expenses, (public transport or fuel for a vehicle), any money received from public speaking was split equally between those that went (often in pairs, though sometimes in threes), regardless of who preached, gave testimony, sang or spoke at Sunday School.

Chapter 13

1. An imminent strike would bring hardship to the village untouched by revival and Rees Howells negotiated credit with two grocers so the villagers could be fed with bread and cheese and have tea and sugar. The promises of God's provision became equal to money in the bank: See *Rees Howells Intercessor* by Norman Grubb, Lutterworth Press, 1952, chapter 7, pages 53-55.
2. Rees Howells gave up the Rechabites Sick Benefit Club as directed by the Holy Spirit, but was later called to pay the arrears of a Benefit Club on behalf of a man who had brought shame on himself and his family: See *Rees Howells Intercessor* by Norman Grubb, Lutterworth Press, 1952, chapter, 14, pages 96-97.

Chapter 14

1. Cf. *Rees Howells Intercessor* by Norman Grubb, Lutterworth Press, 1952, chapter 12, page 87, the gained position of intercession, and 'the grace of faith,' a phrase of George Müller.
2. Rees Howells read the Bible as a book of examples of what can be achieved and accomplished when one believes God. He called the stories and examples the 'plots' of the Bible and would read about Jerusalem being surrounded by enemies, when Britain was surrounded by the expanding Nazis of the Third Reich under Hitler's command. The 'plots' of the Bible are relevant to the tests we experience. We must believe as they believed, trusting God by faith (Hebrews chapter 11).
3. United Nations voting on the nation of Israel being born in a day: See *Rees Howells Intercessor* by Norman Grubb, Lutterworth Press, 1952, chapter 33, pages 237-238. See also *Samuel Rees Howells, A Life of Intercession: The Legacy of Prayer and Spiritual Warfare of an Intercessor* by Richard A. Maton, Paul Backholer and Mathew Backholer, ByFaith Media, 2012, 2018, chapter 10. This includes Kristine Maton's (née Jones) account and that of Dr. Kingsley Priddy, both were present at the College meetings during those vital days and months of prayer and intercession for the nation of Israel.
4. Closing down the Public House on the Glynderwen Estate and forfeiting the valuable alcohol license: See *Rees Howells Intercessor* by Norman Grubb, Lutterworth Press, 1952, chapter 25, pages 189-190.
5. See *A Hunter's Life in South Africa Volume 1* by R. Gordon Cumming, 1850, 1979 facsimile reproduction with an Introduction by James A. Casada, and *A*

Hunter's Life in South Africa Volume 2 by R. Gordon Cumming, 1850, 1979 facsimile reproduction. David Livingstone as a missionary in Southern Africa in the 1840s met Gordon Cumming as Gordon passed through on a one year trek which turned into nearly five! Gordon from Scotland was known as "Africa's Greatest Hunter."

6. 'Man's extremity is God's opportunity' is a quote from Puritan John Flavel (c.1627-1691). There is also a veiled reference in the *1948 Jubilee Conference Hymn Book* 'We've Seen the One on Earth To-day.' This is a unique hymn of victory for the Bible College of Wales (BCW) and is a general overview of some of the victories in intercession accomplished at BCW under Rees Howells and his staff. It dates to no later than summer 1948 and no earlier than summer 1944. It is found in *Rees Howells, Vision Hymns* of Spiritual Warfare, *Intercessory Declarations* by Mathew Backholer, ByFaith Media, 2021, pages 212-213. (Section 3: Bible College of Wales' Hymn Book, 1948, Stanza four of Number 13).

Chapter 15
1. Do not worry or be anxious. Jesus said, "Therefore I say to you, do not worry about your life, what you will eat or what you will drink; nor about your body, what you will put on. Is not life more than food and the body more than clothing? Look at the birds of the air, for they neither sow nor reap nor gather into barns; yet your Heavenly Father feeds them. Are you not of more value than they? Which of you by worrying can add one cubit to his stature? So why do you worry about clothing? Consider the lilies of the field, how they grow: they neither toil nor spin; and yet I say to you that even Solomon in all his glory was not arrayed like one of these. Now if God so clothes the grass of the field, which today is, and tomorrow is thrown into the oven, will He not much more clothe you, O you of little faith? Therefore do not worry, saying, 'What shall we eat?' or 'What shall we drink?' or 'What shall we wear?' For after all these things the Gentiles seek. For your Heavenly Father knows that you need all these things. But seek first the Kingdom of God and His righteousness, and all these things shall be added to you. Therefore do not worry about tomorrow, for tomorrow will worry about its own things. Sufficient for the day is its own trouble" (Matthew 6:25-34).

2. *A Thousand Miles of Miracle In China* by Archibald E. Glover, Pickering & Inglis, 1904, 1926, page 13.

Chapter 16
The story of Rees Howells speaking to a preacher friend in Carmarthen, believing the Bible and trusting the Lord is similar in nature to a story at Livingstone College Hospital. Rees Howells invited a fellow student, a Cambridge graduate to join him in prayer for £20. This student had never seen a direct answer to prayer and Mrs Howells needed this money for her admission for a maternity course in City Road Hospital, London. See *Rees Howells Intercessor* by Norman Grubb, Lutterworth Press, 1952, chapter 23, pages 153-154.

Chapter 17
1. Praying in money for Glynderwen Estate from 1923: See *Rees Howells Intercessor* by Norman Grubb, Lutterworth Press, 1952, chapter 25, pages 188-189.

2. Praying in money for new buildings on the Derwen Fawr Estate from 1930 and then looking to buy Sketty Isha (Isaf) Estate in 1932: See *Rees Howells*

Intercessor by Norman Grubb, Lutterworth Press, 1952, chapter 28, pages 201-202.

3. The first gift from the Treasury of £10,000, a seal on the Every Creature Vision. It arrived in July 1938: See *Rees Howells Intercessor* by Norman Grubb, Lutterworth Press, 1952, chapter 30, pages 214 and 218.

4. From the late 1930s Rees Howells was seeking to give away £10,000 as a seed to the nations so that he could claim the hundredfold, to help fulfil the Great Commission. This amount was later raised to £100,000. Rees was willing to sell all three estates on the Derwen Fawr Road (Glynderwen, Derwen Fawr and Sketty), and to start again on the Penllergaer Estate and announced this at a College meeting. Mrs Howells burst into tears when she heard and other staff members were shocked. Detailed plans of the size of each room in all major buildings were typed up as part of this preparation. However, God was testing Rees Howells to see if he was willing. The British military were buying up and commandeering estates in the Swansea area, but no longer in the westward direction, which was away from the centre of town and towards BCW. Nearing Rees' death, he commissioned his son Samuel to give away £100,000 which he did over a period of years. This story is told in *Samuel Rees Howells, A Life of Intercession: The Legacy of Prayer and Spiritual Warfare of an Intercessor* by Richard A. Maton, Paul Backholer and Mathew Backholer, ByFaith Media, 2012, 2018, chapters 11 and 56.

5. Influenza (Spanish flu) in Southern Africa where Rees Howells turned the chapel into a hospital: See *Rees Howells Intercessor* by Norman Grubb, Lutterworth Press, 1952, chapter 24, pages 173-175.

6. The buying of Derwen Fawr on Christmas Eve 1929, when a small deposit was handed over to its owner: See *Rees Howells Intercessor* by Norman Grubb, Lutterworth Press, 1952, chapter 27, pages 198-199.

Chapter 18

1. The call to submit to the Holy Spirit by 6pm in unconditional surrender, Rees Howells' last chance: See *Rees Howells Intercessor* by Norman Grubb, Lutterworth Press, 1952, chapter 5, pages 34-40. For more about the Holy Spirit entering a Christian in full possession: See *The Baptism of Fire, Personal Revival, Renewal and the Anointing for Supernatural Living* by Paul Backholer, ByFaith Media, 2017.

2. Thursday evening meetings in the consumptive (T.B.) woman's home in Brynamman: See *Rees Howells Intercessor* by Norman Grubb, Lutterworth Press, 1952, chapter 9, pages 68-69.

3. Mrs Lizzie Howells was gravely ill after childbirth, and was told not to take any medicine: 'Have faith in God' in golden letters: See *Rees Howells Intercessor* by Norman Grubb, Lutterworth Press, 1952, chapter 23, pages 154-155. The author has come across an invoice for gold paint from the early 1930s to the Bible College. This receipt was before the purchase of Penllergaer, which to bring it back to its former glory included lavish portions of gold paint for the interior.

4. *Extreme Faith, On Fire Christianity: Hearing from God and Moving in His Grace, Strength & Power, Living in Victory* by Mathew Backholer, ByFaith Media, 2013, 2017, page 35.

Chapter 19

1. Trekking into Portuguese East Africa for mission work and trying to get a foothold in the country by buying land: See *Rees Howells Intercessor* by Norman Grubb, Lutterworth Press, 1952, chapter 24, pages 175-176.

2. Money for a private trip to America: See *Rees Howells Intercessor* by Norman Grubb, Lutterworth Press, 1952, chapter 25, pages 179-180.

3. *Samuel Rees Howells, A Life of Intercession: The Legacy of Prayer and Spiritual Warfare of an Intercessor* by Richard A. Maton, Paul Backholer and Mathew Backholer, ByFaith Media, 2012, 2018, page 73.

Chapter 20

1. Duncan Campbell, following his experience in the Hebridean Revival (1949-1952) was preaching at the College in 1955. The presence of the Holy Spirit was so manifest that the strong stone walls of the Conference Hall trembled! Samuel Rees Howells spoke to Campbell about his burden for global revival. On 7 August he told the College: "Duncan Campbell told me he believed it is God's will to visit us again with an awakening. When people meet God in revival, they do not go back again," said Samuel. "I asked Duncan Campbell if there was any backsliding in the Hebrides; he said, 'There was not one instance.' This is what we need in Wales and everywhere." *Samuel Rees Howells, A Life of Intercession: The Legacy of Prayer and Spiritual Warfare of an Intercessor* by Richard A. Maton, Paul Backholer and Mathew Backholer, ByFaith Media, 2012, 2018, pages 89-90.

2. *Extreme Faith, On Fire Christianity: Hearing from God and Moving in His Grace, Strength & Power, Living in Victory* by Mathew Backholer, ByFaith Media, 2012, 2017, pages 55 and 56. The facts about Duncan Campbell are an addition.

Appendix A

1. Rees Howells said, "During the latter part of the revival, the remark was often heard, that, 'the children born into the Kingdom of God during that time outnumbered the nurses' " (spiritual). This echoes what was written in chapter 4 of *Rees Howells Intercessor* by Norman Grubb, Lutterworth Press, 1952, chapter 4, page 32. 'More children born than there were nurses to tend them. The establishing of the converts became the greatest need, which if not met would be the most dangerous weakness of the revival.'

Appendix B

1. *The South African Pioneer*, November 1916, *Vol xxix, No. 10,* pages 130-131. Note: *The South African Pioneer* magazine had sequential numbering throughout the year. This was so that people could have the magazines bound into a book.

2. *SAGM Pioneer Magazine*, November 1919, *Vol xxxii, No. 11,* pages 86-88. Note: *The South African Pioneer* magazine from 1919 was known as the *SAGM Pioneer Magazine*. It had sequential numbering throughout the year.

ByFaith Media Books

The following ByFaith Media books are available as paperbacks and eBooks, whilst some are available as hardbacks.

Biography and Autobiography
9781907066-13-9. *Samuel Rees Howells A Life of Intercession: The Legacy of Prayer and Spiritual Warfare of an Intercessor* by Richard Maton, Paul Backholer and Mathew Backholer is an in-depth look at the intercessions of Samuel Rees Howells alongside the faith principles that he learnt from his father, Rees Howells, and under the leading and guidance of the Holy Spirit. With 39 black and white photographs. Hardback 9781907066-37-5.

9781907066-14-6. *Samuel, Son and Successor of Rees Howells: Director of the Bible College of Wales – A Biography* by Richard Maton. The life of Samuel and his ministry at the College and the support he received from numerous staff and students as the history of BCW unfolds. With 113 black and white photos. Hardback 9781907066-36-8.

9781907066-41-2. *The Holy Spirit in a Man: Spiritual Warfare, Intercession, Faith, Healings and Miracles* by R. B. Watchman. One man's compelling journey of faith and intercession, a remarkable modern day story of miracles and faith to inspire and encourage. (One chapter relates to the Bible College of Wales and Watchman's visit).

Historical
9781907066-76-4 Hardback. *God Challenges the Dictators, Doom of the Nazis Predicted: The Destruction of the Third Reich Foretold by the Director of Swansea Bible College, An Intercessor from Wales* by Rees Howells and Mathew Backholer. Available for the first time in 80 years – fully annotated and reformatted with twelve digitally enhanced black and white photos. Discover how Rees Howells built a large ministry by faith in times of economic chaos and learn from the predictions he made during times of national crisis, of the destruction of the Third Reich, the end of fascism and the liberation of Christian Europe during World War Two. Paperback 9781907066-77-1.

9781907066-78-8 Hardback. *Rees Howells' God Challenges the Dictators, Doom of Axis Powers Predicted: Victory for Christian England and Release of Europe Through Intercession and Spiritual Warfare, Bible College of Wales* by Mathew Backholer. This is the story behind the story of *God Challenges the Dictators* (GCD), before, during and after publication which is centred around World War Two. Read how extracts of GCD were aired over occupied parts of Europe, and how Hitler and leading Nazi officials were sent copies in 1940! The book includes letters to Winston Churchill and Press Releases from Rees Howells and how he sent copies of his book to Prime Ministers N. Chamberlain and W. Churchill plus government officials, and what the newspapers had to say, at home and abroad, as far away as Australia and the Oceanic Islands! With twenty-four black and white photos. Paperback 9781907066-78-8.

978-1-907066-95-5 Hardback. *Rees Howells, Vision Hymns of Spiritual Warfare, Intercessory Declarations: World War II Songs of Victory, Intercession, Praise and Worship, Israel and the Every Creature Commission* by Mathew Backholer. *Vision Hymns* gives a rare insight into the prophetic declarations, hymns and choruses used in spiritual warfare by Rees Howells and his team of intercessors at the Bible College of Wales (BCW). Spanning the pivotal years of 1936-1948 and brought to life for the first time in more than seventy years. Many of the songs of worship reveal the theology, spiritual battles and history during the dark days of World War II and the years surrounding it. From Emperor Haile Selassie of Ethiopia, Hitler's predicted downfall, to the nation of Israel being born in a day and the glories beyond. With thirty-one black and white photos.

978-1-907066-64-1 Hardback. *Rees Howells, Life of Faith, Intercession, Spiritual Warfare and Walking in the Spirit: Christian Principles, Addresses, Teaching, & Testimonies from an Intercessor & Missionary* by Mathew Backholer and Rees Howells. The famed intercessor and missionary, Rees Howells, preached thousands of times, but until now his authentic voice has not been heard. This book was commissioned by Samuel Rees Howells in the 1960s as the sequel to his dad's biography but was lost in development until now. Discover the wonder as you listen to Rees Howells teach on the ministry of the Holy Spirit and learn how you can open yourselves to Him to become His channel for blessing, faith and intercession. Including anecdotes and contemporary quotes from men and women of God, friends of Rees and Lizzie Howells, with more than 70 digitally enhanced photos and images.

9781907066-45-0. *Britain, A Christian Country, A Nation Defined by Christianity and the Bible and the Social Changes that Challenge this Biblical Heritage* by Paul Backholer. For more than 1,000 years Britain was defined by Christianity, with monarch's dedicating the country to God and national days of prayer. Discover this continuing legacy, how faith defined its nationhood and the challenges from the 1960s till today.

9781907066-02-3. *How Christianity Made the Modern World* by Paul Backholer. Christianity is the greatest reforming force that the world has ever known, yet its legacy is seldom comprehended. But now, using personal observations and worldwide research the author brings this legacy alive by revealing how Christianity helped create the path that led to Western liberty and laid the foundations of the modern world.

9781907066-47-4. *Celtic Christianity and the First Christian Kings in Britain: From St. Patrick and St. Columba, to King Ethelbert and King Alfred* by Paul Backholer. Celtic Christians ignited a Celtic Golden Age of faith and light which spread into Europe. Discover this striking history and what we can learn from the heroes of Celtic Christianity.

Revivals and Spiritual Awakenings
9781907066-01-6. *Revival Fires and Awakenings, Thirty-Six Visitations of the Holy Spirit: A Call to Holiness, Prayer and Intercession for the Nations* by Mathew Backholer. With thirty-six fascinating accounts of revivals in nineteen countries from six continents, plus biblical teaching on revival, prayer and intercession. Hardback 9781907066-38-2.

9781907066-07-8. *Global Revival, Worldwide Outpourings, Forty-Three Visitations of the Holy Spirit: The Great Commission* by Mathew Backholer. How revivals are birthed and the fascinating links between pioneering missionaries and the revivals that they saw as they worked towards the Great Commission, with forty-three accounts of revivals.

9781907066-00-9. *Understanding Revival and Addressing the Issues it Provokes* by Mathew Backholer. Everything you need to know about revival and its phenomena. How to work with the Holy Spirit to see God rend the Heavens and pour out His Spirit on a dry and thirsty land and how not to be taken in by the enemy and his counterfeit tricks, delusions and imitations. Hardback 9781907066-99-3.

9781907066-06-1. *Revival Fire, 150 Years of Revivals, Spiritual Awakenings and Moves of the Holy Spirit* by Mathew Backholer. This book documents in detail, twelve revivals from ten countries on five continents. Be inspired, encouraged and challenged by the wonderful works of God. Hardback 978178822-002-6.

9781907066-15-3. *Revival Answers, True and False Revivals, Genuine or Counterfeit Do not be Deceived* by Mathew Backholer. What is genuine revival and how can we tell the true from the spurious? Drawing from Scripture with examples across Church history, this book will sharpen your senses and take you on a journey of discovery.

9781907066-60-3. *Reformation to Revival, 500 Years of God's Glory: Sixty Revivals, Awakenings and Heaven-Sent visitations of the Holy Spirit* by Mathew Backholer. *Reformation to Revival* traces the Divine thread of God's power from Martin Luther of 1517, through to the Charismatic Movement and into the twenty-first century, with sixty great revivals from twenty nations on five continents. Be encouraged and inspired from the past for the future! Hardback 9781907066-98-6.

Christian Teaching and Inspirational
978-1-78822-003-3. *Spiritual Warfare, Prayers, Declarations and Decrees to Release God's Blessing, Peace and Abundance: 150+ Days of Confessions to Claim Christ's Protection, Break Curses and Receive Freedom from Oppression* by Paul Backholer. Powerfully assert Christ's victory in your life and thrive with daily biblical proclamations, releasing the Lord's blessing. Renew your strength each day with hope, as you set yourself free. Know God's Word, believe God's Word and confess God's Word.

9781907066-35-1. *Jesus Today, Daily Devotional: 100 Days with Jesus Christ* by Paul Backholer. One hundred days of two minutes of Christian inspiration to draw you closer to God to encourage and inspire. Have you ever wished you could have sat at Jesus' feet and heard Him speak? *Jesus Today* is a concise daily devotional defined by Jesus' teaching and how His life can change ours. See the world from God's perspective, learn who Jesus was, what He preached and what it means to live abundantly in Christ.

9781907066-33-7. *Holy Spirit Power: Knowing the Voice, Guidance and Person of the Holy Spirit* by Paul Backholer. Power for Christian living; drawing from the powerful influences of many Christian leaders, including: Rees Howells, Evan Roberts, D. L. Moody, Duncan Campbell and other channels of God's Divine fire. Jesus walked in the power of the Holy Spirit and declared His disciples would do even greater works. Today, God's power can still be released in and through Christians who will meet the Holy Spirit on His terms.

9781907066-43-6. *Tares and Weeds in Your Church: Trouble and Deception in God's House, the End Time Overcomers* by R. B. Watchman. Is there a battle taking place in your house, church or ministry, leading to division? Tares and weeds are counterfeit Christians used to sabotage Kingdom work; learn how to recognise them and neutralise them in the power of the Holy Spirit.

9781907066-56-6. *The Baptism of Fire, Personal Revival, Renewal and the Anointing for Supernatural Living* by Paul Backholer. Jesus will baptise you with the Holy Spirit and fire; that was the promise of John the Baptist. But what is the baptism of fire and how can you experience it? The author unveils the life and ministry of the Holy Spirit, shows how He can transform your life and what supernatural living in Christ means.

Supernatural and Spiritual
9781907066-58-0. *Glimpses of Glory, Revelations in the Realms of God Beyond the Veil in the Heavenly Abode: The New Jerusalem and the*

Eternal Kingdom of God by Paul Backholer. Find a world beyond earth which is real, vivid and eternal. A gripping read!

9781907066-18-4. *Prophecy Now, Prophetic Words and Divine Revelations for You, the Church and the Nations* by Michael Backholer. An enlightening end-time prophetic journal of Visions, prophecies and words from the Holy Spirit to God's people, the Church and the nations. Read about the emptying of stadiums, which was witnessed during the Coronavirus pandemic of 2020!

9781907066-80-1. *Heaven, Paradise is Real, Hope Beyond Death: An Angelic Pilgrimage to Your Future Home* by Paul Backholer. Come on a journey to another world of eternal bliss, joy and light, in this enchanting narrative which pulls you in and shows you Heaven. Meet those who have gone before into paradise and found eternal peace. Enter into the Heavenly Jerusalem, with a man and an angelic guide to discover the truth about immortality, the afterlife and the joy of eternity.

Christian Discipleship
9781907066-16-0. *Extreme Faith, On Fire Christianity: Hearing from God and Moving in His Grace, Strength and Power – Living in Victory* by Mathew Backholer. Discover the powerful biblical foundations for on fire faith in Christ! This book explores biblical truths and routines to shake your world.

9781907066-62-7. *Christianity Rediscovered, in Pursuit of God and the Path to Eternal Life: What you Need to Know to Grow, Living the Christian Life with Jesus Christ, Book 1* by Mathew Backholer. Since the beginning of time mankind has asked, "Why am I alive, does my life matter and is there an afterlife I can prepare for?" *Christianity Rediscovered* has the answers and will help you find meaning, focus, clarity and peace.

9781907066-12-2. *Discipleship For Everyday Living, Christian Growth: Following Jesus Christ and Making Disciples of All Nations* by Mathew Backholer. Engaging biblical teaching to aid Christian believers in maturity, to help make strong disciples with solid biblical foundations who reflect the image of Jesus Christ.

Short-Term Missions (Christian Travel with a Purpose)
9781907066-49-8. *Short-Term Missions, A Christian Guide to STMs: For Leaders, Pastors, Churches, Students, STM Teams and Mission Organizations – Survive and Thrive!* by Mathew Backholer. A concise guide to Short-Term Missions (STMs). What you need to know about planning a STM, or joining a STM team, and considering the options as part of the Great Commission, from the Good News to good works.

9781907066-05-4. *How to Plan, Prepare and Successfully Complete Your Short-Term Mission For Churches, Independent STM Teams and Mission Organizations* by Mathew Backholer. This book will guide you through all you need to know about STMs and includes: mission statistics, cultural issues, where and when to go, what to do and pack, food, accommodation, and more than 140 real-life STM testimonies.

Biblical Adventure and Archaeology
9781907066-52-8. *Lost Treasures of the Bible: Exploration and Pictorial Travel Adventure of Biblical Archaeology* by Paul Backholer. Unveil ancient mysteries as you discover the evidence for Israel's exodus from Egypt, and travel into lost civilisations in search of the Ark of the Covenant. Explore lost worlds with over 160 colour photos and pictures.

978178822-000-2. *The Exodus Evidence In Pictures – The Bible's Exodus: The Hunt for Ancient Israel in Egypt, the Red Sea, the Exodus Route and Mount Sinai* by Paul Backholer. Two brothers and explorers, Paul and Mathew Backholer search for archaeological data to validate the biblical account of Joseph, Moses and the Hebrew Exodus from ancient Egypt. With more than 100 full colour photos and graphics!

978178822-001-9. *The Ark of the Covenant – Investigating the Ten Leading Claims* by Paul Backholer. Join two explorers as they investigate the ten major theories concerning the location of antiquities greatest relic. Combining an on-site travel journal with 80+ colour photographs through Egypt, Ethiopia and beyond.

Budget Travel – Vacation/Holiday
9781907066-54-2. *Budget Travel, a Guide to Travelling on a Shoestring, Explore the World, a Discount Overseas Adventure Trip: Gap Year, Backpacking, Volunteer-Vacation and Overlander* by Mathew Backholer. *Budget Travel* is a practical and concise guide to travelling the world and exploring new destinations with fascinating opportunities and experiences. Full of anecdotes, traveller's advice, informative timelines and testimonies, with suggestions, guidance and ideas.

9781907066-74-0. *Travel the World and Explore for Less than $50 a Day, the Essential Guide: Your Budget Backpack Global Adventure, from Two Weeks to a Gap Year, Solo or with Friends* by Mathew Backholer. A practical guide for the solo backpacker or with friends that will save you time and money with ideas, and need-to-know information so you can have the adventure of a lifetime from two weeks to one year.

ByFaith Media DVDs

Revivals and Spiritual Awakenings
9781907066-03-0. *Great Christian Revivals* on 1 DVD is an inspirational and uplifting account of some of the greatest revivals in Church history. Filmed on location across Britain and beyond, and drawing upon archive information and rare images, the stories of the Welsh Revival (1904-1905), the Hebridean Revival (1949-1952) and the Evangelical Revival (1739-1791) are brought to life in this moving 72-minute documentary. Using computer animation, historic photos and depictions, the events of the past are weaved into the present, to bring these Heaven-sent revivals to life.

Christian Travel (Backpacking Short-Term Missions)
9781907066-04-7. *ByFaith – World Mission* on 1 DVD is a Christian reality TV show that reveals the real experience of backpacking short-term missions in Asia, Europe and North Africa. Two brothers, Paul and Mathew Backholer shoot through fourteen nations, in an 85-minute real-life documentary. Filmed over three years, *ByFaith – World Mission* is the best of ByFaith TV season one.

Historical and Adventure
9781907066-09-2. *Israel in Egypt – The Exodus Mystery* on 1 DVD. A four year quest searching for Joseph, Moses and the Hebrew slaves in Egypt. Join brothers Paul and Mathew Backholer as they hunt through ancient relics and explore the mystery of the biblical exodus, hunt for the Red Sea and climb Mount Sinai. Discover the first reference to Israel outside of the Bible, uncover depictions of people with multicoloured coats, encounter the Egyptian records of slaves making bricks and find lost cities. 110 minutes. The best of *ByFaith – In Search of the Exodus*.

9781907066-10-0. *ByFaith – Quest for the Ark of the Covenant* on 1 DVD. Join two adventurers on their quest for the Ark, beginning at Mount Sinai where it was made, to Pharaoh Tutankhamun's tomb, where Egyptian treasures evoke the majesty of the Ark. The quest proceeds onto the trail of Pharaoh Shishak, who raided Jerusalem. The mission continues up the River Nile to find a lost temple, with clues to a mysterious civilization. Crossing through the Sahara Desert, the investigators enter the underground rock churches of Ethiopia, find a forgotten civilization and examine the enigma of the final resting place of the Ark itself. 100+ minutes.

www.ByFaithDVDs.org

ByFaith Media Downloads and Streaming

The following ByFaith Media productions are based on the DVDs from the previous page and are available to download: to buy, rent or to stream via Amazon.

Revivals and Spiritual Awakenings
Glorious Christian Revival and Holy Spirit Awakenings: The Welsh, Hebridean and Evangelical Revivals, Evan Roberts, Duncan Campbell and John Wesley. 1 hour 12 minutes. Discover the Welsh Revival (1904-1905), the Hebridean Revival (1949-1952) and the Evangelical Revival (1739-1791), with Evan Roberts, Duncan Campbell, John and Charles Wesley, George Whitefield and others. Filmed on location across the UK and beyond. B07N2N762J (UK). B07P1TVY6W (USA).

Christian Revival and Holy Spirit Awakenings. Join revival historian and prolific author Mathew Backholer, as he joins CEO Gordon Pettie in the Revelation TV studios over 7 episodes to examine many powerful Christian revivals which shook the world. Including the: Layman's Prayer Revival of 1857, Ulster Revival 1859-60, Welsh Revival of 1904-05, Azusa Street Revival of 1906-09, Korean Revival of 1907-10, the Hebridean Revival of 1949-52 and more! B07R445S5W (UK), or view on YouTube/ByFaithMedia for free.

Christian Travel (Backpacking Short-Term Missions)
Short-Term Mission Adventures, A Global Christian Missionary STM Expedition with brothers Mathew and Paul Backholer. 1 hour 15 minutes. The mission begins when two adventurers land in Asia, a continent of maximum extremes. After overcoming culture shock and difficult travel, the adventurous missionaries preach in the slums. From India they strike out into Nepal, Bangladesh, Thailand, Myanmar, Cambodia and Vietnam. The mission also touches down in the great cities of Europe: London, Paris, Rome, Dublin, Frankfurt and Amsterdam. B07N2PVZZK (UK). B07PNSWBKN (USA).

Historical and Adventure
The Bible's Lost Ark of the Covenant: Where Is It? Egypt, Ethiopia or Israel? With brothers Mathew and Paul Backholer. 1 hour 10 minutes. The Ark of the Covenant was the greatest treasure in Solomon's Temple, but when Jerusalem fell the Ark vanished from history. Now join two adventurers on their quest for the Ark of the Covenant, beginning at Mount Sinai where it was made, to Pharaoh Tutankhamun's tomb, crossing the Sahara Desert into the underground

rock churches of Ethiopia and beyond in an epic adventure. B07MTTHHZ7 (UK). B07R3BMBW6 (USA).

The Exodus Evidence: Quest for Ancient Israel in Egypt, The Red Sea, The Exodus Route and Mount Sinai. Join two adventurers, brothers Mathew and Paul Backholer as they investigate a three-thousand year old mystery, entering the tombs of ancient Egypt seeking the exodus evidence. Discover the first reference to Israel outside of the Bible in hieroglyphics, uncover ancient depictions of people with multi-colored coats, encounter the Egyptian records of slaves making bricks and find lost cities mentioned in the Bible. 1 hour 15 minutes. B07P63BWZ2 (UK). B07Q3ST613 (USA).

For hundreds of hours of free streaming and various playlists visit our YouTube channel: https://www.youtube.com/ByFaithMedia

Notes

Notes

CPSIA information can be obtained
at www.ICGtesting.com
Printed in the USA
BVHW091921191022
649823BV00001B/1

9 781907 066641